Growth in Mathematics

ORANGE

TEST DESIGN AND EVALUATION

WILLIAM A. MEHRENS
Professor of Educational Measurement
  and Evaluation
Michigan State University
East Lansing, Michigan

ERIC M. GORDON
Assistant Professor of Education
Michigan State University
East Lansing, Michigan

SPECIAL DESIGN FOR INSTRUCTION

JOSEPH F. LOUGHMAN
Art Director
Center for Curriculum Development
New York, New York

Center for Curriculum Development
New York

Growth in Mathematics

ORANGE

CURRICULUM AND WRITING

DAVID W. WELLS
Director of Instruction
  and Mathematics Education
Oakland Schools
Pontiac, Michigan

JANET S. ABBOTT
Coordinator of Mathematics
Chula Vista City School District
Chula Vista, California

MARYANNE E. YACONO
Executive Editor, Elementary Mathematics
Center for Curriculum Development
New York, New York
formerly Mathematics Teacher
Fair Lawn, New Jersey

ROBERT L. SPENCE
Vice President
Center for Curriculum Development
New York, New York
formerly Chairman, Mathematics Department
Haddon Heights, New Jersey

RESEARCH AND CRITIQUE

GEORGE A. SPOONER
Professor of Mathematics
Central Connecticut State College
New Britain, Connecticut

LESLIE S. BEATTY
formerly Mathematics Consultant
Chula Vista City School District
Chula Vista, California

LOLA J. MAY
Mathematics Consultant
Winnetka Public Schools
Winnetka, Illinois

 Harcourt Brace Jovanovich
New York   Chicago   San Francisco   Atlanta   Dallas   *and*   London

CRITICAL READERS

BARBARA BRANCH
Mathematics Consultant for the
  Central Area of Memphis City Schools
Memphis, Tennessee

JAMES DAVIS
Coordinator of Mathematics and
  Specialized Curriculum Services
Clayton County Board of Education
Jonesboro, Georgia

LOUISE GEMAKE
Mathematics Supervisor
Community School District 4
New York, New York

MARJORIE JACKSON
Junior High Mathematics Consultant
Indianapolis Public Schools
Indianapolis, Indiana

DR. RONALD MASSIE
Mathematics Consultant
Lincoln Public Schools
Lincoln, Nebraska

TAYE M. MATOI
Parent
Los Angeles, California

SANDRA McDANIEL
Fourth Grade Teacher
Roll Hill School
Cincinnati, Ohio

TRUDY NAPOLILLO
Mathematics Coordinator
South Stickney School District #111
Burbank, Illinois

DR. M. M. OHMER
Dean, College of Sciences
Nicholls State University
Thibodaux, Louisiana

DR. IRENE ST. CLAIR
formerly Director of Mathematics Program
  for the State of Texas (Levels K-8)
Austin, Texas

DR. HAZEL WAGNER
Director of the Criterion-Reference
  Testing Program
Research and Evaluation Department
Chicago Board of Education
Chicago, Illinois

JOYCE WHITE
Mathematics Supervisor
Cobb County Schools
Marietta, Georgia

MARY FRANCES WILLINGHAM
Fifth Grade Teacher
Summit Drive Elementary School
Greenville, South Carolina

PHOTOGRAPH ACKNOWLEDGMENTS   *Cover:* Ted Demas, DPI   *Text:* E. Maristany, O. Buitrago, and B. Hayward; Harbrace
                      page 40-41, Bohdan Hrynewych/Stock, Boston.
ART ACKNOWLEDGMENTS   *Text:* M. Haller, D. Crews, D. Hampson, and M. Vivo.

TECHNICAL ILLUSTRATIONS AND MECHANICAL PRODUCTION: Pencils Portfolio, Inc.

PRINTED IN THE UNITED STATES OF AMERICA   ISBN 0-15-351280-6

Contents

1 Numeration

A Game For Two

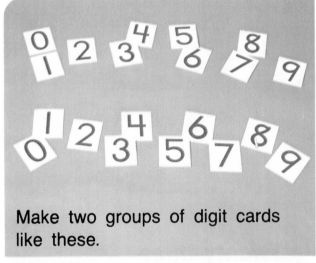

Make two groups of digit cards like these.

Mix the cards.
Place them face down.

Each player draws a card.

The player with the greater number takes both cards.

Continue until all the cards are drawn.
The winner is the one with more cards.

Tens and Ones

You use more than one digit to name numbers greater than 9.

Group by tens:	Use place value:
2 tens **3** ones	tens ¦ ones **2** ¦ **3**

Read the numeral. ⟶ **Twenty-three**

Write the numeral. ⟶ **23**

---

try these

Write the numeral.

1. 4 tens 2 ones

2. 6 tens 3 ones

3. 1 ten 7 ones

4.

tens	ones
7	3

5.

tens	ones
5	0

6.

tens	ones
3	9

7. Sixty-five

8. Ninety-four

9. Forty

Write the numeral.

10. 5 tens 7 ones

11. 7 tens 5 ones

12. 5 tens 0 ones

13. 6 tens 4 ones

14. 4 tens 6 ones

15. 7 tens 9 ones

16.

tens	ones
2	8

17.

tens	ones
8	2

18.

tens	ones
2	0

19.

tens	ones
1	3

20.

tens	ones
3	1

21.

tens	ones
9	9

22. Fifty-six

23. Thirty-two

24. Fifteen

25. Eighty-seven

26. Seventy-eight

27. Thirty

28. Eighteen

29. Thirty-five

30. Ninety

31. Twenty-nine

32. Sixty

33. Forty-four

DOUBLE DIGIT GAME

1. Use twenty digit cards. Place them face down.
2. Each player draws two cards.
3. The player uses the two cards to name a number.
4. The player who names the greater number takes all four cards.
5. When all cards are drawn, the player with the most cards wins.

3

Hundreds, Tens, and Ones

You use more than two digits to name numbers greater than 99.

Group by hundreds and tens:

2 hundreds 4 tens 6 ones

Use place value:

hundreds	tens	ones
2	4	6

Read the numeral. ⟶ **Two hundred forty-six**

Write the numeral. ⟶ **246**

---

try these

Write the numeral.

1. 2 hundreds 3 tens 4 ones

2. 6 hundreds 2 tens 8 ones

3.

hundreds	tens	ones
3	9	4

4.

hundreds	tens	ones
2	3	0

5. Seven hundred twenty-six

6. Eight hundred four

now do these

Write the numeral.

7. 8 hundreds 2 tens 6 ones

8. 5 hundreds 6 tens

9. 3 hundreds 8 ones

10. 7 hundreds

11.

hundreds	tens	ones
2	5	4

12.

hundreds	tens	ones
2	4	5

13.

hundreds	tens	ones
6	1	0

14.

hundreds	tens	ones
9	0	3

15. Nine hundred sixteen

16. Seven hundred twenty

17. Three hundred eight

18. Six hundred fifty-nine

19. Four hundred

20. Two hundred five

21. Eight hundred thirty-four

22. Nine hundred eighty-seven

THREE AT A TIME

1. Use thirty digit cards.
Place them face down.
2. Each player draws three cards.
3. The player uses the three cards
to name a number.
4. The player who names the
greater number takes all six
cards.
5. When all cards are drawn,
the player with the most cards wins.

5

Greater Than and Less Than

Tasty Tuna always eats the greater amount.

3 is greater than **2.**

3 > 2

2 is less than **3.**

2 < 3

73 is greater than 37.
Use > to make a true sentence.

73 ● 37

26 is less than 62.
Use < to make a true sentence.

26 ● 62

645 is greater than 245.
Use > to make a true sentence.

645 ● 245

347 is less than 387.
Use < to make a true sentence.

347 ● 387

Write > or <.
1. 8 ● 5
2. 4 ● 8
3. 12 ● 18
4. 32 ● 23
5. 410 ● 310
6. 155 ● 175

now do these

Write > or <.
7. 9 ● 5
8. 8 ● 9
9. 8 ● 6
10. 9 ● 19
11. 34 ● 14
12. 18 ● 80
13. 14 ● 34
14. 17 ● 71
15. 78 ● 87
16. 433 ● 218
17. 215 ● 205
18. 932 ● 938
19. 514 ● 541
20. 612 ● 512
21. 798 ● 789

Name 10 more.
22. 5
23. 37
24. 90
25. 410
26. 837
27. 495

Name 100 more.
28. 28
29. 39
30. 433
31. 804
32. 714
33. 201

TIP THE SCALES

When you remove your fingers, which side will go down?

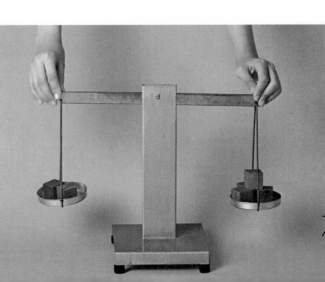

7

Expanded Notation

We use addition to name numbers.

300

IIIII

50

2

```
  300
   50
+   2
-----
  352
```

200

4

```
  200
+   4
-----
  204
```

try these

Write the sum.

1.	2.	3.	4.	5.	6.
500	200	700	400	600	800
80	70	20	+ 3	+ 40	+ 8
+ 1	+ 3	+ 1			

Show the hundreds, tens, and ones that give you the sum.

7. 417   8. 745   9. 389   10. 706   11. 850   12. 307

8

Write the sum.

13. 300	14. 400	15. 700	16. 300	17. 200	18. 100
90	70	30	40	80	60
+ 1	+ 3	+ 4	+ 7	+ 9	+ 6

19. 800	20. 500	21. 100	22. 600	23. 900	24. 300
+ 40	+ 80	+ 90	+ 7	+ 9	+ 3

Show the hundreds, tens, and ones that give you the sum.

25. 488	26. 862	27. 219	28. 311	29. 427	30. 206
31. 560	32. 370	33. 704	34. 860	35. 919	36. 120
37. 198	38. 888	39. 490	40. 601	41. 707	42. 903
43. 604	44. 330	45. 111	46. 789	47. 502	48. 250

THE MARBLE MONSTER

I keep marbles in my bed.
400 are green, 20 are red,
5 are yellow, I do not lie.
How many marbles in bed have I?

9

Thousands

You use more than three digits to name numbers greater than 999.

Group by thousands, hundreds, and tens:

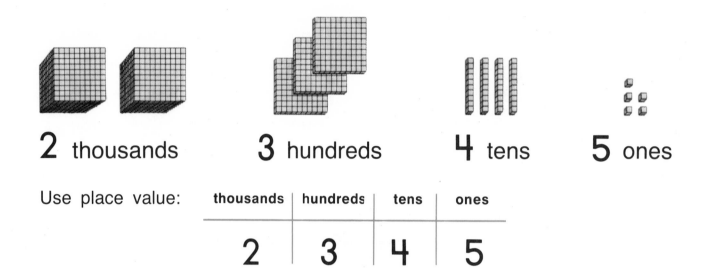

2 thousands   **3** hundreds   **4** tens   **5** ones

Use place value:

thousands	hundreds	tens	ones
2	3	4	5

Two thousand, three hundred forty-five

Read the numeral. ⟶ **2 thousand, 345**

Write the numeral. ⟶ **2345**

---

try these

Write the numeral.

1. 4 thousands 6 hundreds 5 tens 2 ones

2. 8 thousands 2 hundreds 7 tens 1 one

3.

thousands	hundreds	tens	ones
4	0	2	3

4.

thousands	hundreds	tens	ones
7	2	0	3

10

now do these

Write the numeral.

5. 9 thousands 4 hundreds 6 tens 2 ones

6. 8 thousands 7 hundreds

7.

thousands	hundreds	tens	ones
2	6	4	8

8.

thousands	hundreds	tens	ones
7	6	8	0

9.

thousands	hundreds	tens	ones
8	9	0	4

10.

thousands	hundreds	tens	ones
5	0	0	4

11. 3 thousand, 591

12. 7 thousand, 204

13. 4 thousand, 20

14. 8 thousand, 9

Write > or <.

15. 416 ● 742

16. 3416 ● 3742

17. 7894 ● 5894

18. 9002 ● 9007

19. 2468 ● 2648

20. 3788 ● 3748

Name

21. 100 more than 3462.

22. 10 more than 8043.

23. 1000 more than 550.

24. 1000 more than 6582.

CAN YOU DO IT?

Move the digit cards around.
Use all four each time.

Name 24 different numbers.

| 5 | 8 | 2 | 6 |

11

Hundred Thousands

Ten ones make one ten.

Ten tens make one hundred.

Ten hundreds make one thousand.

Ten thousands make one ten thousand.

How many ten thousands
make one hundred thousand?

There are five hundred twenty-five thousand,
six hundred minutes in one year.

hundred thousands	ten thousands	thousands	hundreds	tens	ones
				1	0
			1	0	0
		1	0	0	0
	1	0	0	0	0
1	0	0	0	0	0

hundred thousands	ten thousands	thousands	hundreds	tens	ones
5	2	5	6	0	0

The digit 2 is in the ten-thousands place.
In what places are the other digits?

Read the numeral. ⟶ **525 thousand, 600**

Write the numeral. ⟶ **525,600**

Write the numeral.

1. 322 thousand, 356

2. 45 thousand, 700

3. 700 thousand, 777

4. 203 thousand, 83

now do these

Write the numeral.

5. 28 thousand, 116

6. 62 thousand, 305

7. 428 thousand, 800

8. 37 thousand, 45

9. 801 thousand, 7

10. 600 thousand

In what place is the 2?

11. 472,316

12. 789,002

13. 604,234

14. 273,163

15. 920,004

16. 379,423

17. 92,638

18. 20,001

Use all of the digits. Name the greatest number.

19. 5, 2, 1, 8, 7, 3

20. 2, 3, 4, 6, 7

21. 7, 4, 8, 5, 9, 6

22. 8, 2, 4, 3, 6

Name

23. 10 more than 3047.

24. 10 more than 8192.

25. 100 more than 2468.

26. 100 more than 62,901.

27. 1000 more than 163,841.

28. 1000 more than 39,002.

29. 10,000 more than 473,010.

30. 100,000 more than 630,016.

13

Millions

There are one million, five hundred seventy-six thousand, eight hundred minutes in three years.

millions	hundred thousands	ten thousands	thousands	hundreds	tens	ones
1	5	7	6	8	0	0

How many places are in the numeral?
In what place is the digit 1?
In what place is the 5? the 7? the 6? the 8?

Read the numeral. ⟶ **1 million, 576 thousand, 800**

Write the numeral. ⟶ **1,576,800**

14

Write the numeral.
1. 1 million, 437 thousand, 800
2. 7 million, 860 thousand, 245
3. 9 million, 54 thousand, 388
4. 5 million, 3 thousand, 600

now do these

Write the numeral.
5. 2 million, 475 thousand, 389
6. 7 million, 700 thousand
7. 5 million, 80 thousand, 200
8. 8 million, 204 thousand, 87
9. 6 million, 252
10. 3 million, 4

In what place is the 5?
11. 7,593,421
12. 2,005,326
13. 4,239,750
14. 5,700,428
15. 6,250,786
16. 4,620,508

17. Use all of these digits.   Name the greatest number.   1, 7, 2, 6, 3, 5, 0

18. Name 100,000 more than 7,340,002.

19. Name 1,000,000 more than 6,245,783.

THINK ABOUT IT

There are 1000 gumdrops in this box.

How many of these boxes would you need for one million gumdrops?

Evens and Odds

How many rabbits do you see?

Each rabbit has a partner.
Eight is an **even number.**

How many rabbits do you see?

One rabbit does not have a partner.
Seven is an **odd number.**

These are even numbers. Can you name more?
    2, 4, 6, 8, 10, 22, 34, 56, 78, 200

These are odd numbers. Can you name more?
    1, 3, 5, 7, 9, 31, 43, 65, 97, 119, 251

Names for even numbers end in 0, 2, 4, 6, or 8.
Names for odd numbers end in 1, 3, 5, 7, or 9.

Write EVEN or ODD.

1.

2.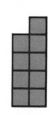

3.

4.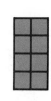

5. 23   **6.** 24   **7.** 475   **8.** 476

now do these

Write EVEN or ODD.

9. 31   **10.** 41   **11.** 305   **12.** 205

13. 343   **14.** 245   **15.** 654   **16.** 630

17. 3578   **18.** 4689   **19.** 9500   **20.** 7003

21. 20,400   **22.** 765,432   **23.** 40,000   **24.** 654,321

List just the even numbers between
25. 11 and 19.   **26.** 42 and 50.

27. 309 and 319.   **28.** 4235 and 4243.

29. 24,689 and 24,694.   **30.** 999 and 1002.

List just the odd numbers between
31. 10 and 20.   **32.** 25 and 35.

33. 402 and 412.   **34.** 9237 and 9247.

35. 9999 and 10,002.   **36.** 100,002 and 100,010.

37. Name the odd number that is 1000 more than 402,647.

38. Name the even number that is 10,000 more than 328,768.

17

Test

Write the numeral.

1. 8 tens 3 ones (p. 2)
2. 4 hundreds 2 tens 6 ones (p. 4)
3. 5 thousands 9 hundreds (p. 10)
4. 4 thousands 1 hundred 2 ones (p. 10)
5. Twenty-five (p. 2)
6. Six hundred thirty-two (p. 4)
7. 2 thousand, 873 (p. 10)
8. 7 million, 32 thousand, 12 (p. 14)

Name

9. 100 more than 7826. (p. 10)
10. 1000 more than 31,524. (p. 12)
11. 100,000 more than 5,032,679. (p. 14)
12. 1,000,000 more than 6,938,570. (p. 14)

Write > or <.

13. 8 ● 6 (p. 6)
14. 21 ● 12 (p. 6)
15. 106 ● 251 (p. 6)
16. 699 ● 782 (p. 6)
17. 8362 ● 8269 (p. 10)
18. 6547 ● 6539 (p. 10)

Write EVEN or ODD.

19. 76 (p. 16)
20. 41,062 (p. 16)
21. 330 (p. 16)
22. 246,821 (p. 16)

Write the sum.

23. 700
      20
    + 4
    (p. 8)

24. 300
    + 60
    (p. 8)

25. 900
    + 9
    (p. 8)

Ordinals

January	**February**	**March**	**April**	**May**
June	**July**	**August**	**September**	
October	**November**	**December**		

We have many national holidays.
The fourth day of the seventh month is one.
What holiday is it?

The first month of the year is January.
Which is the second month?   the sixth month?
Which month is twelfth?

March is the third month of the year.
In which position is April?   June?   September?

Can you name a holiday that comes in the first
month of the year?   the ninth month?
the tenth month?   the eleventh month?

2 Addition and Subtraction

Addition

You add to find how many in all.

4 mice.
3 mice join them.
How many mice in all?

$$4 \quad + \quad 3 \quad = \quad 7$$

Here are two ways to show addition.

addend → 4
addend → +3
sum → 7

$$4 + 3 = 7$$

You can use a number line to find sums.

Start at 0.
Move ahead 4.
Then move ahead 3 more.

$$
\begin{array}{r}
4 \\
+3 \\
\hline
7
\end{array}
$$

20

Add.

1. 9 + 7 = _?_

2. 8 + 7 = _?_

3. 9 + 3 = _?_

4. 8
   +6

5. 6
   +7

6. 9
   +8

7. 6
   +9

8. 3
   +7

9. 5
   +5

now do these

Add.

10. 7 + 4 = _?_

11. 5 + 7 = _?_

12. 6 + 6 = _?_

13. 5
    +9

14. 8
    +8

15. 7
    +9

16. 9
    +6

17. 5
    +4

18. 8
    +5

19. 7
    +5

20. 6
    +8

21. 5
    +8

22. 4
    +7

23. 8
    +9

24. 7
    +8

25. 9
    +5

26. 6
    +5

27. 4
    +9

28. 7
    +6

29. 9
    +4

30. 7
    +7

CLIMB THE MOUNTAIN

Climb the mountain 9 times.
The first time add 1 to each number.
The second time add 2.
The third time add 3, and so on.
The last time, you will add 9.
How fast can you climb?

21

Add in Either Order

Compare the addends in both examples.
Compare the sums.   What do you notice?

3 dimes.
2 nickels.
How many coins?

$$\begin{array}{r} 3 \\ +2 \\ \hline 5 \end{array}$$

2 nickels.
3 dimes.
How many coins?

$$\begin{array}{r} 2 \\ +3 \\ \hline 5 \end{array}$$

**You can add two numbers in either order.
The sum is always the same.**

---

try these

Add.

1. $\begin{array}{r} 5 \\ +2 \\ \hline \end{array}$ $\begin{array}{r} 2 \\ +5 \\ \hline \end{array}$

2. $\begin{array}{r} 4 \\ +3 \\ \hline \end{array}$ $\begin{array}{r} 3 \\ +4 \\ \hline \end{array}$

3. $\begin{array}{r} 4 \\ +6 \\ \hline \end{array}$ $\begin{array}{r} 6 \\ +4 \\ \hline \end{array}$

4. $\begin{array}{r} 9 \\ +4 \\ \hline \end{array}$ $\begin{array}{r} 4 \\ +9 \\ \hline \end{array}$

5. $\begin{array}{r} 4 \\ +8 \\ \hline \end{array}$ $\begin{array}{r} 8 \\ +4 \\ \hline \end{array}$

6. $\begin{array}{r} 8 \\ +7 \\ \hline \end{array}$ $\begin{array}{r} 7 \\ +8 \\ \hline \end{array}$

22

now do these

Add.

7. 9   7
  +7   +9
  ——   ——

8. 6   7
  +7   +6
  ——   ——

9. 8   5
  +5   +8
  ——   ——

10. 9   8
   +8   +9
   ——   ——

11. 6   4
   +4   +6
   ——   ——

12. 7   4
   +4   +7
   ——   ——

13. 5   14. 7   15. 4   16. 7   17. 8   18. 9
   +9   +4   +6   +5   +4   +5
   ——   ——   ——   ——   ——   ——

19. 9   20. 9   21. 8   22. 5   23. 6   24. 4
   +9   +6   +8   +7   +8   +8
   ——   ——   ——   ——   ——   ——

25. 8   26. 7   27. 4   28. 6   29. 5   30. 6
   +7   +7   +9   +9   +6   +6
   ——   ——   ——   ——   ——   ——

SOMETHING ABOUT ZERO

Add.

A. $3 + 0 =$ ___?___   **B.** $8 + 0 =$ ___?___   **C.** $0 + 9 =$ ___?___

D. $0 + 4 =$ ___?___   **E.** $0 + 5 =$ ___?___   **F.** $5 + 0 =$ ___?___

What can you say about the sum
when one of the addends is 0?

23

Using Patterns

Look for a pattern.

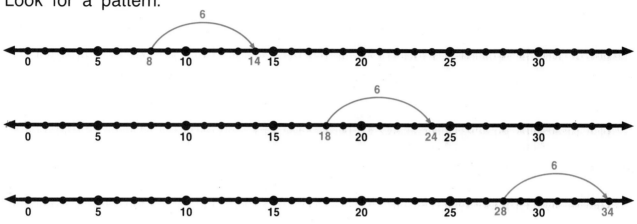

What is the missing sum?

$$\begin{array}{r} 8 \\ +\ 6 \\ \hline 14 \end{array} \qquad \begin{array}{r} 18 \\ +\ 6 \\ \hline 24 \end{array} \qquad \begin{array}{r} 28 \\ +\ 6 \\ \hline 34 \end{array} \qquad \begin{array}{r} 38 \\ +\ 6 \\ \hline ? \end{array}$$

---

try these

Add.

1. $\begin{array}{r} 3 \\ +5 \\ \hline \end{array}$
2. $\begin{array}{r} 13 \\ +\ 5 \\ \hline \end{array}$
3. $\begin{array}{r} 23 \\ +\ 5 \\ \hline \end{array}$
4. $\begin{array}{r} 5 \\ +9 \\ \hline \end{array}$
5. $\begin{array}{r} 15 \\ +\ 9 \\ \hline \end{array}$
6. $\begin{array}{r} 25 \\ +\ 9 \\ \hline \end{array}$

7. $\begin{array}{r} 8 \\ +7 \\ \hline \end{array}$
8. $\begin{array}{r} 18 \\ +\ 7 \\ \hline \end{array}$
9. $\begin{array}{r} 28 \\ +\ 7 \\ \hline \end{array}$
10. $\begin{array}{r} 38 \\ +\ 7 \\ \hline \end{array}$
11. $\begin{array}{r} 48 \\ +\ 7 \\ \hline \end{array}$
12. $\begin{array}{r} 58 \\ +\ 7 \\ \hline \end{array}$

now do these

Add.

13. 9
    +4

14. 19
    + 4

15. 29
    + 4

16. 7
    +9

17. 37
    + 9

18. 57
    + 9

19. 6
    +8

20. 16
    + 8

21. 26
    + 8

22. 36
    + 8

23. 46
    + 8

24. 56
    + 8

25. 28
    + 8

26. 35
    + 6

27. 18
    + 4

28. 36
    + 6

29. 27
    + 5

30. 49
    + 6

31. 57
    + 7

32. 48
    + 4

33. 37
    + 6

34. 67
    + 4

35. 16
    + 9

36. 46
    + 4

37. 18
    + 3

38. 55
    + 9

39. 82
    + 8

40. 48
    + 8

41. 79
    + 9

42. 34
    + 7

AMAZO

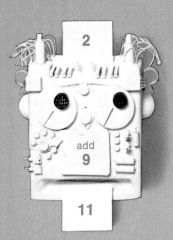

Put in a number.
Amazo adds 9.
Out comes the answer.

Copy and complete
the chart.

ADD 9

IN	OUT
2	11
5	?
8	?
7	?
6	?

25

Grouping Addends

$(9 + 2) + 8 = ?$ $9 + (2 + 8) = ?$

$11 + 8 = 19$ $9 + 10 = 19$

You can group addends differently.
The sum is always the same.

You can group addends differently.
You can add in either order.
So, you can add down   or   you can add up.

$$\left.\begin{array}{r} 8 \\ 6 \end{array}\right\} 14$$
$$\begin{array}{r} +7 \\ \hline 21 \end{array}$$

$$\begin{array}{r} 8 \\ \left.\begin{array}{r} 6 \\ +7 \end{array}\right\} 13 \\ \hline 21 \end{array}$$

26

Add.

| 1. 8
4
+5 | 2. 6
8
+5 | 3. 9
8
+7 | 4. 6
3
2
+4 | 5. 7
3
4
+5 | 6. 8
6
7
+5 |

now do these

Add.

| 7. 9
3
+7 | 8. 8
4
+8 | 9. 9
5
+7 | 10. 6
4
+8 | 11. 8
5
+9 | 12. 6
3
+9 |

| 13. 7
6
+8 | 14. 6
8
+6 | 15. 9
1
+7 | 16. 8
7
+8 | 17. 9
9
+6 | 18. 8
6
+5 |

| 19. 6
4
3
+8 | 20. 8
7
3
+5 | 21. 6
7
5
+4 | 22. 5
2
2
+9 | 23. 2
3
3
+7 | 24. 6
5
2
+4 |

| 25. 8
2
3
+9 | 26. 2
9
2
+5 | 27. 3
4
3
+8 | 28. 6
4
6
+9 | 29. 6
5
6
+7 | 30. 8
9
7
+6 |

27

Adding Greater Numbers

Step 1	Step 2	Step 3	Step 4
3764 +2105 9	3764 +2105 69	3764 +2105 869	3764 +2105 5869
Add the ones.	Add the tens.	Add the hundreds.	Add the thousands.

Add amounts of money as if you were adding whole numbers.
Remember to write the dollar sign and the cents point in the answer.

Step 1	Step 2	Step 3	Step 4
$37.64 +21.05 9	$37.64 +21.05 69	$37.64 +21.05 8 69	$37.64 +21.05 $58.69

Add.

1. 8234
   +1342

2. 6432
   + 401

3. $62.70
   + 53.25

4. $63.00
   + 6.45

5. $54.61
   + .38

now do these

Add.

6. 7330
   +2459

7. 4234
   +8003

8. 6342
   + 535

9. 7354
   + 240

10. 4603
    + 92

11. 3245
    +4543

12. 4460
    + 108

13. 8110
    +2621

14. 5821
    + 41

15. 9242
    + 145

16. $72.25
    + 13.14

17. $32.35
    + 90.02

18. $ 2.75
    + 25.24

19. $18.03
    + 1.95

20. $24.07
    + .60

21. 2234
    7301
    +3224

22. 42
    133
    7000
    +2824

23. $ 4.03
    1.02
    + 33.92

24. $ .32
    65.21
    .03
    + 82.30

25. $ 6.10
    .03
    1.42
    + 32.04

quick check

Add.

1. 8
   +9

2. 7
   +6

3. 9
   +0

4. 9
   2
   +4

5. 7
   6
   5
   +2

6. 65
   + 7

7. 46
   + 4

8. 78
   + 8

9. 5843
   + 126

10. $60.52
    + 9.40

Subtraction

You subtract to find how many are left.

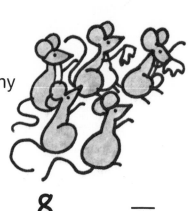

8 mice.
3 go away.
How many are left?

$$8 - 3 = 5$$

Here are two ways to show subtraction.

$$8 - 3 = 5$$

$$
\begin{array}{r}
8 \\
-3 \\
\hline
5
\end{array}
$$

You can use a number line to find answers.

Start at 0.
Move ahead 8.
Then move back 3.

$$
\begin{array}{r}
8 \\
-3 \\
\hline
5
\end{array}
$$

Subtract.

1. $13 - 4 = \underline{\ ?\ }$

2. $14 - 7 = \underline{\ ?\ }$

3. $12 - 8 = \underline{\ ?\ }$

4. $\begin{array}{r} 13 \\ -\ 5 \\ \hline \end{array}$

5. $\begin{array}{r} 11 \\ -\ 2 \\ \hline \end{array}$

6. $\begin{array}{r} 12 \\ -\ 3 \\ \hline \end{array}$

7. $\begin{array}{r} 15 \\ -\ 6 \\ \hline \end{array}$

8. $\begin{array}{r} 14 \\ -\ 5 \\ \hline \end{array}$

9. $\begin{array}{r} 11 \\ -\ 7 \\ \hline \end{array}$

now do these

Subtract.

10. $12 - 7 = \underline{\ ?\ }$

11. $14 - 6 = \underline{\ ?\ }$

12. $13 - 9 = \underline{\ ?\ }$

13. $\begin{array}{r} 16 \\ -\ 7 \\ \hline \end{array}$

14. $\begin{array}{r} 15 \\ -\ 8 \\ \hline \end{array}$

15. $\begin{array}{r} 14 \\ -\ 9 \\ \hline \end{array}$

16. $\begin{array}{r} 12 \\ -\ 6 \\ \hline \end{array}$

17. $\begin{array}{r} 11 \\ -\ 8 \\ \hline \end{array}$

18. $\begin{array}{r} 16 \\ -\ 9 \\ \hline \end{array}$

19. $\begin{array}{r} 13 \\ -\ 7 \\ \hline \end{array}$

20. $\begin{array}{r} 16 \\ -\ 8 \\ \hline \end{array}$

21. $\begin{array}{r} 11 \\ -\ 6 \\ \hline \end{array}$

22. $\begin{array}{r} 15 \\ -\ 9 \\ \hline \end{array}$

23. $\begin{array}{r} 13 \\ -\ 8 \\ \hline \end{array}$

24. $\begin{array}{r} 17 \\ -\ 9 \\ \hline \end{array}$

25. $\begin{array}{r} 18 \\ -\ 9 \\ \hline \end{array}$

26. $\begin{array}{r} 12 \\ -\ 4 \\ \hline \end{array}$

27. $\begin{array}{r} 15 \\ -\ 7 \\ \hline \end{array}$

28. $\begin{array}{r} 13 \\ -\ 6 \\ \hline \end{array}$

29. $\begin{array}{r} 12 \\ -\ 9 \\ \hline \end{array}$

30. $\begin{array}{r} 14 \\ -\ 8 \\ \hline \end{array}$

CHECK IT OUT

Use addition to check your answer.

Subtract   Check

$\begin{array}{r} 14 \\ -\ 9 \\ \hline 5 \end{array}$ ⟵ These should be the same. ⟶ $\begin{array}{r} 5 \\ +\ 9 \\ \hline 14 \end{array}$

31

Related Facts

You can write four related facts using these three numbers.

5 nickels in all.

3 show Thomas Jefferson.

2 show Monticello.

---

3 nickels show Jefferson.

2 show Monticello.

How many nickels in all?

$$\begin{array}{r} 3 \\ +2 \\ \hline 5 \end{array}$$

2 nickels show Monticello.

3 show Jefferson.

How many nickels in all?

$$\begin{array}{r} 2 \\ +3 \\ \hline 5 \end{array}$$

---

5 nickels in all.

3 show Jefferson.

How many show Monticello?

$$\begin{array}{r} 5 \\ -3 \\ \hline 2 \end{array}$$

5 nickels in all.

2 show Monticello.

How many show Jefferson?

$$\begin{array}{r} 5 \\ -2 \\ \hline 3 \end{array}$$

try these

Add. Then use the same numbers to write another addition fact.

1. 9
   +8

2. 8
   +5

3. 6
   +9

4. 7
   +8

5. 6
   +5

6. 3
   +8

Subtract. Then use the same numbers to write another subtraction fact.

7. 16
   − 9

8. 11
   − 7

9. 17
   − 8

10. 15
    − 6

11. 13
    − 4

12. 10
    − 7

now do these

Add. Then write another addition fact.

13. 5
    +8

14. 6
    +8

15. 4
    +9

16. 7
    +6

17. 3
    +7

18. 2
    +9

Subtract. Then write another subtraction fact.

19. 12
    − 4

20. 14
    − 5

21. 11
    − 2

22. 11
    − 3

23. 11
    − 5

24. 10
    − 8

Use the three numbers.
Write two addition facts and two subtraction facts.

25. 8, 5, 13

26. 6, 8, 14

27. 5, 7, 12

28. 3, 9, 12

29. 4, 6, 10

30. 7, 8, 15

AMAZO

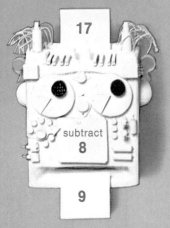

Put in a number.
Amazo subtracts 8.
Out comes the answer.

Copy and complete
the chart.

SUBTRACT 8

IN	OUT
17	9
14	?
16	?
13	?
15	?

33

Be Sure of Your Facts

Drive the car around the track without making a mistake.
Can you do it?   How fast are you?

First, drive car number 9.
(Subtract 9 from each number.)
Then try it with car number 8.

Drive car number 7.
(Subtract 7 from each number.)
Then try it with car number 6.

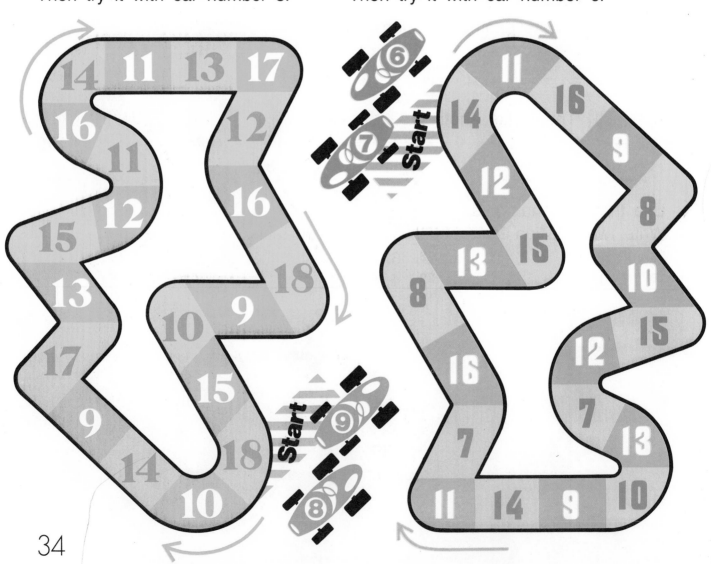

Drive car number 5.
(Subtract 5 from each number.)
Then try it with car number 4.

Drive car number 3.
(Subtract 3 from each number.)
Then try it with car number 2.

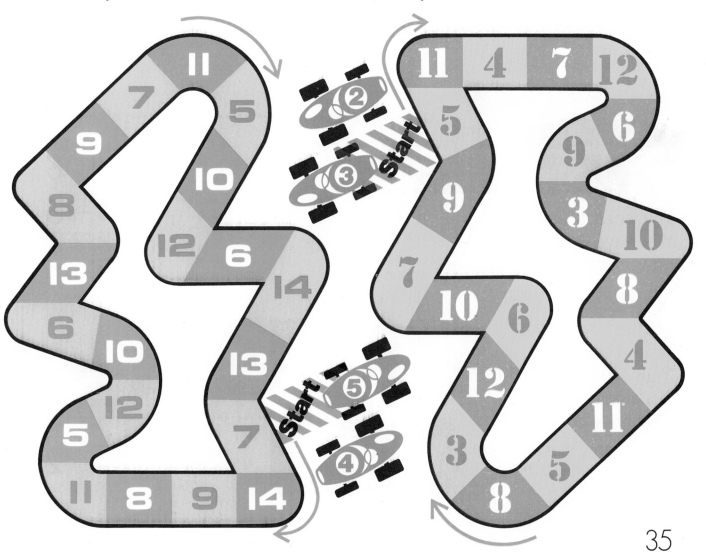

When to Subtract

Subtract to find how many are left.

You have 7 stamps.
You give 3 away.
How many do you have left?

$$\begin{array}{r} 7 \\ -3 \\ \hline 4 \end{array}$$

Subtract to find how many more you need.

You need 8 stamps.
You have 5.
How many more do you need?

$$\begin{array}{r} 8 \\ -5 \\ \hline 3 \end{array}$$

Subtract to compare.

Your friend has
5 stamps.
You have 3.
How many more does
your friend have?

   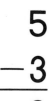

$$\begin{array}{r} 5 \\ -3 \\ \hline 2 \end{array}$$

try these

Solve the problem.

1. You have 12 stamps.
You lose 8 of them.
How many do
you have left?

2. You want 16 stamps.
You have 8.
How many more
do you need?

3. You have 7 stamps.
Jill has 15.
How many more
does Jill have?

now do these

Solve the problem.

4. 18 stamps are needed
for a package.
You have 9.
How many more
do you need?

5. Barney has 16 stamps.
He uses 7.
How many are left?

6. George has 9 stamps
from Europe.
Jane has 17. How
many more does
Jane have?

7. 14 stamps are
needed for a letter.
You have 7.
How many more
do you need?

8. 13 stamps are red.
6 are blue.
How many more
are red?

9. You have 11 stamps.
You use 7.
How many were
not used?

Subtracting Greater Numbers

Step 1	Step 2	Step 3	Step 4
4865 −1703 —— 2	4865 −1703 —— 62	4865 −1703 —— 162	4865 −1703 —— 3162
Subtract the ones.	Subtract the tens.	Subtract the hundreds.	Subtract the thousands.

Subtract amounts of money as if you were subtracting whole numbers. Remember to write the dollar sign and the cents point in the answer.

Step 1	Step 2	Step 3	Step 4
$48.65 −17.03 —— 2	$48.65 −17.03 —— 62	$48.65 −17.03 —— 162	$48.65 −17.03 —— $31.62

try these

Subtract.

1. 7835
−4215

2. 1689
− 530

3. 8790
−8600

4. 9876
−9843

5. 1778
− 362

6. $59.78
− 23.58

7. $18.75
− 6.20

8. $94.30
− 93.20

9. $19.69
− .45

10. $47.83
− 6.40

now do these

Subtract.

11. 5370
−3250

12. 1438
− 337

13. 1900
− 800

14. 9368
−6003

15. 7348
−5103

16. 8056
− 23

17. 7891
−6541

18. 9460
−5320

19. 8652
− 101

20. 5407
− 405

21. $89.76
− 87.42

22. $67.09
− 47.05

23. $19.65
− 7.65

24. $16.64
− .24

25. $78.87
− 65.47

HIDE AND SEEK

Some digits are hidden.
The digit under ■ is 6.
Do you see why?
Which digit is under ■?

```
  5 9 ■
− 3 1 4
  ■ 8 2
```

Which digits are hidden?

A.
```
  1 9 ■
−   2 3
  1 ■ 6
```

B.
```
  9 8 7
− ■ 4 ■
  2 4 2
```

C.
```
  1 7 ■
− 1 2 0
    ■ 0
```

D.
```
  9 9 ■
− 6 ■ 4
  3 8 2
```

39

add or subtract?

Some elevators in the Sears Tower are double-deck elevators. The first deck holds 30 people. The second deck holds 30 people. How many people does the elevator hold?

Think: Joining two groups.

Add.

$$\begin{array}{r} 30 \\ +30 \\ \hline 60 \end{array}$$

The elevator holds 60 people.

There are 89 elevators in the Sears Tower. 14 are double-deck elevators. The rest are single-deck elevators. How many single-deck elevators are there?

Think: Separating a group.

Subtract.

$$\begin{array}{r} 89 \\ -14 \\ \hline 75 \end{array}$$

There are 75 single-deck elevators.

How would you solve? Write ADD or SUBTRACT.

1. An express elevator goes to the Skydeck. It takes 55 seconds. You have already ridden for 14 seconds. How many more seconds are there to go?

2. There are 110 floors in the Sears Tower. The Skydeck is on floor 103. How many floors are above the Skydeck?

3. 18 people get on an empty elevator. 10 more get on. How many people are on the elevator now?

4. 24 people are in the top cab of a double-deck elevator. 19 people are in the bottom cab. How many people in all are on the elevator?

436 meters high

skydeck

89 elevators

stepback

over 16,000 windows

stepback

1500 person cafeteria

Solve the problem.

5. The Sears Tower has over 16,000 windows. The windows have been cleaned 3 times this year. They will be cleaned 5 more times. How many times in all will they be cleaned this year?

6. The top of the Sears Tower is 436 meters from the ground. The Skydeck is 406 meters from the ground. You are standing on the Skydeck. How far is it from you to the top of the tower?

7. The Sears Tower has 3 stepbacks. There are 50 floors from the ground to the first stepback. There are 66 floors from the ground to the second stepback. How many floors are there between the first stepback and the second stepback?

8. There are 90 floors from the ground to the third stepback. There are 20 more floors to the top. How many floors is this in all?

9. The cafeteria can seat 1500 people. 1200 people are already seated. How many more can be seated?

10. The Sears Tower is in Chicago. It is 436 meters tall. The World Trade Center is in New York City. It is 405 meters tall. Which is taller? How much taller?

41

Test

Add.

1. $9 + 6 = \underline{\ ?\ }$ (p. 20)   **2.** $4 + 8 = \underline{\ ?\ }$ (p. 20)

3. $\begin{array}{r} 7 \\ +8 \\ \hline \end{array}$ (p. 20)

4. $\begin{array}{r} 5 \\ +9 \\ \hline \end{array}$ (p. 20)

5. $\begin{array}{r} 3 \\ +8 \\ \hline \end{array}$ (p. 20)

6. $\begin{array}{r} 4 \\ 7 \\ +6 \\ \hline \end{array}$ (p. 26)

7. $\begin{array}{r} 5 \\ 3 \\ 8 \\ +2 \\ \hline \end{array}$ (p. 26)

8. $\begin{array}{r} 26 \\ +\ 4 \\ \hline \end{array}$ (p. 24)

9. $\begin{array}{r} 37 \\ +\ 9 \\ \hline \end{array}$ (p. 24)

10. $\begin{array}{r} 9642 \\ +\ 257 \\ \hline \end{array}$ (p. 28)

11. $\begin{array}{r} \$74.80 \\ +\ 13.05 \\ \hline \end{array}$ (p. 28)

12. $\begin{array}{r} \$71.43 \\ 1.33 \\ +\ 22.10 \\ \hline \end{array}$ (p. 28)

Subtract.

13. $16 - 8 = \underline{\ ?\ }$ (p. 30)   **14.** $12 - 5 = \underline{\ ?\ }$ (p. 30)

15. $\begin{array}{r} 18 \\ -\ 9 \\ \hline \end{array}$ (p. 30)

16. $\begin{array}{r} 11 \\ -\ 3 \\ \hline \end{array}$ (p. 30)

17. $\begin{array}{r} 17 \\ -\ 8 \\ \hline \end{array}$ (p. 30)

18. $\begin{array}{r} 13 \\ -\ 7 \\ \hline \end{array}$ (p. 30)

19. $\begin{array}{r} 12 \\ -\ 4 \\ \hline \end{array}$ (p. 30)

20. $\begin{array}{r} 2600 \\ -\ 300 \\ \hline \end{array}$ (p. 38)

21. $\begin{array}{r} 6087 \\ -\ 54 \\ \hline \end{array}$ (p. 38)

22. $\begin{array}{r} 9632 \\ -4501 \\ \hline \end{array}$ (p. 38)

23. $\begin{array}{r} \$53.62 \\ -\ 12.52 \\ \hline \end{array}$ (p. 38)

24. $\begin{array}{r} \$87.30 \\ -\ 77.10 \\ \hline \end{array}$ (p. 38)

Subtract.   Then use the same numbers to write another subtraction fact.

25. $\begin{array}{r} 14 \\ -\ 5 \\ \hline \end{array}$ (p. 32)

26. $\begin{array}{r} 16 \\ -\ 9 \\ \hline \end{array}$ (p. 32)

27. $\begin{array}{r} 11 \\ -\ 7 \\ \hline \end{array}$ (p. 32)

28. $\begin{array}{r} 15 \\ -\ 8 \\ \hline \end{array}$ (p. 32)

29. $\begin{array}{r} 12 \\ -\ 7 \\ \hline \end{array}$ (p. 32)

Use the three numbers.
Write two addition facts and two subtraction facts.

30. 4, 6, 10 (p. 32)   **31.** 5, 6, 11 (p. 32)

32. 5, 8, 13 (p. 32)   **33.** 6, 8, 14 (p. 32)

More Than One Correct Answer

Which numbers from 1 to 18 make this sentence true?

$$5 + 8 < \;?$$

13 does not. (5 + 8 is not less than 13.)
12 does not. (5 + 8 is not less than 12.)
14 does.   (5 + 8 is less than 14.)
So does 15.   (5 + 8 is less than 15.)
What about 16, 17, and 18?

Find the numbers that make this sentence true.

$$5 + 8 > \;?$$

The checks show the numbers that make the sentence true.

1	2	3	4	5	6	7	8	9	10	11	12	13	14	15	16	17	18
✔	✔	✔	✔	✔	✔	✔	✔	✔	✔	✔	✔						

Find the numbers from 1 to 18 that make the sentence true.

1. $6 + 4 > \underline{\;?\;}$ 2. $7 + 7 < \underline{\;?\;}$ 3. $13 - 6 > \underline{\;?\;}$ 4. $16 - 7 < \underline{\;?\;}$

5. $8 - 6 < \underline{\;?\;}$ 6. $3 + 4 > \underline{\;?\;}$ 7. $18 - 9 < \underline{\;?\;}$ 8. $4 + 8 > \underline{\;?\;}$

9. $14 - 5 > \underline{\;?\;}$ 10. $6 + 5 < \underline{\;?\;}$ 11. $17 - 9 > \underline{\;?\;}$ 12. $12 - 9 < \underline{\;?\;}$

3 Measurement

Once upon a time, parts of the body were used as units to measure things.

A person's outstretched arms make a **fathom.**

Another unit is the **hand.**

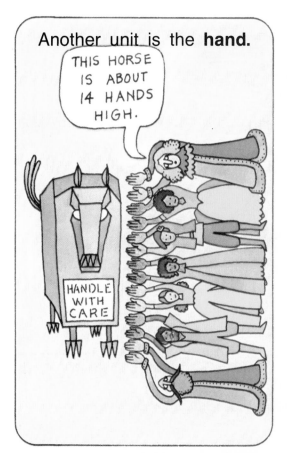

An open hand is a **span.**

And a foot is a **foot.**

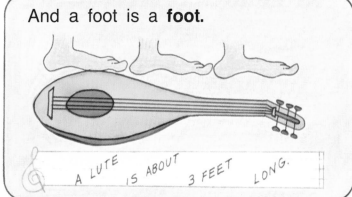

Projects for you and your friends.

1. Each of you use your fathom to measure the length of the classroom. Do you all get the same answer?

2. Use your hand to measure the width of a desk. Do you all get the same answer?

3. Use your span to measure the length of a desk. Do you all get the same answer?

4. Use your foot to measure the width of the classroom. Do you all get the same answer?

Centimeter

We use **standard units** to measure things.
Then everyone knows how long something is.
A **centimeter (cm)** is a standard unit of length.

Line up the end of the ruler with the end of the object.
The toothbrush is 14 cm long.

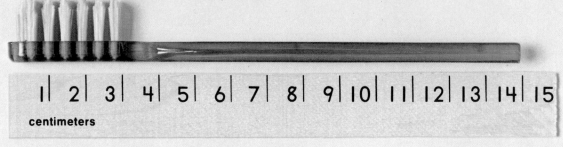

The length of this pencil is nearer to 11 cm than to 12 cm.
The length is 11 cm to the nearest centimeter.

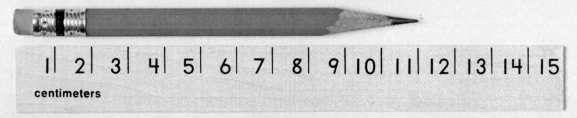

The length of this pencil seems to be midway between 12 and 13.
Most people think big and use 13.

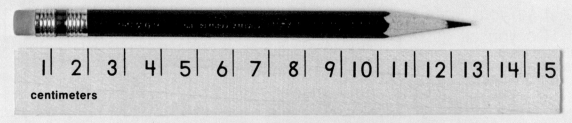

46

Measure the length to the nearest centimeter.

1.

2.

now do these

Measure the length to the nearest centimeter.

3.

4.

5.

6.

Millimeter

2 centimeters

20 millimeters

A **millimeter (mm)** is another standard unit.
A nickel is about 2 centimeters across.
A nickel is about 20 millimeters across.

10 millimeters make 1 centimeter.

Each mark on this ruler is for a millimeter.

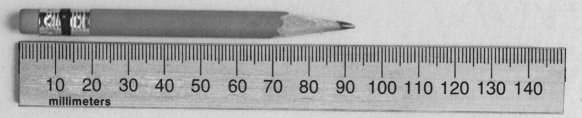

The pencil is about 93 mm long.

Suppose we sharpen the pencil.

Now the pencil is about 87 mm long.

48

Measure the length to the nearest millimeter.

1.
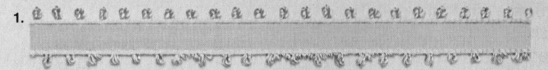

2.

Measure the length to the nearest millimeter.

3.

4.

5.

6.

Meter and Kilometer

A **meter (m)** is a standard unit.
A meter stick is 100 centimeters long.
Jack and Jenny are measuring
things with a meter stick.

About how many meters
high is the stove?

About how many meters
high is a door?

A **kilometer (km)** is a
standard unit.
**1000 meters make a
kilometer.**

It takes Jack and Jenny
about 12 minutes to walk
one kilometer.

Which unit would you use to measure?
Write MILLIMETER, CENTIMETER, METER, or KILOMETER.

1. Length of an ant.

2. Height of a person.

3. Height of a barn from the ground to the peak.

4. Distance from Atlanta, Georgia, to Chicago, Illinois.

now do these

Write YES or NO.

5. Are you taller than a meter?

6. Is your arm longer than a meter?

7. Is your desk wider than a meter?

8. Is your desk higher than a meter?

Choose the correct unit.

9. Kim is about 160 (centimeters, meters) tall.

10. Andrew's room is about 4 (centimeters, meters) wide.

11. A car is about 4 (centimeters, meters) long.

12. Jenny's window is about 78 (centimeters, meters) wide.

About how far is it from
13. San Francisco to New York?

14. San Francisco to Miami?

15. Miami to Chicago?

16. Chicago to San Francisco?

17. Chicago to New York?

18. New York to Miami?

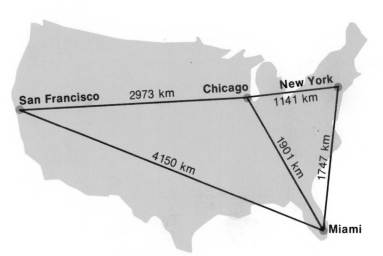

San Francisco   2973 km   Chicago   New York
1141 km
4150 km
1901 km
1747 km
Miami

51

Perimeter

The distance around a figure is its **perimeter.**

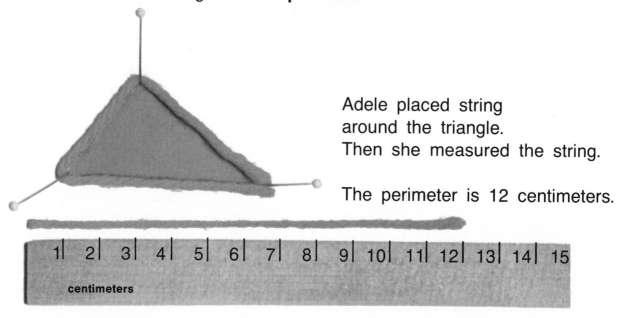

Adele placed string
around the triangle.
Then she measured the string.

The perimeter is 12 centimeters.

Adam measured each side.   Then he added the measures.

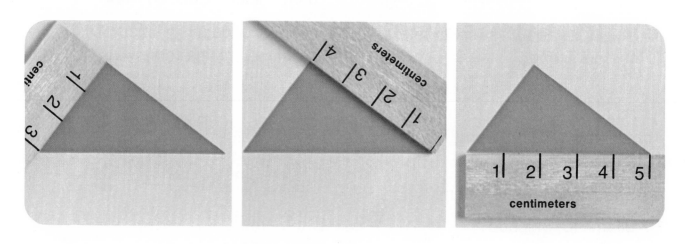

$$3 + 4 + 5 = 12$$

The perimeter is 12 centimeters.

Find the perimeter in centimeters.

1.

2.

now do these

Find the perimeter in centimeters.

3.

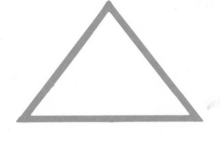

4.

5.

6.

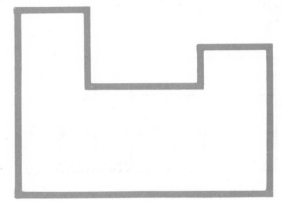

Area

The shape of the table top
is a rectangle.
The shape of each tile
is a square.
How many tiles are needed
to cover the table top?

To measure a surface,
we use square units.
The number of square units
is the **area** of the surface.
A **square centimeter**
is a unit of area.

try these

Find the area in square centimeters.

1.

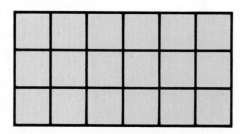

2.

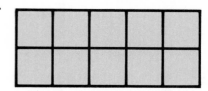

54

Find the area in square centimeters.

3.

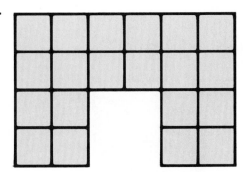

4.

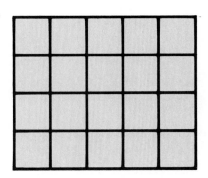

5.

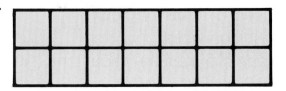

6.

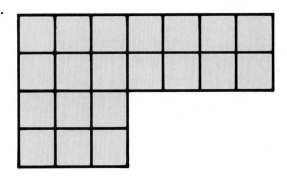

THINK ABOUT IT

How many square
centimeters of paper would it
take to cover all 6
sides of this box?

55

Gram and Kilogram

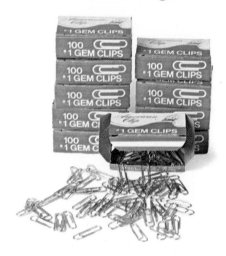

A **gram** is a standard unit.
It is used to measure how
much things weigh.
A paper clip weighs about one gram.

Think of 1000 paper clips.
They weigh about one **kilogram.**

1000 grams make 1 kilogram.

---

try these

Is each group GREATER THAN or LESS THAN a kilogram?

1.

680 grams

2.

312 grams each

3.

315 grams each

4.

737 grams each

now do these

Choose the answer that is reasonable.

5.

100 grams
100 kilograms

6.

2 grams
2 kilograms

7.

168 grams
168 kilograms

8.

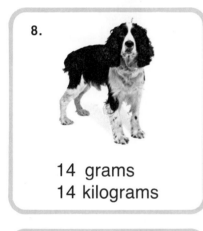

14 grams
14 kilograms

9.

310 grams
310 kilograms

10.

5 grams
5 kilograms

11.

896 grams
896 kilograms

12.

7 grams
7 kilograms

13.

54 grams
54 kilograms

Liter and Cup

A **liter** is a standard unit.
It is used to measure liquids.

4 metric cups make 1 liter.

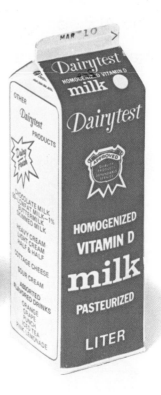

---

try these

Which holds more?

1.	2.	3.

2 cups or 1 liter	5 cups or 1 liter	7 cups or 2 liters

now do these

How many cups in each group?

4.

5.

6.

How many liters in each group?

7.

8.

9.

Choose the answer that is reasonable.

10.

A full gasoline
tank holds about

38 cups.
38 liters.

11.

The amount of water
Jack drinks each day
is about

5 cups.
5 liters.

12.

The amount of
water in this
fishtank is about

100 cups.
100 liters.

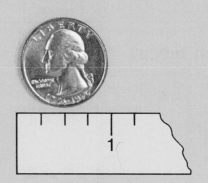

An **inch** is a standard
unit of length.
A quarter measures
about one inch across.

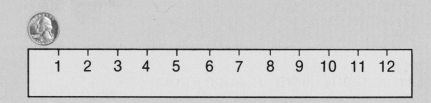

A **foot** is a standard
unit of length.
12 inches make 1 foot.

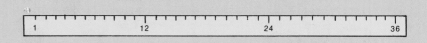

A **yard** is a standard
unit of length.
3 feet make 1 yard.
36 inches make 1 yard.

How many inches are in 4 feet?
You can add. ⟶ 12 + 12 + 12 + 12 = 48
You can also use this table.

yards			1			2			3			4			5
feet	1	2	3	4	5	6	7	8	9	10	11	12	13	14	15
inches	12	24	36	48	60	72	84	96	108	120	132	144	156	168	180

Find the missing number. Use the table.

1. 5 feet = _?_ inches   2. 7 feet = _?_ inches   3. 10 feet = _?_ inches

4. 1 yard = _?_ feet   5. 2 yards = _?_ feet   6. 3 yards = _?_ feet

7. 1 yard = _?_ inches   8. 2 yards = _?_ inches   9. 3 yards = _?_ inches

60 *Problem-solving Help*

Solve the problem.

10. Betsy is 6 feet tall.
How many inches is that?

11. Carl is 4 feet tall.
How many inches is that?

12. The backboard measures
72 inches across.
How many yards is that?

13. It is 120 inches from the
floor to the top of the basket.
How many feet is that?

14. The free throw line is 12 feet long.
How many inches is that?

15. It is 15 feet from the
free throw line to the
backboard.
How many yards is that?

16. The free throw circle is
4 yards across.
How many feet is that?

17. The target area is
24 inches wide.
How many feet is that?

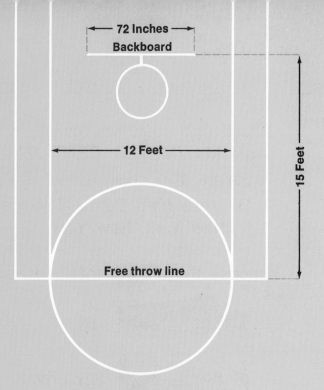

72 Inches
Backboard

12 Feet

15 Feet

Free throw line

Test

Which unit would you use to measure?
Write MILLIMETER, CENTIMETER, METER, or KILOMETER.

1. Height of a chair. (p. 50)

2. Height of an elephant. (p. 50)

3. Distance from Detroit, Michigan, to New York, New York. (p. 50)

4. Length of an apple seed. (p. 50)

Choose the answer that is reasonable.

5.

227 grams
227 kilograms
(p. 56)

6.

31 grams
31 kilograms
(p. 56)

7. How many cups? (p. 58)

8. How many liters? (p. 58)

9. Find the perimeter in centimeters. (p. 52)

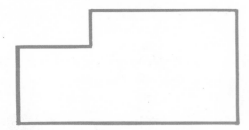

10. Find the area in square centimeters. (p. 54)

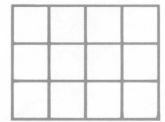

Other Units of Measure

A **quart** is a unit of
liquid measure.
It is slightly less than a liter.

2 pints make 1 quart.
4 quarts make 1 gallon.

pint   **quart**   **gallon**

Use the table to complete the sentences.

gallons				1				2				3
quarts	1	2	3	4	5	6	7	8	9	10	11	12
pints	2	4	6	8	10	12	14	16	18	20	22	24

1. 2 quarts = _?_ pints   2. 4 quarts = _?_ pints   3. 9 quarts = _?_ pints

4. 1 gallon = _?_ quarts   5. 2 gallons = _?_ quarts   6. 3 gallons = _?_ quarts

7. 1 gallon = _?_ pints   8. 2 gallons = _?_ pints   9. 3 gallons = _?_ pints

Try it the other way.

10. 4 pints = _?_ quarts   11. 10 pints = _?_ quarts   12. 22 pints = _?_ quarts

13. 8 pints = _?_ gallons   14. 24 pints = _?_ gallons   15. 16 pints = _?_ gallons

Enrichment 63

Thermometer

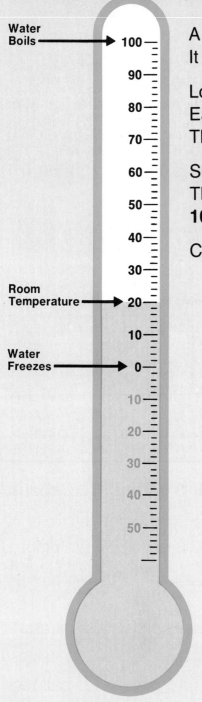

Water Boils — 100
90
80
70
60
50
40
30
Room Temperature — 20
10
Water Freezes — 0
10
20
30
40
50

A **degree Celsius** is a standard unit.
It is used to measure temperature.

Look at this thermometer.
Each mark stands for 2 degrees Celsius.
The temperature is **20 degrees Celsius above zero.**

Suppose the temperature falls 30 degrees.
The new temperature would be
10 degrees Celsius below zero.

Copy and complete this chart.

temperature (degrees Celsius)	change (degrees Celsius)	new temperature (degrees Celsius)
20 above 0	rises 9	29 above 0
4 above 0	falls 8	4 below 0
35 above 0	rises 4	?
24 above 0	falls 16	?
12 above 0	rises 15	?
3 below 0	rises 10	?
8 below 0	falls 15	?
20 below 0	falls 16	?
32 below 0	rises 22	?

4 Addition with Renaming

The Nearest Ten

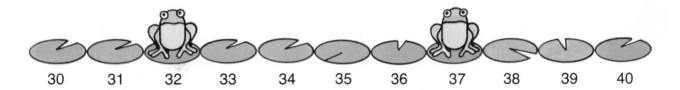

30   31   32   33   34   35   36   37   38   39   40

One frog is on 32.
Is it nearer to 30 or to 40?
  It is 2 hops from 30.
  It is 8 hops from 40.
The nearest ten is 30.

Another frog is on 37.
Is it nearer to 30 or to 40?
  It is 7 hops from 30.
  It is 3 hops from 40.
The nearest ten is 40.

Can you tell how to complete the chart?

the frog is on	hops from 30	hops from 40	the nearest ten
31	1	9	30
32	2	8	30
33	3	?	?
34	?	?	?
35	5	5	40
36	6	4	40
37	?	3	40
38	8	?	?
39	?	?	?

35 is halfway. Think big. Use 40.

65

Estimating Sums

Alan has 34 peppermint candies.
He has 27 spearmint candies.
How many candies does he have in all?

You can add the nearest tens to estimate sums.

NUMBERS		NEAREST TENS

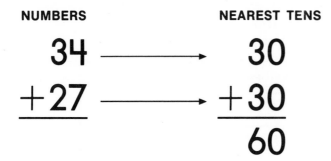

$$
\begin{array}{r}
34 \\
+27 \\
\hline
\end{array}
\longrightarrow
\begin{array}{r}
30 \\
+30 \\
\hline
60
\end{array}
$$

Alan has **about** 60 candies.

try these

Estimate the sum. Use the nearest tens.

1. $\begin{array}{r} 45 \\ +32 \\ \hline \end{array}$
2. $\begin{array}{r} 73 \\ +17 \\ \hline \end{array}$
3. $\begin{array}{r} 44 \\ +38 \\ \hline \end{array}$
4. $\begin{array}{r} 43 \\ 22 \\ +47 \\ \hline \end{array}$
5. $\begin{array}{r} 27 \\ 35 \\ +48 \\ \hline \end{array}$
6. $\begin{array}{r} 42 \\ 9 \\ +57 \\ \hline \end{array}$

66

now do these

Estimate the sum.   Use the nearest tens.

7. 28	8. 54	9. 46	10. 61	11. 45	12. 82
+38	+15	+49	+29	+67	+68

13. 56	14. 79	15. 72	16. 58	17. 84	18. 92
+66	+95	+83	+74	+35	+82

19. 62	20. 65	21. 91	22. 60	23. 87	24. 65
+58	+72	+73	+42	+42	+82

25. 25	26. 43	27. 18	28. 32	29. 18	30. 21
60	22	72	41	43	25
+62	+91	+13	+42	+25	+28

31. 55	32. 71	33. 17	34. 51	35. 32	36. 55
21	22	51	35	44	13
+43	+83	+62	+92	+15	+82

HIDE AND SEEK

Some digits are hidden.
The digit under ■ is 9.
Do you see why?
Which digit is under ■ ?

```
  4 ■ 2
+ 1 5 7
-------
  5 8 ■
```

Which digits are hidden?

A. ■ 7 3
    + 4 1 2
    ----
    1 1 ■ 5

B. 1 2 3
    + 4 ■ 6

    ■ 7 9

C. ■ 2 1
    + 6 5 ■
    ----
    1 5 7 5

D. ■ 1 ■
    + 6 4 5
    ----
    1 2 5 8

67

The Nearest Hundred and Estimating

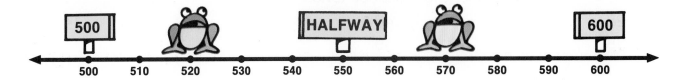

500   510   520   530   540   550   560   570   580   590   600

Find the frog on 520.
It is nearer to 500 than to 600.
The nearest hundred is 500.

Find the frog on 570.
It is nearer to 600 than to 500.
The nearest hundred is 600.

550 is halfway between 500 and 600.
Think big and use 600.

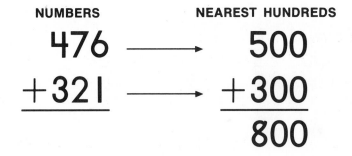

476 frogs in one pond.
321 in another pond.
How many frogs in both ponds?

You can add the nearest hundreds to estimate sums.

NUMBERS		NEAREST HUNDREDS
476	⟶	500
+321	⟶	+300
		800

There are **about** 800 frogs.

Choose the nearest hundred for the frog.

1.

300   334   350   400

2.

100   150   172   200

Estimate the sum. Use the nearest hundreds.

3. 325	4. 175	5. 232	6. 395	7. 365	8. 480
+434	+750	+589	143	550	99
			+201	+286	+210

---

now do these

Choose the nearest hundred for the frog.

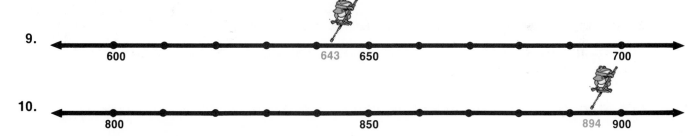

9.

600   643   650   700

10.

800   850   894   900

Estimate the sum. Use the nearest hundreds.

11. 425	12. 450	13. 735	14. 502	15. 224	16. 155
+113	+567	+152	+350	+667	+450

17. 235	18. 348	19. 259	20. 100	21. 179	22. 310
247	162	307	324	402	172
+262	+225	+350	+515	+250	+245

69

More Than Ten Ones

Count the ones.	Group ten ones to make one ten.	Write the numeral.
 15 ones	 1 ten 5 ones	15

Count the tens and ones.	Group ten ones to make one more ten.	Write the numeral.
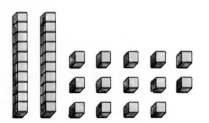 2 tens 14 ones	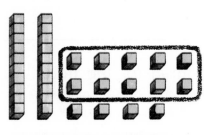 3 tens 4 ones	34

try these

Write the numeral to show tens and ones.

1.

2.

3.

70

Write the numeral to show tens and ones.

4.

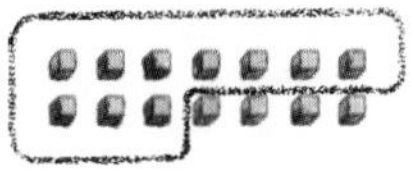

5.

6.

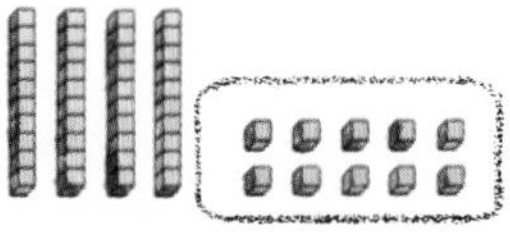

7.

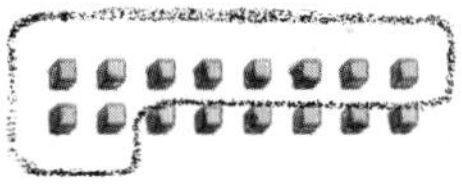

8.

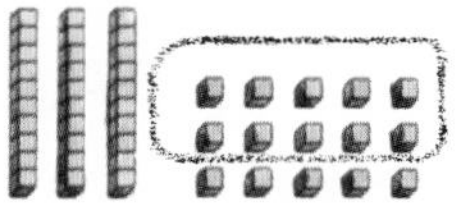

9.

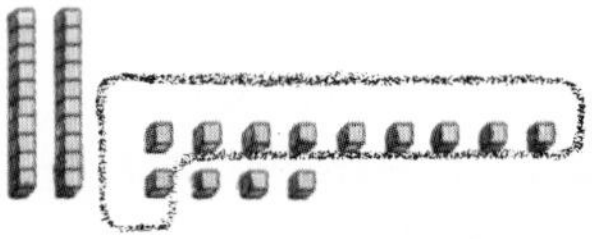

10.

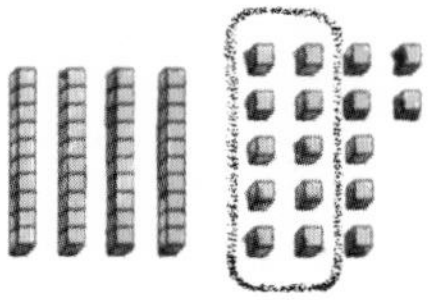

11.

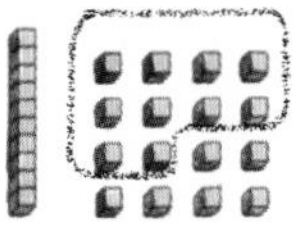

12.

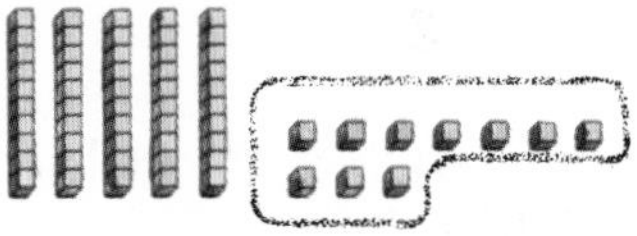

13.

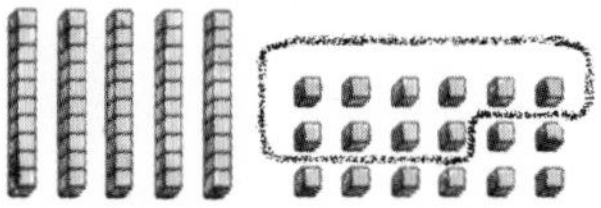

14.

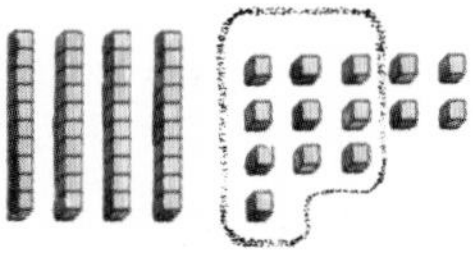

15.

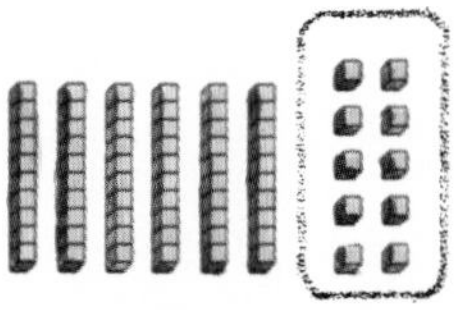

71

Addition With Renaming

Step 1

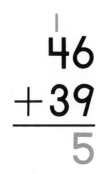

Add the ones.
Rename: Group ten ones to make one more ten.

Step 2

$$\begin{array}{r} 1 \\ 46 \\ +39 \\ \hline 85 \end{array}$$

Add the tens.

---

try these

Copy and complete.

1. 1 37 +48 5	2. 1 9 +23 2	3. 1 68 + 9 7	4. 1 94 +67 1	5. 1 5 +19 4	6. 1 49 + 9 8

Add.

7. 56 +48	8. 29 +34	9. 8 +94	10. 7 +38	11. 96 +65	12. 66 +54

72

Add.

13. 27
    +54

14. 79
    +58

15. 76
    +16

16. 87
    +98

17. 86
    +15

18. 18
    +68

19. 69
    +57

20. 27
    +65

21. 48
    +36

22. 27
    +47

23. 49
    +34

24. 65
    + 9

25. 7
    +56

26. 8
    +94

27. 58
    +27

28. 55
    + 8

29. 94
    +86

30. 27
    +44

31. 9
    +76

32. 47
    +45

33. 35
    +27

34. 4
    +95

35. 24
    + 9

36. 98
    +66

37. 4
    +88

38. 35
    +96

39. 4
    +96

40. 34
    + 9

41. 63
    +49

42. 8
    +48

I HAVE A PROBLEM

Decide: ADD or SUBTRACT.
Then solve the problem.

A. 47 peanut bars.
26 raisin bars.
How many in all?

B. 47 peanut bars.
26 given away.
How many left?

73

More Than Ten Tens

Count the tens and ones.

14 tens 3 ones

Group ten tens
to make one hundred.

1 hundred 4 tens 3 ones

Write the numeral.

143

Count the hundreds, tens,
and ones.

3 hundreds 12 tens 6 ones

Group ten tens
to make one more hundred.

4 hundreds 2 tens 6 ones

Write the numeral.

426

try these

Write the numeral to show hundreds, tens, and ones.

1.

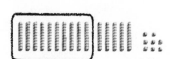

2.

Write the numeral to show hundreds, tens, and ones.

3.

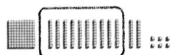

4.

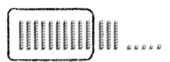

5.

6.

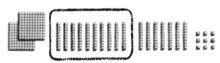

7.

8.

9.

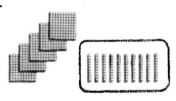

10.

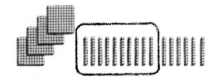

Addition With Renaming

Step 1

$$\begin{array}{r} 463 \\ +295 \\ \hline 8 \end{array}$$

Add the ones.

Step 2

$$\begin{array}{r} {\scriptstyle 1} \\ 463 \\ +295 \\ \hline 58 \end{array}$$

Add the tens.
Rename: Group ten tens
to make one more hundred.

Step 3

$$\begin{array}{r} {\scriptstyle 1} \\ 463 \\ +295 \\ \hline 758 \end{array}$$

Add the hundreds.

try these

Copy and complete.

1.
$$\begin{array}{r} {\scriptstyle 1} \\ 582 \\ +293 \\ \hline 75 \end{array}$$

2.
$$\begin{array}{r} {\scriptstyle 1} \\ 863 \\ +671 \\ \hline 34 \end{array}$$

3.
$$\begin{array}{r} {\scriptstyle 1} \\ 52 \\ +982 \\ \hline 34 \end{array}$$

4.
$$\begin{array}{r} {\scriptstyle 1} \\ 63 \\ +644 \\ \hline 07 \end{array}$$

5.
$$\begin{array}{r} {\scriptstyle 1} \\ 970 \\ +\ 30 \\ \hline 00 \end{array}$$

6.
$$\begin{array}{r} {\scriptstyle 1} \\ 31 \\ +998 \\ \hline 29 \end{array}$$

Add.

7.
$$\begin{array}{r} 52 \\ +955 \\ \hline \end{array}$$

8.
$$\begin{array}{r} 582 \\ +774 \\ \hline \end{array}$$

9.
$$\begin{array}{r} 991 \\ +\ 35 \\ \hline \end{array}$$

10.
$$\begin{array}{r} 40 \\ +860 \\ \hline \end{array}$$

11.
$$\begin{array}{r} 872 \\ +682 \\ \hline \end{array}$$

12.
$$\begin{array}{r} 513 \\ +590 \\ \hline \end{array}$$

Add.

13. 472 +543	**14.** 396 +240	**15.** 684 +185	**16.** 467 +351	**17.** 493 +670	**18.** 584 +763
19. 866 +563	**20.** 699 +690	**21.** 72 +973	**22.** 87 +652	**23.** 40 +398	**24.** 63 +786
25. 953 + 52	**26.** 862 + 44	**27.** 973 + 35	**28.** 987 + 22	**29.** 990 + 10	**30.** 382 +243
31. 770 +149	**32.** 60 +940	**33.** 492 +487	**34.** 773 +690	**35.** 42 +975	**36.** 70 +530
37. 794 +753	**38.** 75 +961	**39.** 381 +265	**40.** 365 +454	**41.** 460 + 63	**42.** 365 +454

quick check

Estimate the sum.
Use the nearest tens.

1. 43 +65	**2.** 15 32 +47

Estimate the sum.
Use the nearest hundreds.

3. 497 +350	**4.** 227 +559	**5.** 150 285 +435

Add.

6. 47 +35	**7.** 63 + 9	**8.** 408 + 39	**9.** 542 +371	**10.** 963 + 92

Renaming Twice

Step 1

$$\begin{array}{r} \overset{1}{5}38 \\ +296 \\ \hline 4 \end{array}$$

Add the ones.
Rename: Group ten ones to make one more ten.

Step 2

$$\begin{array}{r} \overset{1\;1}{5}38 \\ +296 \\ \hline 34 \end{array}$$

Add the tens.
Rename: Group ten tens to make one more hundred.

Step 3

$$\begin{array}{r} \overset{1\;1}{5}38 \\ +296 \\ \hline 834 \end{array}$$

Add the hundreds.

---

try these

Copy and complete.

1. $\begin{array}{r} \overset{1\;1}{6}57 \\ +267 \\ \hline 24 \end{array}$

2. $\begin{array}{r} \overset{1\;1}{6}76 \\ +489 \\ \hline 65 \end{array}$

3. $\begin{array}{r} \overset{1\;1}{7}05 \\ +597 \\ \hline 02 \end{array}$

4. $\begin{array}{r} \overset{1}{9}4 \\ +768 \\ \hline 2 \end{array}$

5. $\begin{array}{r} \overset{1}{9}68 \\ +\;85 \\ \hline 3 \end{array}$

6. $\begin{array}{r} \overset{1}{\;}43 \\ +657 \\ \hline 0 \end{array}$

Add.

7. $\begin{array}{r} 508 \\ +694 \\ \hline \end{array}$

8. $\begin{array}{r} 569 \\ +959 \\ \hline \end{array}$

9. $\begin{array}{r} 94 \\ +877 \\ \hline \end{array}$

10. $\begin{array}{r} 37 \\ +978 \\ \hline \end{array}$

11. $\begin{array}{r} 379 \\ +447 \\ \hline \end{array}$

12. $\begin{array}{r} 986 \\ +\;34 \\ \hline \end{array}$

now do these

Add.

13. 369
  +394

14. 457
  +274

15. 276
  +549

16. 288
  +688

17. 435
  +879

18. 558
  +487

19. 846
  +457

20. 575
  +666

21. 704
  +599

22. 796
  +709

23. 409
  +898

24. 794
  +407

25. 94
  +876

26. 985
  + 57

27. 94
  +638

28. 55
  +986

29. 287
  +267

30. 569
  +769

31. 305
  +698

32. 984
  + 78

33. 508
  +594

34. 47
  +954

35. 377
  +295

36. 754
  +879

37. 96
  +846

38. 476
  +475

39. 957
  + 48

40. 686
  +878

41. 356
  + 46

42. 89
  +417

DO YOU HAVE THE TIME?

The time is 3:05.
30 minutes from now, the time will be 3:35.

Look at the clock.
Tell what time it will be 30 minutes later.

A.

B.

C.

D.

79

More Than Two Addends

Step 1	Step 2	Step 3
2 458 329 +687 — 4	1 2 458 329 +687 — 74	1 2 458 329 +687 — 1474
Add the ones. Rename.	Add the tens. Rename.	Add the hundreds.

try these

Copy and complete.

	1 2		2 1		1 2		2		1		1
1.	877	**2.**	76	**3.**	408	**4.**	867	**5.**	836	**6.**	46
	417		863		707		56		979		370
	+738		+798		+385		+629		+ 13		+996
	32		37		00		2		8		2

Add.

7.	528	**8.**	807	**9.**	73	**10.**	854	**11.**	667	**12.**	35
	788		605		93		825		79		835
	+ 47		+796		+856		+945		+974		+735

80

now do these

Add.

13.	237	14.	283	15.	813	16.	353	17.	86	18.	94
	328		462		915		473		737		374
	+279		+379		+895		+198		+458		+667

19.	709	20.	98	21.	934	22.	583	23.	670	24.	893
	88		609		40		363		580		74
	+269		+295		+987		+ 72		+ 66		+844

25.	308	26.	106	27.	205	28.	89	29.	137	30.	538
	409		267		207		207		43		92
	+595		+398		+ 98		+587		+280		+705

31.	269	32.	973	33.	106	34.	458	35.	326	36.	43
	348		84		806		535		24		273
	253		63		583		647		215		683
	+315		+312		+353		+238		+ 83		+ 13

BE ON TIME

The time is 4:00.
You must be somewhere in 15 minutes.
You must be there at 4:15.

Look at the clock.
You must be somewhere in 15 minutes.
What time must you be there?

A.   **B.**   **C.**    **D.**

Renaming More Than Twice

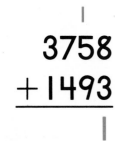

Step 1

```
   I
  3758
 +1493
     I
```

Add the ones.
Rename.

Step 2

```
   I I
  3758
 +1493
    51
```

Add the tens.
Rename.

Step 3

```
  I I I
  3758
 +1493
   251
```

Add the hundreds.
Rename.

Step 4

```
  I I I
  3758
 +1493
  5251
```

Add the thousands.

try these

Copy and complete.

1. 1 1 1	2. 1 1 1	3. 1 1	4. 1	5. 1
3769	4676	4069	86	4789
+2756	+5964	+7985	+7948	+ 789
525	640	54	4	8

Add.

6.	7.	8.	9.	10.
7054	66	8676	4769	9675
+5949	+8975	+8649	+2957	+ 435

82

now do these

Add.

| 11. 7369 +4394 | 12. 4578 +2749 | 13. 8828 +4868 | 14. 4356 +8792 | 15. 5548 +4837 |

| 16. 8469 +4578 | 17. 7046 +5997 | 18. 7964 +7092 | 19. 9794 +9407 | 20. 94 +2876 |

| 21. 947 +6382 | 22. 55 +6986 | 23. 2874 +2674 | 24. 5692 +7609 | 25. 3052 +6985 |

| 26. 5087 +9948 | 27. 476 +9457 | 28. 3776 +2953 | 29. 7342 + 768 | 30. 9324 + 678 |

| 31. 5526 7317 + 883 | 32. 8072 5065 +3969 | 33. 2654 49 +7972 | 34. 23 795 + 58 | 35. 834 264 +7454 |

HIDE AND SEEK

Some digits are hidden.
The digit under ■ is 6.
Do you see why?
The digit under ▨ is 8.
Do you see why?

```
  4 5 8
+ 3 7 ■
▨ 3 4
```

Which digits are hidden?

A.
```
  6 7 ■
+ 9 7 6
1 ▨ 5 4
```

B.
```
  7 5 ■
+ 8 ▨ 9
1 6 3 3
```

C.
```
  9 5 ■
+   4 8
1 0 ▨ 5
```

D.
```
  3 7 4 2
+ 2 ■ 7 8
▨ 7 2 0
```

83

Adding Amounts of Money

Add amounts of money as if you were adding whole numbers.
Remember to write the dollar sign and the cents point in the answer.

Step 1	Step 2	Step 3	Step 4
I	I	I I	I I
$27.38	$27.38	$27.38	$27.38
+14.56	+14.56	+14.56	+14.56
4	94	I 94	$41.94

Don't forget to write the dollar sign and the cents point in the answer.

Step 1	Step 2	Step 3	Step 4
I	I I	I I I	I I I
$15.25	$15.25	$15.25	$15.25
32.61	32.61	32.61	32.61
+14.98	+14.98	+14.98	+14.98
4	84	2 84	$62.84

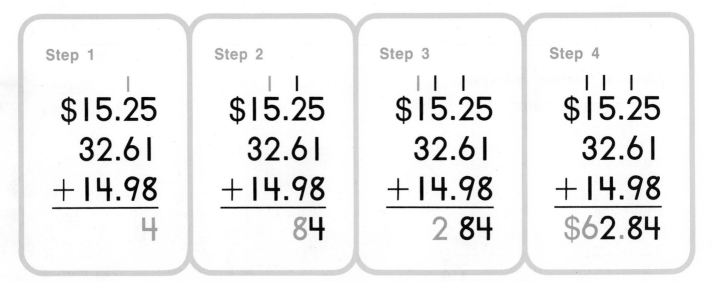

try these

Copy and complete.

1. $\begin{array}{r} {}^{1\ 1}\\ \$88.82 \\ +\ \ 48.86 \\ \hline 68 \end{array}$

2. $\begin{array}{r} {}^{1\ 1\ 1}\\ \$48.57 \\ +\ \ 29.74 \\ \hline 31 \end{array}$

3. $\begin{array}{r} {}^{\ \ \ 1}\\ \$70.39 \\ +\ \ 49.34 \\ \hline 73 \end{array}$

4. $\begin{array}{r} {}^{1\ 1\ 1}\\ \$23.05 \\ 36.00 \\ +\ \ 45.95 \\ \hline 0 \end{array}$

5. $\begin{array}{r} {}^{1\ 1\ 1}\\ \$\ \ 1.06 \\ 55.63 \\ +\ \ 93.94 \\ \hline 3 \end{array}$

Add.

6. $\begin{array}{r} \$\ \ \ .69 \\ +\ \ 43.71 \\ \hline \end{array}$

7. $\begin{array}{r} \$43.71 \\ +\ \ \ 6.89 \\ \hline \end{array}$

8. $\begin{array}{r} \$70.47 \\ +\ \ 50.46 \\ \hline \end{array}$

9. $\begin{array}{r} \$17.02 \\ 5.02 \\ +\ \ \ \ .96 \\ \hline \end{array}$

10. $\begin{array}{r} \$77.01 \\ .49 \\ +\ \ \ 3.78 \\ \hline \end{array}$

now do these

Add.

11. $\begin{array}{r} \$28.92 \\ +\ \ 76.09 \\ \hline \end{array}$

12. $\begin{array}{r} \$26.74 \\ +\ \ 56.92 \\ \hline \end{array}$

13. $\begin{array}{r} \$\ \ \ .49 \\ +\ \ 28.76 \\ \hline \end{array}$

14. $\begin{array}{r} \$\ \ 4.76 \\ +\ \ 74.75 \\ \hline \end{array}$

15. $\begin{array}{r} \$80.17 \\ +\ \ \ 8.90 \\ \hline \end{array}$

16. $\begin{array}{r} \$60.46 \\ +\ \ 39.97 \\ \hline \end{array}$

17. $\begin{array}{r} \$\ \ 9.47 \\ +\ \ 83.62 \\ \hline \end{array}$

18. $\begin{array}{r} \$69.73 \\ +\ \ 94.43 \\ \hline \end{array}$

19. $\begin{array}{r} \$78.45 \\ +\ \ 49.27 \\ \hline \end{array}$

20. $\begin{array}{r} \$\ \ 6.39 \\ +\ \ 38.59 \\ \hline \end{array}$

21. $\begin{array}{r} \$\ \ 2.32 \\ 73.28 \\ +\ \ 85.72 \\ \hline \end{array}$

22. $\begin{array}{r} \$93.42 \\ 82.22 \\ +\ \ 71.93 \\ \hline \end{array}$

23. $\begin{array}{r} \$63.11 \\ 5.12 \\ +\ \ 75.89 \\ \hline \end{array}$

24. $\begin{array}{r} \$33.37 \\ 4.53 \\ +\ \ 81.70 \\ \hline \end{array}$

25. $\begin{array}{r} \$32.43 \\ .86 \\ +\ \ \ 7.14 \\ \hline \end{array}$

26. $\begin{array}{r} \$\ \ 9.45 \\ 20.40 \\ +\ \ 30.89 \\ \hline \end{array}$

27. $\begin{array}{r} \$\ \ 9.73 \\ 10.48 \\ +\ \ 80.90 \\ \hline \end{array}$

28. $\begin{array}{r} \$61.06 \\ 78.06 \\ +\ \ 85.80 \\ \hline \end{array}$

29. $\begin{array}{r} \$\ \ 4.58 \\ 5.35 \\ +\ \ 76.42 \\ \hline \end{array}$

30. $\begin{array}{r} \$\ \ 9.73 \\ 29.40 \\ +\ \ \ 2.12 \\ \hline \end{array}$

85

do you have enough money?

Allison Wonderland wants to buy these tickets.
She has $2.00. Does she have enough money?

SWISS
FAMILY
ROBINSON
$.25

IT'S A
SMALL
WORLD
$.85

You can estimate.   You can add.

$ .30 $ .25
+ .90   + .85
———   ———
$1.20 $1.10

Yes, Allison has enough money.

1. Is $2.00 enough to buy the tickets?
   Write YES or NO.

SWISS
FAMILY
ROBINSON
$.25

PETER
PAN
FLIGHT
$.40

CANOES
$.70

2. Is $2.00 enough to buy the tickets?
   Write YES or NO.

DUMBO'S
FLYING
ELEPHANTS
$.40

COUNTRY
BEAR
JAMBOREE
$.85

AMERICA
SINGS
$.85

Do you have enough money? Write YES or NO.

3. You have $2.00.

| TOM SAWYER'S ISLAND **$.70** | IT'S A SMALL WORLD **$.85** |

4. You have $2.00.

| CANOES **$.70** | STORY BOOK CANAL BOAT **$.70** | AMERICA SINGS **$.85** |

5. You have $.50.

| SLEEPING BEAUTY CASTLE **$.10** | PETER PAN FLIGHT **$.40** |

6. You have $.50.

| MOTORBOAT CRUISE **$.25** | MAD TEA PARTY **$.40** |

7. You have $1.50.

| IT'S A SMALL WORLD **$.85** | AMERICA SINGS **$.85** |

8. You have $2.25.

| KING ARTHUR'S CAROUSEL **$.10** | TOM SAWYER'S ISLAND **$.70** | AMERICA SINGS **$.85** |

9. You have $1.50.

| STORY BOOK CANAL BOAT **$.70** | COUNTRY BEAR JAMBOREE **$.85** |

10. You have $2.25.

| IT'S A SMALL WORLD **$.85** | COUNTRY BEAR JAMBOREE **$.85** | AMERICA SINGS **$.85** |

Problem-solving Help 87

Test

Estimate the sum.
Use the nearest tens.

1. 45
  +32
  (p. 66)

2. 17
  43
  +28
  (p. 66)

Estimate the sum.
Use the nearest hundreds.

3. 403
  +580
  (p. 68)

4. 176
  234
  +350
  (p. 68)

5. 299
  443
  +550
  (p. 68)

Add.

6. 8
  +65
  (p. 72)

7. 34
  + 7
  (p. 72)

8. 136
  + 54
  (p. 72)

9. 847
  + 62
  (p. 76)

10. 70
  +460
  (p. 76)

11. 555
  + 76
  (p. 78)

12. 834
  +388
  (p. 78)

13. 365
  +498
  (p. 78)

14. 721
  +999
  (p. 78)

15. 698
  +143
  (p. 78)

16. 123
  456
  +789
  (p. 80)

17. 768
  439
  +124
  (p. 80)

18. 548
  386
  +254
  (p. 80)

19. 103
  405
  976
  +283
  (p. 80)

20. 647
  85
  13
  +349
  (p. 80)

21. 7618
  +4986
  (p. 82)

22. 9575
  + 688
  (p. 82)

23. $35.07
  + 54.96
  (p. 84)

24. $38.27
  14.05
  + 9.92
  (p. 84)

25. $66.13
  2.18
  + 77.87
  (p. 84)

bonus

Solve the problem.

26. 25 adults.
    37 children.
    How many people in all?
    (p. 72)

27. A book costs $4.85.
    Another book costs $3.71.
    What is the total cost of both books?
    (p. 84)

Magic Squares

This is a magic square.
Add down each column. Add across each row. Add along each diagonal.

25	11	21
15	19	23
17	27	13

25	11	21
15	19	23
17	27	13

25	11	21
15	19	23
17	27	13

All the sums are the same. It is a magic square.
Which of these are magic squares?

A.

19	12	17
14	16	18
15	20	13

B.

21	22	23
23	21	22
22	23	21

C.

32	39	34
37	35	33
36	31	38

Try to make these into magic squares.

1.

4	9	2
3	5	?
?	1	?

2.

15	1	11
?	9	?
7	?	3

3.

8	1	?
?	5	7
4	?	2

5 Subtraction with Renaming

Estimating Answers

You can subtract the nearest tens to estimate answers.

	NUMBERS		NEAREST TENS
Julie has 58 boxes of candy. She sells 22. How many boxes are left?	58 -22	$\longrightarrow$ $\longrightarrow$	60 -20 40

Julie has **about** 40 boxes left.

You can subtract the nearest hundreds to estimate answers.

	NUMBERS		NEAREST HUNDREDS
Jim has 432 candy bars. He sells 185. How many are left?	432 -185	$\longrightarrow$ $\longrightarrow$	400 -200 200

Jim has **about** 200 left.

Estimate. Use the nearest tens.

1. 44	2. 73	3. 64	4. 62	5. 35	6. 87
−23	−54	−54	−33	−15	−75

Estimate. Use the nearest hundreds.

7. 643	8. 432	9. 782	10. 943	11. 525	12. 439
−235	−253	−653	−722	−210	−248

now do these

Estimate. Use the nearest tens.

13. 27	14. 85	15. 43	16. 32	17. 63	18. 79
−13	−63	−24	−25	−42	−32

Estimate. Use the nearest hundreds.

19. 758	20. 492	21. 346	22. 683	23. 879	24. 587
−296	−235	−255	−357	−267	−324

HIDE AND SEEK

Some digits are hidden.
The digit under ▒ is 3.
Do you see why?
The digit under ■ is 7.
Do you see why?

```
  5 ▒ 4
− 2 5 1
  3 2 ■
```

Which digits are hidden?

A. 8 3 ▒	B. ■ 9 9	C. 8 ▒ 9	D. 5 6 ▒
− 7 0 4	− 6 ■	− ■ 0 7	− ■ 7
1 ■ 1	9 3 6	3 2	5 3 1

91

Renaming Tens as Ones

Rename: Show one fewer ten and ten more ones.

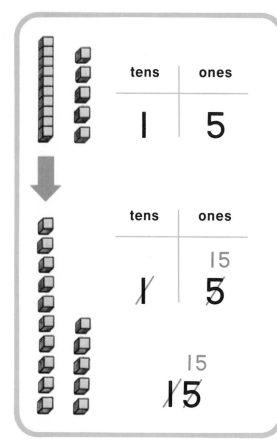

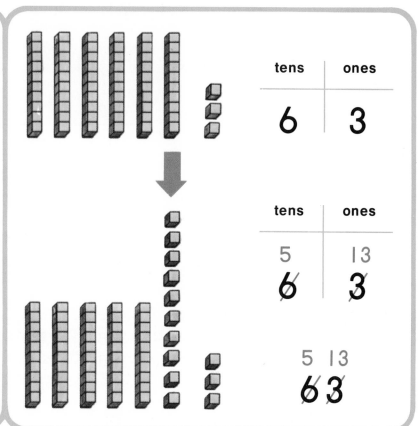

---

try these

Copy. Rename: Show one fewer ten and ten more ones.

1.

tens	ones
3	6

2.

tens	ones
8	9

3.

tens	ones
6	0

4. 73   5. 26   6. 30   7. 94   8. 53   9. 20

92

Copy. Rename: Show one fewer ten and ten more ones.

10.	tens	ones
	5	6

11.	tens	ones
	8	7

12.	tens	ones
	6	5

13.	tens	ones
	7	8

14.	tens	ones
	9	0

15.	tens	ones
	3	4

16. 67   17. 32   18. 74   19. 23   20. 59   21. 60

22. 12   23. 80   24. 18   25. 51   26. 77   27. 11

28. 20   29. 48   30. 99   31. 41   32. 66   33. 50

PATTERNS

Each number is five greater than the number named before it. What are the next two numbers?

3	8	13	?	?

What are the next two numbers in the pattern?

A.
4	11	18	?	?

B.
5	25	45	?	?

C.
6	47	88	?	?

D.
9	139	269	?	?

Subtraction With Renaming

Step 1	Step 2	Step 3
$$\begin{array}{r} {\scriptstyle 7\ 12} \\ 58\!\!\!/2 \\ -147 \\ \hline 5 \end{array}$$	$$\begin{array}{r} {\scriptstyle 7\ 12} \\ 58\!\!\!/2 \\ -147 \\ \hline 35 \end{array}$$	$$\begin{array}{r} {\scriptstyle 7\ 12} \\ 58\!\!\!/2 \\ -147 \\ \hline 435 \end{array}$$
Rename: Show one fewer ten and ten more ones. Subtract the ones.	Subtract the tens.	Subtract the hundreds.

try these

Copy and complete.

$\scriptstyle 7\ 13$	$\scriptstyle 5\ 14$	$\scriptstyle 5\ 12$	$\scriptstyle 6\ 11$	$\scriptstyle 8\ 10$	$\scriptstyle 1\ 10$
1. $8\!\!\!/3$	**2.** $6\!\!\!/4$	**3.** $56\!\!\!/2$	**4.** $57\!\!\!/1$	**5.** $39\!\!\!/0$	**6.** $62\!\!\!/0$
-47	-58	$-\ 46$	-264	-379	$-\ 8$
6	6	6	7	1	2

Subtract.

7. 94	**8.** 63	**9.** 473	**10.** 156	**11.** 753	**12.** 430
-87	-39	-468	$-\ 49$	-346	$-\ 25$

94

now do these

Subtract.

13. 78
   −39

14. 84
   −56

15. 62
   −57

16. 91
   −78

17. 43
   −35

18. 70
   −39

19. 82
   −74

20. 64
   −49

21. 75
   −67

22. 52
   −43

23. 81
   −36

24. 92
   − 7

25. 764
   − 35

26. 571
   −267

27. 396
   − 48

28. 853
   −644

29. 642
   − 28

30. 810
   − 3

31. 671
   −365

32. 855
   −446

33. 252
   − 39

34. 796
   −287

35. 865
   − 38

36. 640
   −327

37. 867
   −858

38. 391
   −252

39. 452
   −224

40. 393
   −385

41. 983
   −656

42. 451
   − 38

A RIDDLE

Each sum stands for a letter.
Find the sums. Then solve the riddle.

27	39	44	61	38	47	32	52
+25	+26	+28	+19	+19	+37	+21	+46
E	I	D	S	O	U	T	H

53 − 98 − 52   57 − 84 − 53 − 80 − 65 − 72 − 52

Which side of a chicken
has the most feathers?

95

Renaming Hundreds as Tens

Rename: Show one fewer hundred and ten more tens.

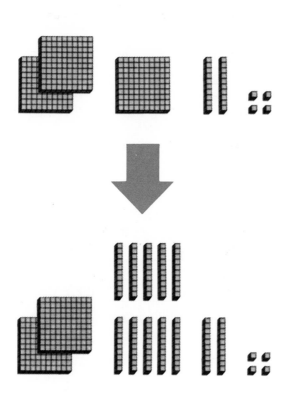

hundreds	tens	ones
3	2	4

hundreds	tens	ones
2	12	
3	2	4

2 12
324

---

try these

Copy. Rename: Show one fewer hundred and ten more tens.

1.

hundreds	tens	ones
3	4	5

2.

hundreds	tens	ones
4	5	6

3.

hundreds	tens	ones
8	0	9

4. 373   **5.** 644   **6.** 425   **7.** 617   **8.** 904   **9.** 831

Copy. Rename: Show one fewer hundred and ten more tens.

10.

hundreds	tens	ones
4	8	7

11.

hundreds	tens	ones
8	6	7

12.

hundreds	tens	ones
5	1	8

13.

hundreds	tens	ones
9	0	2

14.

hundreds	tens	ones
1	0	3

15.

hundreds	tens	ones
1	5	0

16. 684   **17.** 204   **18.** 719   **19.** 125   **20.** 433   **21.** 666

22. 108   **23.** 301   **24.** 505   **25.** 700   **26.** 538   **27.** 300

28. 107   **29.** 662   **30.** 857   **31.** 501   **32.** 400   **33.** 809

PATTERNS

Each number is five less than the number named before it. What are the next two numbers?

24	19	14	?	?

What are the next two numbers in the pattern?

A.

35	27	19	?	?

B.

77	60	43	?	?

C.

389	376	363	?	?

D.

678	575	472	?	?

97

Subtraction With Renaming

Step 1

$$\begin{array}{r} 628 \\ -152 \\ \hline 6 \end{array}$$

Look at the ones.
No need to
rename.
Subtract the ones.

Step 2

$$\begin{array}{r} {\scriptstyle 5\ 12} \\ 6\!\!\!/28 \\ -152 \\ \hline 6 \end{array}$$

Look at the tens.
5 is greater
than 2.
Rename: Show
one fewer hundred
and ten more tens.

Step 3

$$\begin{array}{r} {\scriptstyle 5\ 12} \\ 6\!\!\!/28 \\ -152 \\ \hline 76 \end{array}$$

Subtract the
tens.

Step 4

$$\begin{array}{r} {\scriptstyle 5\ 12} \\ 6\!\!\!/28 \\ -152 \\ \hline 476 \end{array}$$

Subtract the
hundreds.

---

try these

Copy and complete.

1.
$$\begin{array}{r} {\scriptstyle 4\ 13} \\ 5\!\!\!/39 \\ -273 \\ \hline 66 \end{array}$$

2.
$$\begin{array}{r} {\scriptstyle 8\ 17} \\ 9\!\!\!/78 \\ -498 \\ \hline 80 \end{array}$$

3.
$$\begin{array}{r} {\scriptstyle 1\ 14} \\ 2\!\!\!/46 \\ -\ 83 \\ \hline 63 \end{array}$$

4.
$$\begin{array}{r} {\scriptstyle 7\ 13} \\ 8\!\!\!/35 \\ -760 \\ \hline 5 \end{array}$$

5.
$$\begin{array}{r} {\scriptstyle 8\ 12} \\ 9\!\!\!/27 \\ -\ 57 \\ \hline 0 \end{array}$$

6.
$$\begin{array}{r} {\scriptstyle 4\ 10} \\ 5\!\!\!/06 \\ -186 \\ \hline 0 \end{array}$$

Subtract.

7.
$$\begin{array}{r} 746 \\ -696 \\ \hline \end{array}$$

8.
$$\begin{array}{r} 159 \\ -\ 73 \\ \hline \end{array}$$

9.
$$\begin{array}{r} 627 \\ -503 \\ \hline \end{array}$$

10.
$$\begin{array}{r} 643 \\ -\ 73 \\ \hline \end{array}$$

11.
$$\begin{array}{r} 858 \\ -380 \\ \hline \end{array}$$

12.
$$\begin{array}{r} 702 \\ -\ 41 \\ \hline \end{array}$$

now do these

Subtract.

13. 987 −694	14. 716 −683	15. 844 −662	16. 529 −471	17. 918 −347	18. 608 −415
19. 126 − 53	20. 867 −473	21. 715 −665	22. 132 − 92	23. 728 −283	24. 926 − 73
25. 216 −136	26. 748 − 73	27. 457 −393	28. 929 −767	29. 123 − 52	30. 405 − 31
31. 752 −160	32. 825 − 71	33. 630 −580	34. 968 −778	35. 169 − 87	36. 800 −250
37. 426 − 55	38. 774 −492	39. 516 −231	40. 307 −145	41. 525 − 72	42. 450 −160

quick check

Estimate.
Use the nearest tens.

1. 34 −12	2. 85 −62

Estimate.
Use the nearest hundreds.

3. 476 −335	4. 850 −250	5. 916 −798

Subtract.

6. 73 −18	7. 60 −25	8. 876 −439	9. 394 − 57	10. 482 −190

Renaming Twice

Step 1

$$
\begin{array}{r}
{\scriptstyle 3\;12} \\
8\cancel{4}\cancel{2} \\
-367 \\
\hline
5
\end{array}
$$

Look at the ones.
7 is greater than 2.
Rename: Show one
fewer ten and ten
more ones.
Subtract the ones.

Step 2

$$
\begin{array}{r}
{\scriptstyle 13} \\
{\scriptstyle 7\;3\;12} \\
\cancel{8}\cancel{4}\cancel{2} \\
-367 \\
\hline
75
\end{array}
$$

Look at the tens.
6 is greater than 3.
Rename: Show one
fewer hundred and
ten more tens.
Subtract the tens.

Step 3

$$
\begin{array}{r}
{\scriptstyle 13} \\
{\scriptstyle 7\;3\;12} \\
\cancel{8}\cancel{4}\cancel{2} \\
-367 \\
\hline
475
\end{array}
$$

Subtract the
hundreds.

Use addition to check your answers.

Subtract		Check
842		475
−367	These should	+367
475	be the same.	842

try these

Copy and complete.

1.
```
    14
  5 4 13
  6 5 3
-2 8 7
───────
    6 6
```

2.
```
    16
  5 6 11
  6 7 1
-5 8 9
───────
      2
```

3.
```
     12
  7 2 10
  8 3 0
-   3 7
───────
    9 3
```

4.
```
    13
  6 3 16
  7 4 6
-3 6 8
───────
    7 8
```

5.
```
    10
  6 0 13
  7 1 3
-   5 7
───────
      6
```

6.
```
    11
  3 1 15
  4 2 5
-1 6 7
───────
      8
```

Subtract.

7.
```
 946
-847
────
```

8.
```
 542
- 75
────
```

9.
```
 561
-478
────
```

10.
```
 512
-346
────
```

11.
```
 635
- 57
────
```

12.
```
 250
- 58
────
```

now do these

Subtract.

13.
```
 787
-389
────
```

14.
```
 421
-367
────
```

15.
```
 674
-376
────
```

16.
```
 438
-359
────
```

17.
```
 263
-166
────
```

18.
```
 954
- 68
────
```

19.
```
 542
-467
────
```

20.
```
 953
- 68
────
```

21.
```
 986
-389
────
```

22.
```
 960
-468
────
```

23.
```
 563
-489
────
```

24.
```
 721
-386
────
```

25.
```
 814
-575
────
```

26.
```
 832
- 48
────
```

27.
```
 753
-555
────
```

28.
```
 724
-259
────
```

29.
```
 535
-489
────
```

30.
```
 732
-484
────
```

31.
```
 340
-289
────
```

32.
```
 721
- 45
────
```

33.
```
 570
-478
────
```

34.
```
 394
- 96
────
```

35.
```
 561
-277
────
```

36.
```
 636
-559
────
```

37.
```
 947
- 79
────
```

38.
```
 622
-368
────
```

39.
```
 531
-478
────
```

40.
```
 842
- 49
────
```

41.
```
 650
- 54
────
```

42.
```
 820
-571
────
```

101

Zero in Subtraction

Step 1

$$\begin{array}{r} {}^{6\ 10}\!\!\!\!\!\!\!\!\!\!\!\! \\ 7\cancel{0}4 \\ -236 \\ \hline \end{array}$$

6 is greater than 4. You must rename. There are 0 tens. Rename: Show one fewer hundred and ten more tens.

Step 2

$$\begin{array}{r} {}^{9}\!\!\!\!\!\!\!\!\!\!\!\! \\ {}^{6\ 10\ 14} \\ \cancel{7}\cancel{0}\cancel{4} \\ -236 \\ \hline 8 \end{array}$$

Now rename the tens. Show one fewer ten and ten more ones. Subtract the ones.

Step 3

$$\begin{array}{r} {}^{9}\!\!\!\!\!\!\!\!\!\!\!\! \\ {}^{6\ 10\ 14} \\ \cancel{7}\cancel{0}\cancel{4} \\ -236 \\ \hline 68 \end{array}$$

Subtract the tens.

Step 4

$$\begin{array}{r} {}^{9}\!\!\!\!\!\!\!\!\!\!\!\! \\ {}^{6\ 10\ 14} \\ \cancel{7}\cancel{0}\cancel{4} \\ -236 \\ \hline 468 \end{array}$$

Subtract the hundreds.

Step 1

$$\begin{array}{r} {}^{4\ 10}\!\!\!\!\!\!\!\!\!\!\!\! \\ 5\cancel{0}0 \\ -198 \\ \hline \end{array}$$

8 is greater than 0. You must rename. There are 0 tens. Rename: Show one fewer hundred and ten more tens.

Step 2

$$\begin{array}{r} {}^{9}\!\!\!\!\!\!\!\!\!\!\!\! \\ {}^{4\ 10\ 10} \\ \cancel{5}\cancel{0}\cancel{0} \\ -198 \\ \hline 2 \end{array}$$

Now rename the tens. Show one fewer ten and ten more ones. Subtract the ones.

Step 3

$$\begin{array}{r} {}^{9}\!\!\!\!\!\!\!\!\!\!\!\! \\ {}^{4\ 10\ 10} \\ \cancel{5}\cancel{0}\cancel{0} \\ -198 \\ \hline 02 \end{array}$$

Subtract the tens.

Step 4

$$\begin{array}{r} {}^{9}\!\!\!\!\!\!\!\!\!\!\!\! \\ {}^{4\ 10\ 10} \\ \cancel{5}\cancel{0}\cancel{0} \\ -198 \\ \hline 302 \end{array}$$

Subtract the hundreds.

Copy and complete.

1. $\begin{array}{r} \overset{9}{\overset{6\ \cancel{10}\ 10}{\cancel{700}}} \\ -346 \\ \hline 54 \end{array}$

2. $\begin{array}{r} \overset{9}{\overset{3\ \cancel{10}\ 15}{\cancel{405}}} \\ -238 \\ \hline 67 \end{array}$

3. $\begin{array}{r} \overset{9}{\overset{4\ \cancel{10}\ 16}{\cancel{506}}} \\ -\ 97 \\ \hline 09 \end{array}$

4. $\begin{array}{r} \overset{9}{\overset{7\ \cancel{10}\ 10}{\cancel{800}}} \\ -\ 37 \\ \hline 3 \end{array}$

5. $\begin{array}{r} \overset{9}{\overset{5\ \cancel{10}\ 13}{\cancel{603}}} \\ -\ 19 \\ \hline 4 \end{array}$

6. $\begin{array}{r} \overset{9}{\overset{2\ \cancel{10}\ 14}{\cancel{304}}} \\ -297 \\ \hline \end{array}$

Subtract.

7. $\begin{array}{r} 607 \\ -199 \\ \hline \end{array}$

8. $\begin{array}{r} 806 \\ -\ 59 \\ \hline \end{array}$

9. $\begin{array}{r} 704 \\ -698 \\ \hline \end{array}$

10. $\begin{array}{r} 802 \\ -406 \\ \hline \end{array}$

11. $\begin{array}{r} 600 \\ -123 \\ \hline \end{array}$

12. $\begin{array}{r} 500 \\ -465 \\ \hline \end{array}$

Subtract.

13. $\begin{array}{r} 905 \\ -349 \\ \hline \end{array}$

14. $\begin{array}{r} 502 \\ -194 \\ \hline \end{array}$

15. $\begin{array}{r} 800 \\ -\ 35 \\ \hline \end{array}$

16. $\begin{array}{r} 504 \\ -499 \\ \hline \end{array}$

17. $\begin{array}{r} 307 \\ -199 \\ \hline \end{array}$

18. $\begin{array}{r} 900 \\ -\ 18 \\ \hline \end{array}$

19. $\begin{array}{r} 307 \\ -108 \\ \hline \end{array}$

20. $\begin{array}{r} 805 \\ -\ 37 \\ \hline \end{array}$

21. $\begin{array}{r} 603 \\ -599 \\ \hline \end{array}$

22. $\begin{array}{r} 800 \\ -248 \\ \hline \end{array}$

23. $\begin{array}{r} 206 \\ -198 \\ \hline \end{array}$

24. $\begin{array}{r} 300 \\ -\ 42 \\ \hline \end{array}$

25. $\begin{array}{r} 803 \\ -\ 96 \\ \hline \end{array}$

26. $\begin{array}{r} 509 \\ -302 \\ \hline \end{array}$

27. $\begin{array}{r} 601 \\ -597 \\ \hline \end{array}$

28. $\begin{array}{r} 404 \\ -295 \\ \hline \end{array}$

29. $\begin{array}{r} 605 \\ -127 \\ \hline \end{array}$

30. $\begin{array}{r} 100 \\ -\ 75 \\ \hline \end{array}$

31. $\begin{array}{r} 808 \\ -179 \\ \hline \end{array}$

32. $\begin{array}{r} 503 \\ -194 \\ \hline \end{array}$

33. $\begin{array}{r} 500 \\ -\ 64 \\ \hline \end{array}$

34. $\begin{array}{r} 401 \\ -209 \\ \hline \end{array}$

35. $\begin{array}{r} 403 \\ -125 \\ \hline \end{array}$

36. $\begin{array}{r} 200 \\ -131 \\ \hline \end{array}$

37. $\begin{array}{r} 700 \\ -357 \\ \hline \end{array}$

38. $\begin{array}{r} 506 \\ -\ 99 \\ \hline \end{array}$

39. $\begin{array}{r} 600 \\ -246 \\ \hline \end{array}$

40. $\begin{array}{r} 604 \\ -129 \\ \hline \end{array}$

41. $\begin{array}{r} 606 \\ -309 \\ \hline \end{array}$

42. $\begin{array}{r} 707 \\ -\ 99 \\ \hline \end{array}$

Renaming Thousands

Step 1	Step 2	Step 3	Step 4

Step 1

$$\begin{array}{r} 4268 \\ -1723 \\ \hline 5 \end{array}$$

Subtract the ones.

Step 2

$$\begin{array}{r} 4268 \\ -1723 \\ \hline 45 \end{array}$$

Subtract the tens.

Step 3

$$\begin{array}{r} \overset{3\ \ 12}{\cancel{4}268} \\ -1723 \\ \hline 545 \end{array}$$

Look at the hundreds.
Rename: Show one fewer thousand and ten more hundreds. Subtract the hundreds.

Step 4

$$\begin{array}{r} \overset{3\ \ 12}{\cancel{4}268} \\ -1723 \\ \hline 2545 \end{array}$$

Subtract the thousands.

---

try these

Copy and complete.

1.
$$\begin{array}{r} \overset{8\ \ 15}{\cancel{9}575} \\ -3623 \\ \hline 952 \end{array}$$

2.
$$\begin{array}{r} \overset{1\ \ 13}{2\cancel{3}86} \\ -\ 942 \\ \hline 44 \end{array}$$

3.
$$\begin{array}{r} \overset{6\ \ 10}{7\cancel{0}67} \\ -5234 \\ \hline 33 \end{array}$$

4.
$$\begin{array}{r} \overset{6\ \ 15}{7\cancel{5}94} \\ -6823 \\ \hline 1 \end{array}$$

5.
$$\begin{array}{r} \overset{4\ \ 16}{5\cancel{6}72} \\ -1861 \\ \hline 1 \end{array}$$

Subtract.

6.
$$\begin{array}{r} 6072 \\ -2351 \\ \hline \end{array}$$

7.
$$\begin{array}{r} 4278 \\ -3953 \\ \hline \end{array}$$

8.
$$\begin{array}{r} 1456 \\ -\ 723 \\ \hline \end{array}$$

9.
$$\begin{array}{r} 3745 \\ -2832 \\ \hline \end{array}$$

10.
$$\begin{array}{r} 8536 \\ -4921 \\ \hline \end{array}$$

104

now do these

Subtract.

11. 1587
    − 926

12. 7683
    − 841

13. 7356
    −6623

14. 3259
    −2426

15. 8254
    −7732

16. 9321
    −6510

17. 7038
    −5900

18. 9253
    −3621

19. 6478
    −5625

20. 2054
    −1432

21. 1467
    − 852

22. 1178
    − 721

23. 7132
    −2911

24. 1388
    − 765

25. 6478
    −5555

26. 4373
    −2421

27. 69,027
    −28,701

28. 85,186
    −53,921

29. 48,329
    − 6,807

30. 71,477
    − 535

A RIDDLE

Each answer stands for a letter.
Find the answers. Then solve the riddle.

58	62	91	75	83	46
−23	−18	−42	−35	−57	−19
R	**U**	**N**	**T**	**O**	**M**

34	57	29	60	83
−15	−20	− 4	−14	−23
E	**D**	**K**	**Y**	**A**

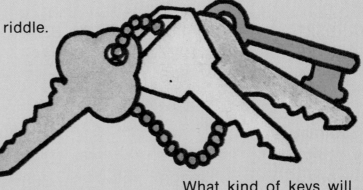

What kind of keys will
not open locked doors?

27 − 26 − 49 − 25 − 19 − 46, 40 − 44 − 35 − 25 − 19 − 46,

60 − 49 − 37   37 − 26 − 49 − 25 − 19 − 46

105

Renaming More Than Twice

Step 1	Step 2	Step 3	Step 4

Step 1

$$\begin{array}{r} 0\ 13 \\ 52\cancel{1}\cancel{3} \\ -2845 \\ \hline 8 \end{array}$$

Look at the ones.
Rename.
Subtract the ones.

Step 2

$$\begin{array}{r} 10 \\ 1\ 0\ 13 \\ 52\cancel{1}\cancel{3} \\ -2845 \\ \hline 68 \end{array}$$

Look at the tens.
Rename.
Subtract the tens.

Step 3

$$\begin{array}{r} 1\ 1\ 10 \\ 4\ 1\ 0\ 13 \\ \cancel{5}\cancel{2}\cancel{1}\cancel{3} \\ -2845 \\ \hline 368 \end{array}$$

Look at the
hundreds. Rename.
Subtract the
hundreds.

Step 4

$$\begin{array}{r} 1\ 1\ 10 \\ 4\ 1\ 0\ 13 \\ \cancel{5}\cancel{2}\cancel{1}\cancel{3} \\ -2845 \\ \hline 2368 \end{array}$$

Subtract the
thousands.

try these

Copy and complete.

1.
$$\begin{array}{r} {\scriptstyle 12\ 11} \\ {\scriptstyle 8\ 2\ 1\ 11} \\ \cancel{9}\cancel{3}\cancel{2}\cancel{1} \\ -6786 \\ \hline 535 \end{array}$$

2.
$$\begin{array}{r} {\scriptstyle 10\ 10} \\ {\scriptstyle 6\ 0\ 0\ 13} \\ \cancel{7}\cancel{1}\cancel{1}\cancel{3} \\ -4287 \\ \hline 826 \end{array}$$

3.
$$\begin{array}{r} {\scriptstyle 4\ 12\ 4\ 14} \\ \cancel{5}\cancel{2}\cancel{5}\cancel{4} \\ -3847 \\ \hline 07 \end{array}$$

4.
$$\begin{array}{r} {\scriptstyle 9\ 9} \\ {\scriptstyle 8\ 10\ 10\ 11} \\ \cancel{9}\cancel{0}\cancel{0}\cancel{1} \\ -\ 736 \\ \hline 5 \end{array}$$

5.
$$\begin{array}{r} {\scriptstyle 9\ 13} \\ {\scriptstyle 5\ 10\ 3\ 10} \\ \cancel{6}\cancel{0}\cancel{4}\cancel{0} \\ -3275 \\ \hline 5 \end{array}$$

Subtract.

6.
$$\begin{array}{r} 7768 \\ -2879 \\ \hline \end{array}$$

7.
$$\begin{array}{r} 4004 \\ -2796 \\ \hline \end{array}$$

8.
$$\begin{array}{r} 6114 \\ -\ 358 \\ \hline \end{array}$$

9.
$$\begin{array}{r} 5763 \\ -2697 \\ \hline \end{array}$$

10.
$$\begin{array}{r} 1136 \\ -\ 728 \\ \hline \end{array}$$

Subtract.

11. 9454 −8569	12. 6547 −2798	13. 7346 −6687	14. 9005 − 236	15. 3048 −2563
16. 7189 − 763	17. 7004 −3545	18. 9113 −2674	19. 7242 −3868	20. 3888 − 999
21. 7825 −7766	22. 1765 − 357	23. 3762 −1284	24. 7239 −1807	25. 4000 − 321
26. 5462 −5286	27. 9001 − 381	28. 5055 − 888	29. 6132 −5764	30. 8462 − 739
31. 4236 −2478	32. 8704 −1325	33. 6438 −4659	34. 5452 − 536	35. 2783 −2697

TWO RIDDLES

Each answer stands for a letter.
Find the answers. Then solve the riddle.

80 −68 **T**	65 −51 **R**	27 −11 **I**	52 −39 **S**	36 −18 **H**	91 −74 **O**	44 −29 **N**	73 −54 **E**

A. What word becomes shorter when you
add two letters?   13−18−17−14−12

B. If two is company and three is a crowd,
what are four and five?   15−16−15−19

107

Subtracting Amounts of Money

Subtract amounts of money as if you were subtracting whole numbers. Remember to write the dollar sign and the cents point in the answer.

Step 1	Step 2	Step 3	Step 4
$^{4\,10}$ $\$47.50$ $-\ 17.85$ $\overline{\hspace{1.2em}5}$	^{14} $^{6\ 4\,10}$ $\$47.50$ $-\ 17.85$ $\overline{\hspace{0.8em}65}$	$^{16\,14}$ $^{3\,6\ 4\,10}$ $\$47.50$ $-\ 17.85$ $\overline{9\ 65}$	$^{16\,14}$ $^{3\,6\ 4\,10}$ $\$47.50$ $-\ 17.85$ $\overline{\$29.65}$

---

try these

Copy and complete.

1. $^{11\,10}_{7\ \not{8}\ \not{9}\ 10}$
    $\$82.10$
    $-\ 56.75$
    $\overline{\hspace{1.4em}35}$

2. $^{10\,10}_{4\ \not{0}\ \not{0}\ 13}$
    $\$51.13$
    $-\ 22.36$
    $\overline{\hspace{1.4em}77}$

3. $^{9\ \ 9}_{6\ 10\,10\,12}$
    $\$70.02$
    $-\ 37.46$
    $\overline{\hspace{1.4em}56}$

4. $^{5\ 13\ 5\ 15}$
    $\$63.65$
    $-\ 58.47$
    $\overline{\hspace{2.0em}8}$

5. $^{12}_{6\ \not{2}\ 10}$
    $\$17.30$
    $-\ 6.64$
    $\overline{\hspace{2.0em}6}$

Subtract.

6. $\$66.57$
    $-\ \ \ 8.68$

7. $\$50.05$
    $-\ 38.97$

8. $\$51.13$
    $-\ 23.48$

9. $\$46.52$
    $-\ \ \ 6.86$

10. $\$18.00$
    $-\ \ \ 9.43$

108

— **now do these** —

Subtract.

11. $61.18 − 38.59	12. $16.56 − 8.21	13. $94.66 − 39.87	14. $90.05 − 26.46	15. $73.44 − 69.65
16. $53.67 − 7.22	17. $87.33 − 27.37	18. $91.13 − 26.75	19. $51.02 − 42.94	20. $63.73 − 14.21
21. $12.78 − 7.21	22. $81.13 − 36.74	23. $50.03 − 35.49	24. $70.27 − 67.01	25. $67.23 − 66.55
26. $80.00 − 12.34	27. $24.68 − 15.97	28. $84.36 − 34.29	29. $21.13 − 9.25	30. $12.34 − 5.67
31. $60.00 − 25.52	32. $72.10 − 35.60	33. $40.07 − 8.55	34. $90.05 − 3.98	35. $17.52 − 10.73

I HAVE A PROBLEM

Decide: ADD or SUBTRACT.
Then solve the problem.

A. In 1928, a sled cost $1.39.
It now costs $9.95.
How much more does it cost now?

B. Last week's food bill was $34.25.
This week's bill is $35.45.
How much was spent in all?

C. A walkie-talkie costs $14.50.
On sale it costs $9.95.
How much do you save if
you buy it on sale?

D. A book costs $7.95.
The sales tax is $.56.
How much do you pay in all?

109

making change

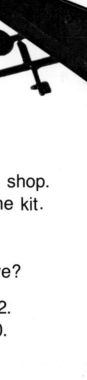

You are working in a hobby shop.
A person buys a model plane kit.
It costs $3.32.
The person gives you $5.00.
What change should you give?

Start with the cost, $3.32.
Count on to reach $5.00.

Start ⟶	$3.32
3 pennies ⟶	3.35
1 nickel ⟶	3.40
1 dime ⟶	3.50
2 quarters ⟶	4.00
1 dollar ⟶	5.00

What change should you give?

1. A bead kit costs $2.25.
   You are given $5.00.

Start ⟶	$2.25
_?_ quarters ⟶	3.00
_?_ dollars ⟶	5.00

2. A candle kit costs $4.29.
   You are given $5.00.

Start ⟶	$4.29
_?_ pennies ⟶	4.30
_?_ dimes ⟶	4.50
_?_ quarters ⟶	5.00

110   *Problem-solving Help*

Start with the cost.
Count on to reach the amount given.
Exercises 3 and 4 are done for you.

ITEM	COST	GIVEN					
3. lacing	$ .28	$1.00	2		2	2	
4. candlewax	$1.45	$5.00		1		2	3
5. beads	$ .34	$ .50					
6. plaster mold	$ .52	$1.00					
7. colored sand	$1.98	$2.00					
8. flower kit	$1.56	$2.00					
9. water colors	$1.17	$5.00					
10. model boat	$2.25	$3.00					
11. string art kit	$3.78	$5.00					
12. leather kit	$4.03	$5.00					
13. science kit	$7.41	$10.00					

Test

Estimate.
Use the nearest tens.

1. 37
−12
(p. 90)

2. 65
−57
(p. 90)

Estimate.
Use the nearest hundreds.

3. 833
−450
(p. 90)

4. 716
−598
(p. 90)

5. 450
−137
(p. 90)

Subtract.

6. 87
−38
(p. 94)

7. 66
−29
(p. 94)

8. 573
− 16
(p. 94)

9. 741
− 23
(p. 94)

10. 174
− 93
(p. 98)

11. 635
−452
(p. 98)

12. 942
− 81
(p. 98)

13. 752
−369
(p. 100)

14. 613
−287
(p. 100)

15. 240
− 63
(p. 100)

16. 300
−126
(p. 102)

17. 502
−264
(p. 102)

18. 6258
−2430
(p. 104)

19. 9530
−4720
(p. 104)

20. 2365
− 753
(p. 104)

21. 7423
−4285
(p. 106)

22. 8963
− 786
(p. 106)

23. 4511
−4297
(p. 106)

24. $60.60
− 38.95
(p. 108)

25. $23.00
− 15.99
(p. 108)

bonus

Solve the problem.

26. 42 people.
15 go on a boat trip.
How many do not go?
(p. 94)

27. You have $29.58.
You spend $7.75.
How much do you have left?
(p. 108)

112

Choose the Coins

68¢	2	1	1	3
14¢				
15¢				
28¢				
37¢				
49¢				
56¢				
61¢				
74¢				
82¢				
90¢				
99¢				
$1.00				
$1.32				
$1.57				

What is the least number of coins that could be used to make each amount?

Copy and complete the chart.

6 Graphing

Pictographs

kinds of books read by the class
Each 📖 stands for 5 books.

Mystery	📖 📖
Adventure	📖 📖 📖 📖 📖
Biography	📖 📖 📖 📖
Science Fiction	📖

Brian's class made a **pictograph**.
It shows how many books of each kind were read.

Adventure books were read the most.
Which kind of book was read the least?

They read more mystery books than science fiction.
Did they read more biography or more adventure?

Eric recorded the number of people who visited his town's park.

Visitors to Morris Park Each ♀ stands for 25 people.	
Monday	♀ ♀ ♀
Tuesday	♀ ♀ ♀ ♀
Wednesday	♀ ♀
Thursday	♀ ♀ ♀ ♀
Friday	♀ ♀ ♀ ♀ ♀ ♀

1. On which day were there the most visitors?
2. On which day were there the least?
3. Did more people visit on Wednesday or on Thursday?
4. On which two days were there the same number of visitors?

now do these

Claire recorded the number of planes that landed at an airport.

Flights Landing at the County Airport Each ✈ stands for 10 airplanes.	
Monday	✈ ✈ ✈ ✈ ✈ ✈ ✈ ✈
Tuesday	✈ ✈ ✈
Wednesday	✈ ✈ ✈ ✈ ✈ ✈ ✈
Thursday	✈ ✈ ✈ ✈ ✈
Friday	✈ ✈ ✈ ✈ ✈ ✈ ✈ ✈ ✈ ✈

5. On which day did the most planes use the airport?
6. On which day did the least number use it?
7. Did more planes use the airport on Wednesday or on Thursday?
8. Did more planes use the airport on Monday or on Friday?

115

Bar Graphs

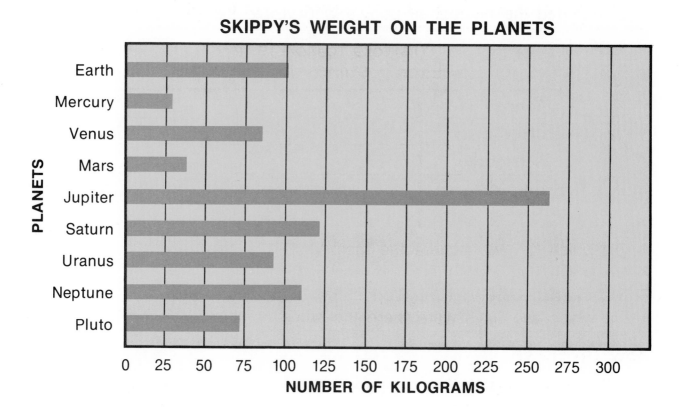

SKIPPY'S WEIGHT ON THE PLANETS

Michael is studying the planets.

He learned that his pony Skippy would weigh different amounts on the different planets.

He made a **bar graph** to show this.

Skippy weighs 100 kilograms on earth.
Skippy would weigh less on Mercury.
Skippy would weigh more on Jupiter.

Would Skippy weigh more or less on Pluto?

Skippy would weigh the most on Jupiter.
On which planet would Skippy weigh the least?

116

Juan used a balance scale to measure different things.
He made a bar graph to show the results.

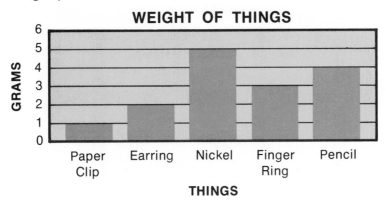

WEIGHT OF THINGS

1. Which item weighs the most?
2. Which item weighs the least?
3. Which weighs more, the paper clip or the pencil?
4. Which weighs less, the earring or the finger ring?

now do these

Steven made a bar graph to show about
how long some animals live.

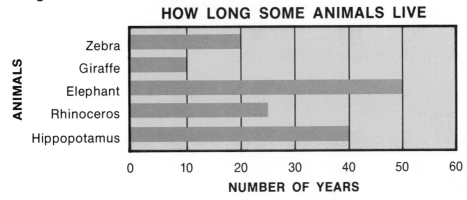

HOW LONG SOME ANIMALS LIVE

5. Which animal usually has the longest life?
6. Which animal usually has the shortest life?
7. Which usually lives longer, a zebra or a hippopotamus?
8. Which usually lives longer, an elephant or a rhinoceros?

Streets and Avenues

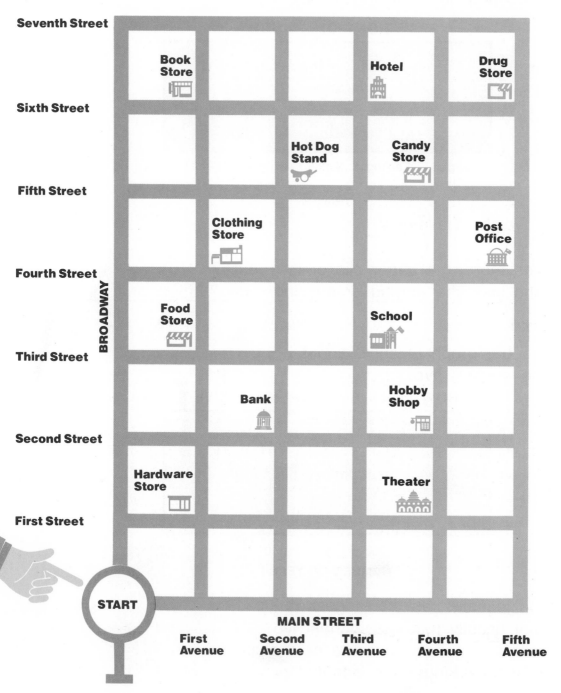

You are on the corner of Main Street and Broadway.
Walk on Main Street to Fourth Avenue.
Turn. Walk up Fourth Avenue to First Street.
Do you see a theater on the corner?

Go back to START. Walk on Main Street to Third Avenue.
Walk up Third Avenue to Third Street.
Did you come to the school?

try these

What do you find on the corner?
1. Second Avenue and Fifth Street.
2. Fourth Avenue and Second Street.

now do these

What do you find on the corner?
3. Fourth Avenue and Fifth Street.

4. First Avenue and Sixth Street.

5. Fifth Avenue and Fourth Street.

6. First Avenue and Third Street.

7. Third Avenue and Sixth Street.

8. First Avenue and First Street.

9. Fifth Avenue and Sixth Street.

10. First Avenue and Fourth Street.

11. Second Avenue and Second Street.

Graphing

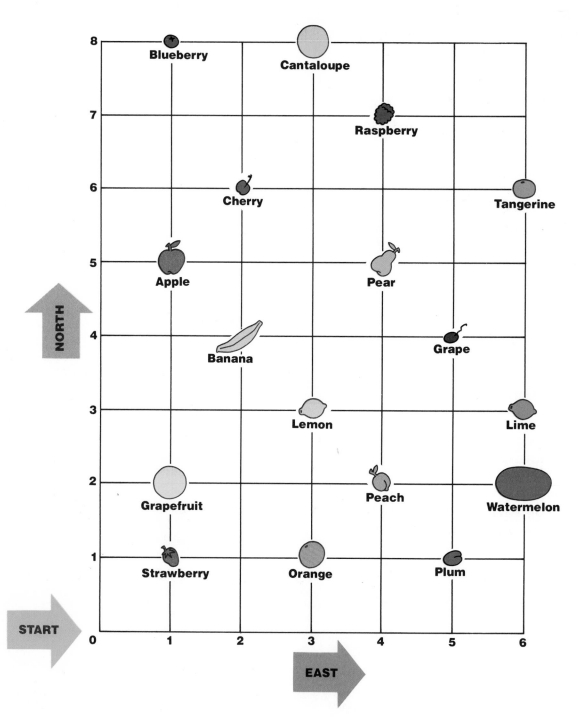

Start at 0. Go EAST 4, NORTH 2.
You should find a peach.

Start at 0. Go EAST 1, NORTH 5.
You should find an apple.

try these

Start at 0. Follow the directions. What fruit do you find?
1. EAST 3, NORTH 1   2. EAST 1, NORTH 2   3. EAST 4, NORTH 5

now do these

Start at 0. Follow the directions. What fruit do you find?

4. EAST 5, NORTH 1   5. EAST 2, NORTH 4   6. EAST 1, NORTH 8

7. EAST 4, NORTH 7   8. EAST 3, NORTH 3   9. EAST 6, NORTH 2

10. EAST 1, NORTH 1   11. EAST 2, NORTH 6   12. EAST 6, NORTH 6

13. EAST 6, NORTH 3   14. EAST 3, NORTH 8   15. EAST 5, NORTH 4

Giving Directions

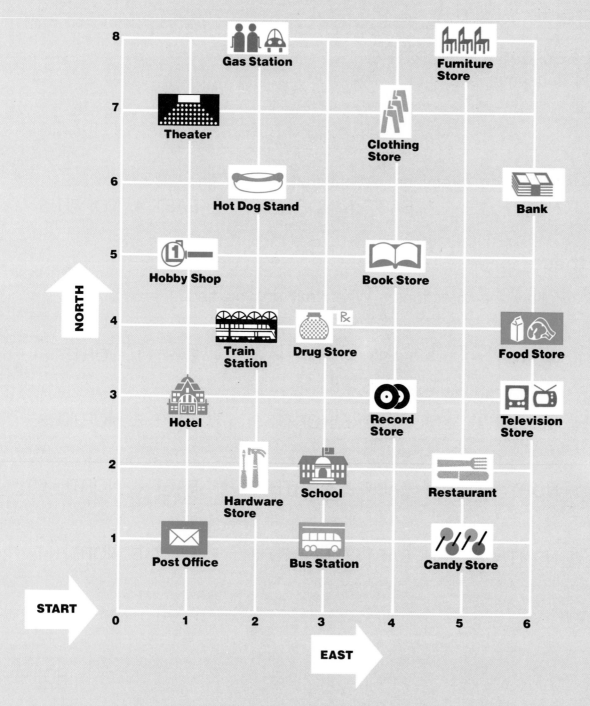

You and two friends are at 0.
One friend wants to find the book store.
You give the friend directions.
You say: EAST 4, NORTH 5.

Your other friend wants to find the school.
Which directions should you give?

EAST 2, NORTH 3 or EAST 3, NORTH 2

try these

Give directions to find the place.

1. Hotel
2. Drug Store
3. Hot Dog Stand

now do these

Give directions to find the place.

4. Candy Store
5. Clothing Store
6. Food Store

7. Post Office
8. Hobby Shop
9. Hardware Store

10. Bank
11. Theater
12. Record Store

13. Gas Station
14. Bus Station
15. Restaurant

16. Train Station
17. Furniture Store
18. Television Store

reading maps

ADAMS COUNTY PARK

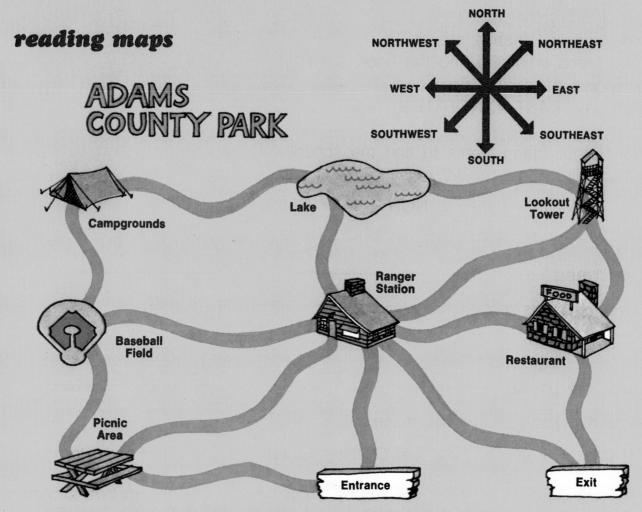

NORTH
NORTHWEST NORTHEAST
WEST EAST
SOUTHWEST SOUTHEAST
SOUTH

Campgrounds

Lake

Lookout Tower

Ranger Station

Baseball Field

Restaurant

Picnic Area

Entrance

Exit

Connie and Carl are park rangers. They help visitors in the park. They also see that the visitors obey the rules. Their work day begins at the ranger station.

To get to the lake, they would go NORTH.

To get to the picnic area, they would go SOUTHWEST.

In which direction should Connie and Carl go?

1. From the ranger station to the baseball field.
2. From the ranger station to the lookout tower.
3. From the ranger station to the campgrounds.
4. From the ranger station to the restaurant.

Problem-solving Help

You visit the park. In which direction should you go?

5. From the entrance to the ranger station.

6. From the ranger station to the lookout tower.

7. From the lookout tower to the restaurant.

8. From the restaurant to the baseball field.

9. From the baseball field to the picnic area.

10. From the picnic area to the campgrounds.

11. From the campgrounds to the lake.

12. From the lake to the ranger station.

13. From the ranger station to the exit.

14. From the campgrounds to the exit.

Test

1. Of which color marble does Michael have the most? (p. 114)

2. Of which color marble does he have the least? (p. 114)

3. Does he have more orange marbles or blue marbles? (p. 114)

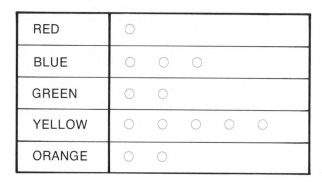

MICHAEL'S MARBLE COLLECTION
Each ○ stands for 5 marbles.

RED	○
BLUE	○ ○ ○
GREEN	○ ○
YELLOW	○ ○ ○ ○ ○
ORANGE	○ ○

4. Who drew more pictures, the fifth grade or the fourth grade? (p. 116)

5. How many pictures did the third grade draw? (p. 116)

6. Who drew the least number of pictures? (p. 116)

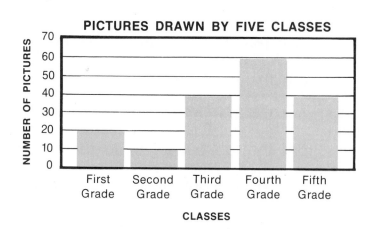

Which letter do you find at the point? Always start at 0.

7. EAST 5, NORTH 1 (p. 120)

8. EAST 6, NORTH 5 (p. 120)

9. EAST 3, NORTH 3 (p. 120)

10. EAST 7, NORTH 2 (p. 120)

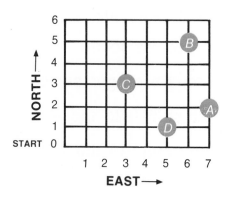

126

Treasure Hunt Game

You need 18 slips of paper.
Number 9 of them 1 to 9. Number the rest the same way.
Mix them up and place them upside down.
A player draws two slips.
One slip tells how far to go EAST. The other tells how far to go NORTH.
You can put the slips in any order.
You want to land on the greatest amount of money possible.
Record how much you land on.
Return the slips to the bottom of the pile.
When the game ends, the winner is the one with the most money.

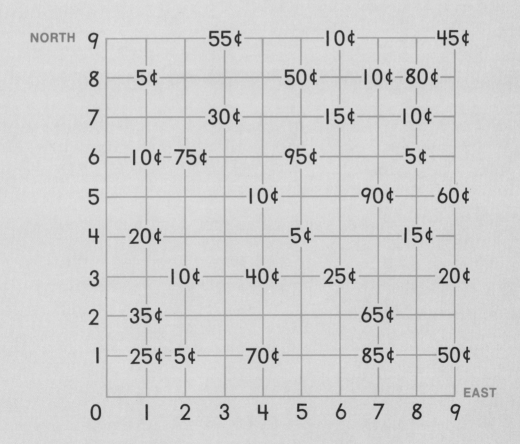

ROMAN NUMERALS

The ancient Romans used these symbols to name numbers.

I	V	X	L	C	D
1	5	10	50	100	500

They added or subtracted the values of the symbols.

When the values were the same, they added.

III	XX	CCC
1 + 1 + 1	10 + 10	100 + 100 + 100
3	20	300

When the symbol for a greater value came first, they added.

VII	XV	LXII	CXI	DCCXV
5 + 1 + 1	10 + 5	50 + 10 + 1 + 1	100 + 10 + 1	500 + 100 + 100 + 10 + 5
7	15	62	111	715

When the symbol for a smaller value came first, they subtracted.

IV	IX	XL	CXIV	XC
5 − 1	10 − 1	50 − 10	100 + 10 + (5 − 1)	100 − 10
4	9	40	114	90

What number is named?

1. LXV   2. XLVI   3. XXIX   4. CXXIV

5. CCCXXXIII   6. LXXIX   7. DCCCX   8. DXC

Counting Groups

Count to find the answer.

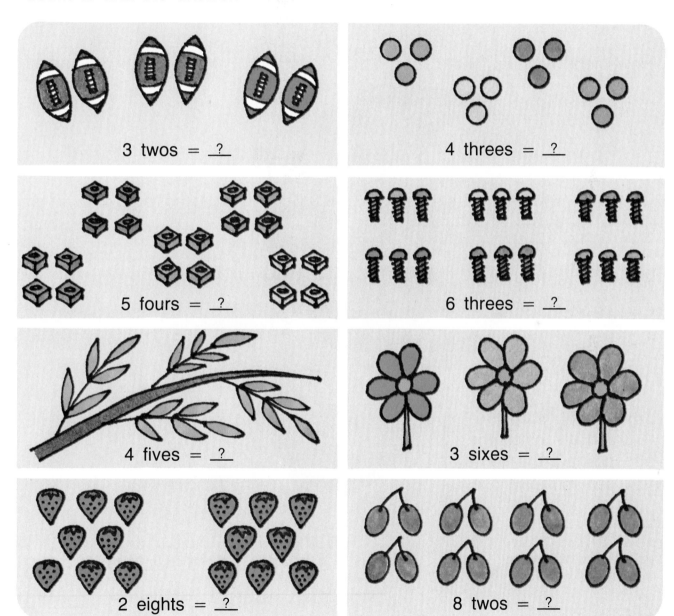

3 twos = ___?___

4 threes = ___?___

5 fours = ___?___

6 threes = ___?___

4 fives = ___?___

3 sixes = ___?___

2 eights = ___?___

8 twos = ___?___

Multiplication

Marsha decorates cupcakes.
She puts 5 candies on each.

She decorates 3 cupcakes.
3 times she puts on 5 candies.

How many candies in all?

3 times 5 equals 15.

$$3 \times 5 = 15$$

factor   factor   product

You add to find how many in all. When the addends are the same, you can multiply.

4 cups.

2 candies on each.

8 candies in all.

$$2 + 2 + 2 + 2 = 8$$

$$4 \times 2 = 8$$

Write an addition sentence and a multiplication sentence.

1.

2.

3.

Write an addition sentence and a multiplication sentence.

4.

5.

6.

7.

8.

9.

10.

11.

12.

2 and 5 as Factors

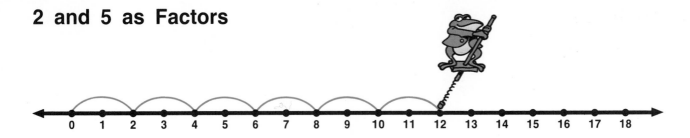

The frog makes 6 hops of 2 lily pads each.

$$6 \times 2 = 12$$

$$
\begin{array}{r}
2 \\
\times 6 \\
\hline
12
\end{array}
$$

2 ← factor

×6 ← factor

12 ← product

Count by twos to find 9×2.

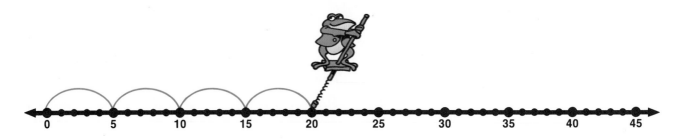

The frog makes 4 hops of 5 lily pads each.

$$4 \times 5 = 20$$

$$
\begin{array}{r}
5 \\
\times 4 \\
\hline
20
\end{array}
$$

Count by fives to find 9×5.

Find the product.

| 1. 2
 ×2 | 2. 5
 ×3 | 3. 2
 ×4 | 4. 5
 ×5 | 5. 5
 ×6 | 6. 2
 ×8 |

now do these

Find the product.

| 7. 5
 ×8 | 8. 2
 ×3 | 9. 5
 ×7 | 10. 2
 ×9 | 11. 5
 ×2 | 12. 2
 ×6 |

| 13. 2
 ×5 | 14. 5
 ×4 | 15. 5
 ×6 | 16. 5
 ×9 | 17. 2
 ×7 | 18. 2
 ×1 |

| 19. 2
 ×4 | 20. 5
 ×3 | 21. 5
 ×1 | 22. 2
 ×7 | 23. 5
 ×8 | 24. 2
 ×9 |

| 25. 2
 ×6 | 26. 5
 ×7 | 27. 2
 ×3 | 28. 5
 ×4 | 29. 2
 ×8 | 30. 5
 ×9 |

Solve the problem.

31. 6 bags.
    5 carrots in each.
    How many carrots in all?

32. 3 packs.
    5 pieces of cheese in each.
    How many pieces in all?

33. He eats 2 carrots.
    9 times a day.
    How many carrots in all?

34. She eats 5 pieces of cheese.
    8 times a day.
    How many pieces in all?

3 as a Factor

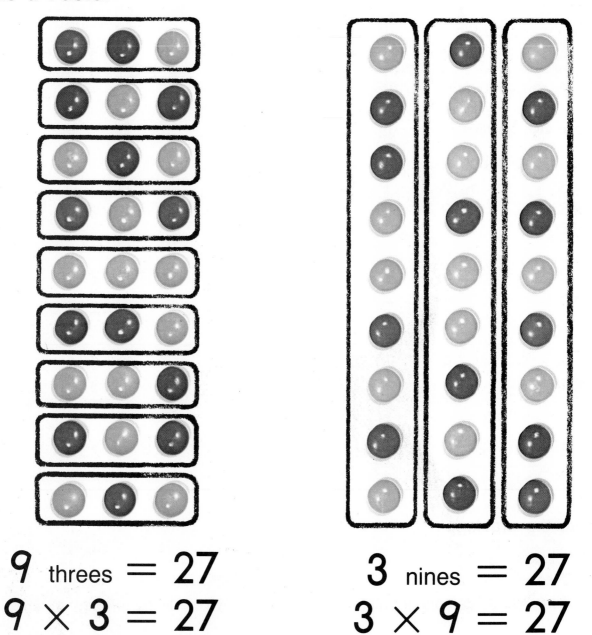

9 threes $= 27$

$9 \times 3 = 27$

3 nines $= 27$

$3 \times 9 = 27$

You can multiply two numbers in either order. The product is always the same.

134

Find the product.

1. 7
   ×3

2. 3
   ×7

3. 4
   ×3

4. 3
   ×4

5. 9
   ×3

6. 3
   ×9

now do these

Find the product.

7. 3
   ×3

8. 2
   ×3

9. 3
   ×5

10. 8
    ×3

11. 3
    ×6

12. 3
    ×8

13. 9
    ×3

14. 6
    ×3

15. 3
    ×2

16. 7
    ×3

17. 5
    ×3

18. 4
    ×3

19. 5
    ×8

20. 8
    ×5

21. 9
    ×2

22. 2
    ×9

23. 6
    ×5

24. 5
    ×6

25. 7
    ×2

26. 2
    ×7

27. 5
    ×9

28. 9
    ×5

29. 5
    ×7

30. 7
    ×5

Solve the problem.

31. 7 puppies.
    2 ears on each.
    How many ears in all?

32. 7 puppies.
    3 toys for each.
    How many toys in all?

33. 2 tails.
    Each wags 4 times.
    How many wags in all?

34. 3 tails.
    Each wags 5 times.
    How many wags in all?

135

4 as a Factor

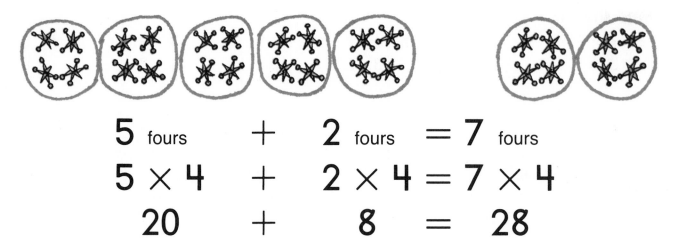

$$5 \text{ fours} \quad + \quad 2 \text{ fours} \quad = 7 \text{ fours}$$
$$5 \times 4 \quad + \quad 2 \times 4 = 7 \times 4$$
$$20 \quad + \quad 8 \quad = \quad 28$$

Suppose you know these facts: $5 \times 4 = 20$ and $2 \times 4 = 8$.
You can use them to find another product: $7 \times 4 = \underline{\ ?\ }$.

$$\begin{array}{c} 4 \\ \times 5 \\ \hline 20 \end{array} + \begin{array}{c} 4 \\ \times 2 \\ \hline 8 \end{array} = \begin{array}{c} 4 \\ \times 7 \\ \hline 28 \end{array}$$

---

try these

Multiply.

1.
$$\begin{array}{r} 4 \\ \times 2 \\ \hline \end{array} \qquad \begin{array}{r} 4 \\ \times 1 \\ \hline \end{array} \qquad \begin{array}{r} 4 \\ \times 3 \\ \hline \end{array}$$

2.
$$\begin{array}{r} 4 \\ \times 5 \\ \hline \end{array} \qquad \begin{array}{r} 4 \\ \times 1 \\ \hline \end{array} \qquad \begin{array}{r} 4 \\ \times 6 \\ \hline \end{array}$$

3.
$$\begin{array}{r} 4 \\ \times 4 \\ \hline \end{array} \qquad \begin{array}{r} 4 \\ \times 4 \\ \hline \end{array} \qquad \begin{array}{r} 4 \\ \times 8 \\ \hline \end{array}$$

4.
$$\begin{array}{r} 4 \\ \times 4 \\ \hline \end{array} \qquad \begin{array}{r} 4 \\ \times 5 \\ \hline \end{array} \qquad \begin{array}{r} 4 \\ \times 9 \\ \hline \end{array}$$

Multiply.

5. 4 ×4	6. 6 ×4	7. 4 ×9	8. 7 ×4	9. 4 ×5	10. 8 ×4
11. 2 ×4	12. 9 ×4	13. 5 ×4	14. 3 ×4	15. 1 ×4	16. 2 ×5
17. 4 ×7	18. 5 ×5	19. 3 ×6	20. 5 ×3	21. 4 ×6	22. 4 ×3
23. 9 ×3	24. 4 ×2	25. 5 ×9	26. 3 ×7	27. 8 ×3	28. 6 ×5
29. 5 ×7	30. 9 ×5	31. 3 ×8	32. 3 ×9	33. 7 ×3	34. 4 ×8

Solve the problem.

35. 3 hats.
    4 rabbits in each.
    How many rabbits in all?

36. 2 magicians.
    5 wands each.
    How many wands in all?

37. 4 birds in a cage.
    4 times as many appear.
    How many birds in all?

38. 6 scarves in the sleeve.
    4 times as many in
    the pocket.
    How many scarves in
    the pocket?

6 as a Factor

Cover the answers.
How fast can you name the products?

$$\begin{array}{c} 6 \\ \times 1 \\ \hline 6 \end{array} \qquad \begin{array}{c} 6 \\ \times 2 \\ \hline 12 \end{array} \qquad \begin{array}{c} 6 \\ \times 3 \\ \hline 18 \end{array} \qquad \begin{array}{c} 6 \\ \times 4 \\ \hline 24 \end{array} \qquad \begin{array}{c} 6 \\ \times 5 \\ \hline 30 \end{array}$$

Use facts you know to find other facts.

$$\begin{array}{c} 6 \\ \times 3 \\ \hline 18 \end{array} + \begin{array}{c} 6 \\ \times 3 \\ \hline 18 \end{array} = \begin{array}{c} 6 \\ \times 6 \\ \hline 36 \end{array} \qquad\qquad \begin{array}{c} 6 \\ \times 3 \\ \hline 18 \end{array} + \begin{array}{c} 6 \\ \times 4 \\ \hline 24 \end{array} = \begin{array}{c} 6 \\ \times 7 \\ \hline 42 \end{array}$$

$$\begin{array}{c} 6 \\ \times 3 \\ \hline 18 \end{array} + \begin{array}{c} 6 \\ \times 5 \\ \hline 30 \end{array} = \begin{array}{c} 6 \\ \times 8 \\ \hline 48 \end{array} \qquad\qquad \begin{array}{c} 6 \\ \times 4 \\ \hline 24 \end{array} + \begin{array}{c} 6 \\ \times 5 \\ \hline 30 \end{array} = \begin{array}{c} 6 \\ \times 9 \\ \hline 54 \end{array}$$

try these

Multiply.

1. $\begin{array}{c} 6 \\ \times 6 \\ \hline \end{array}$	2. $\begin{array}{c} 3 \\ \times 6 \\ \hline \end{array}$	3. $\begin{array}{c} 6 \\ \times 7 \\ \hline \end{array}$	4. $\begin{array}{c} 4 \\ \times 6 \\ \hline \end{array}$	5. $\begin{array}{c} 6 \\ \times 8 \\ \hline \end{array}$	6. $\begin{array}{c} 9 \\ \times 6 \\ \hline \end{array}$
7. $\begin{array}{c} 8 \\ \times 6 \\ \hline \end{array}$	8. $\begin{array}{c} 2 \\ \times 6 \\ \hline \end{array}$	9. $\begin{array}{c} 6 \\ \times 9 \\ \hline \end{array}$	10. $\begin{array}{c} 6 \\ \times 4 \\ \hline \end{array}$	11. $\begin{array}{c} 5 \\ \times 6 \\ \hline \end{array}$	12. $\begin{array}{c} 7 \\ \times 6 \\ \hline \end{array}$

Multiply.

13. 4 ×6	14. 9 ×6	15. 2 ×6	16. 6 ×6	17. 6 ×8	18. 6 ×3
19. 6 ×9	20. 6 ×4	21. 7 ×6	22. 6 ×2	23. 8 ×6	24. 6 ×7
25. 3 ×6	26. 6 ×5	27. 5 ×6	28. 3 ×7	29. 5 ×5	30. 8 ×3
31. 5 ×4	32. 4 ×4	33. 9 ×4	34. 3 ×3	35. 4 ×7	36. 8 ×4
37. 3 ×9	38. 7 ×3	39. 7 ×5	40. 5 ×9	41. 5 ×3	42. 5 ×8

139

GOING SHOPPING

Buy 6 of the items.
How much will they cost?

 A.

3¢

B.

C.

1¢

D.

5¢

6¢

E.

8¢

F. ○

2¢

G.

9¢

H. ○

4¢

I.

7¢

7 as a Factor

Cover the answers.
How fast can you name the products?

$$
\begin{array}{ccccc}
7 & 7 & 7 & 7 & 7 \\
\times 1 & \times 2 & \times 3 & \times 4 & \times 5 \\
\hline
7 & 14 & 21 & 28 & 35
\end{array}
$$

Use facts you know to find other facts.

$$
\begin{array}{ccc}
7 & 7 & 7 \\
\times 3 & \times 3 & \times 6 \\
\hline
21 & + \quad 21 & = \quad 42
\end{array}
\qquad
\begin{array}{ccc}
7 & 7 & 7 \\
\times 2 & \times 5 & \times 7 \\
\hline
14 & + \quad 35 & = \quad 49
\end{array}
$$

$$
\begin{array}{ccc}
7 & 7 & 7 \\
\times 3 & \times 5 & \times 8 \\
\hline
21 & + \quad 35 & = \quad 56
\end{array}
\qquad
\begin{array}{ccc}
7 & 7 & 7 \\
\times 4 & \times 5 & \times 9 \\
\hline
28 & + \quad 35 & = \quad 63
\end{array}
$$

---

try these

Multiply.

1.	2.	3.	4.	5.	6.
7 $\times 2$	7 $\times 6$	8 $\times 7$	7 $\times 4$	7 $\times 7$	7 $\times 3$

7.	8.	9.	10.	11.	12.
4 $\times 7$	7 $\times 9$	6 $\times 7$	7 $\times 5$	9 $\times 7$	7 $\times 8$

140

now do these

Multiply.

13. 3 ×7	**14.** 7 ×2	**15.** 7 ×9	**16.** 7 ×5	**17.** 7 ×8	**18.** 9 ×7
19. 7 ×4	**20.** 2 ×7	**21.** 7 ×7	**22.** 4 ×7	**23.** 5 ×7	**24.** 7 ×6
25. 6 ×7	**26.** 8 ×7	**27.** 7 ×3	**28.** 5 ×4	**29.** 6 ×3	**30.** 4 ×4
31. 8 ×5	**32.** 6 ×6	**33.** 9 ×6	**34.** 8 ×5	**35.** 8 ×6	**36.** 6 ×4
37. 2 ×9	**38.** 9 ×4	**39.** 5 ×5	**40.** 6 ×9	**41.** 6 ×8	**42.** 5 ×6

quick check

Multiply.

1. 9 ×2	**2.** 3 ×6	**3.** 6 ×5	**4.** 4 ×7	**5.** 8 ×6
6. 7 ×9	**7.** 9 ×4	**8.** 6 ×9	**9.** 8 ×3	**10.** 5 ×7

141

8 as a Factor

Cover the answers.
How fast can you name the products?

$$
\begin{array}{ccccc}
8 & 8 & 8 & 8 & 8 \\
\times 1 & \times 2 & \times 3 & \times 4 & \times 5 \\
\hline
8 & 16 & 24 & 32 & 40
\end{array}
$$

Use facts you know to find other facts.

$$
\begin{array}{ccc}
8 & 8 & 8 \\
\times 3 & \times 3 & \times 6 \\
\hline
24 + & 24 = & 48
\end{array}
\qquad
\begin{array}{ccc}
8 & 8 & 8 \\
\times 2 & \times 5 & \times 7 \\
\hline
16 + & 40 = & 56
\end{array}
$$

$$
\begin{array}{ccc}
8 & 8 & 8 \\
\times 3 & \times 5 & \times 8 \\
\hline
24 + & 40 = & 64
\end{array}
\qquad
\begin{array}{ccc}
8 & 8 & 8 \\
\times 4 & \times 5 & \times 9 \\
\hline
32 + & 40 = & 72
\end{array}
$$

---

try these

Multiply.

$$
\begin{array}{llllll}
\text{1.} \ 8 & \text{2.} \ 8 & \text{3.} \ 8 & \text{4.} \ 8 & \text{5.} \ 7 & \text{6.} \ 8 \\
\ \ \times 6 & \ \ \times 2 & \ \ \times 8 & \ \ \times 4 & \ \ \times 8 & \ \ \times 3
\end{array}
$$

$$
\begin{array}{llllll}
\text{7.} \ 4 & \text{8.} \ 8 & \text{9.} \ 6 & \text{10.} \ 8 & \text{11.} \ 9 & \text{12.} \ 8 \\
\ \ \times 8 & \ \ \times 9 & \ \ \times 8 & \ \ \ \times 5 & \ \ \ \times 8 & \ \ \ \times 7
\end{array}
$$

Multiply.

13. 8 ×9	**14.** 8 ×2	**15.** 3 ×8	**16.** 8 ×5	**17.** 8 ×8	**18.** 9 ×8
19. 8 ×4	**20.** 2 ×8	**21.** 8 ×7	**22.** 4 ×8	**23.** 5 ×8	**24.** 8 ×6
25. 6 ×8	**26.** 8 ×3	**27.** 7 ×8	**28.** 7 ×7	**29.** 9 ×6	**30.** 7 ×9
31. 6 ×7	**32.** 5 ×5	**33.** 9 ×7	**34.** 6 ×6	**35.** 4 ×7	**36.** 4 ×4
37. 7 ×6	**38.** 7 ×4	**39.** 6 ×7	**40.** 6 ×9	**41.** 5 ×7	**42.** 9 ×4

PRACTICE YOUR FACTS

8 ×1	8 ×7	8 ×2	8 ×5	8 ×3	8 ×6	8 ×8	8 ×9	8 ×4
8	56	16	40	24	48	64	72	32

Copy these facts.

8 ×1	8 ×7	8 ×2	8 ×5	8 ×3	8 ×6	8 ×8	8 ×9	8 ×4
8								

Fold the paper.
Write the products.
Check your answers.

8 ×1	8 ×7	8 ×2	8 ×5	8 ×3	8 ×6	8 ×8	8 ×9	8 ×4
8								

Fold the paper again.
Write the products.
Continue until you are
sure you know them all.

143

9 as a Factor

You know many facts with 9 as a factor.
Here is a way to help you remember .all of them.

$$
\begin{array}{cccccccc}
9 & 9 & 9 & 9 & 9 & 9 & 9 & 9 \\
\times 2 & \times 3 & \times 4 & \times 5 & \times 6 & \times 7 & \times 8 & \times 9 \\
\hline
18 & 27 & 36 & 45 & 54 & 63 & 72 & 81
\end{array}
$$

Look at the red digits in each fact.
The digit in the tens place of the product is 1 less than the factor.

Add the digits in the product.
You always get 9 as the sum.

try these

Write the digit in the tens place.

1.	2.	3.	4.	5.	6.
9	9	9	9	9	9
×4	×9	×6	×3	×7	×5
□6	□1	□4	□7	□3	□5

Write the digit in the ones place.

7.	8.	9.	10.	11.	12.
9	9	9	9	9	9
×2	×8	×4	×6	×9	×7
1□	7□	3□	5□	8□	6□

144

— **now do these** —

Multiply.

13.   9
  ×5
	14. 9
	  ×9
		15. 9
		  ×2
			16. 3
			  ×9
				17. 9
				  ×8
					18. 6
					  ×9

19.   9
  ×4
	20. 2
	  ×9
		21. 9
		  ×7
			22. 9
			  ×6
				23. 5
				  ×9
					24. 4
					  ×9

25.   7
  ×9
	26. 9
	  ×3
		27. 8
		  ×9
			28. 5
			  ×5
				29. 8
				  ×7
					30. 5
					  ×8

31.   7
  ×5
	32. 8
	  ×8
		33. 7
		  ×4
			34. 7
			  ×7
				35. 6
				  ×8
					36. 8
					  ×6

37.   4
  ×4
	38. 6
	  ×7
		39. 6
		  ×6
			40. 7
			  ×8
				41. 3
				  ×7
					42. 2
					  ×8

145

GOING SHOPPING

Buy 9 of the items.
How much will they cost?

C.  1¢

E.  8¢

G.  9¢

I. 7¢

3¢

B. 5¢

D.  6¢

F. 2¢

H.  4¢

Going Shopping

8¢
each

You buy 5.
How much will they cost?

$$\frac{\begin{array}{r} 8 \\ \times 5 \end{array}}{40}$$

They will cost 40¢.

---

try these

How much will they cost?

1. **2¢**	2. **5¢**	3. **9¢**	4. **6¢**
Buy 8.	Buy 6.	Buy 4.	Buy 3.
5. **8¢**	6. **3¢**	7. **7¢**	8. **4¢**
Buy 2.	Buy 9.	Buy 7.	Buy 5.

now do these

How much will they cost?

9. **9¢** Buy 3.	10. **4¢** Buy 6.	11. **8¢** Buy 4.	12. **4¢** Buy 7.
13. **9¢** Buy 4.	14. **5¢** Buy 9.	15. **3¢** Buy 7.	16. **6¢** Buy 5.
17. **6¢** Buy 4.	18. **4¢** Buy 8.	19. **9¢** Buy 5.	20. **7¢** Buy 4.
21. **8¢** Buy 3.	22. **7¢** Buy 5.	23. **4¢** Buy 9.	24. **5¢** Buy 6.

147

1 and 0 as Factors

  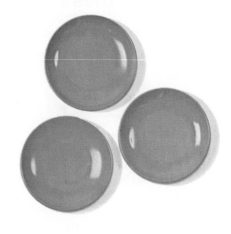

3 plates.
2 crackers on each.
6 crackers in all.

$$3 \times 2 = 6$$

3 plates.
1 cracker on each.
3 crackers in all.

$$3 \times 1 = 3$$

3 plates.
0 crackers on each.
0 crackers in all.

$$3 \times 0 = 0$$

The product of any number and 1 is that number.

The product of any number and 0 is 0.

---

try these

Multiply.

1. $\begin{array}{r} 4 \\ \times 0 \\ \hline \end{array}$	2. $\begin{array}{r} 9 \\ \times 1 \\ \hline \end{array}$	3. $\begin{array}{r} 1 \\ \times 8 \\ \hline \end{array}$	4. $\begin{array}{r} 6 \\ \times 0 \\ \hline \end{array}$	5. $\begin{array}{r} 7 \\ \times 1 \\ \hline \end{array}$	6. $\begin{array}{r} 5 \\ \times 0 \\ \hline \end{array}$
7. $\begin{array}{r} 0 \\ \times 9 \\ \hline \end{array}$	8. $\begin{array}{r} 1 \\ \times 5 \\ \hline \end{array}$	9. $\begin{array}{r} 0 \\ \times 7 \\ \hline \end{array}$	10. $\begin{array}{r} 8 \\ \times 0 \\ \hline \end{array}$	11. $\begin{array}{r} 6 \\ \times 1 \\ \hline \end{array}$	12. $\begin{array}{r} 1 \\ \times 4 \\ \hline \end{array}$

now do these

Multiply.

13. 7
×6

14. 9
×9

15. 8
×7

16. 8
×8

17. 6
×7

18. 1
×2

19. 6
×8

20. 8
×4

21. 9
×6

22. 7
×4

23. 7
×8

24. 7
×7

25. 5
×8

26. 0
×4

27. 6
×9

28. 2
×0

29. 9
×7

30. 4
×7

31. 8
×6

32. 4
×8

33. 9
×3

34. 7
×9

35. 1
×7

36. 8
×9

37. 0
×8

38. 6
×9

39. 9
×4

40. 6
×6

41. 8
×9

42. 6
×4

Solve the problem.

43. 9 on a team.
5 teams.
How many people
in all?

44. 3 players at bat.
3 strikes each.
How many strikes
in all?

45. 9 innings in a game.
2 games played.
How many innings in all?

149

A Chart and a Game

×	0	1	2	3	4	5	6	7	8	9
0	0	0	0	0	0	0	0	0	0	0
1	0	1	2	3	4	5	6	7	8	9
2	0	2	4	6	8	10	12	14	16	18
3	0	3	6	9	12	15	18	21	24	27
4	0	4	8	12	16	20	24	28	32	36
5	0	5	10	15	20	25	30	35	40	45
6	0	6	12	18	24	30	36	42	48	54
7	0	7	14	21	28	35	42	49	56	63
8	0	8	16	24	32	40	48	56	64	72
9	0	9	18	27	36	45	54	63	72	81

The chart shows

$7 \times 6 = 42.$

Use the chart to find this product.

$5 \times 8 = ?$

try these

Multiply. Use the chart when you need it.

1.	2.	3.	4.	5.	6.
9	4	8	7	9	8
×5	×7	×3	×6	×9	×6

now do these

Multiply.

7.	8.	9.	10.	11.	12.
6	4	5	8	4	9
×6	×9	×8	×9	×8	×6

150

Each player circles the track 9 times.
The first time multiply each number by 1.
The second time multiply by 2.
The third time multiply by 3, and so on.
The last time, multiply by 9.

The first player to circle the track 9 times without making a mistake is the winner.

If more than one player circles the track with no errors, the one who did it faster is the winner.

add or multiply?

2 male flight attendants.
3 female flight attendants.
How many in all?

Groups are being joined.
The addends are different.
You add.
2 + 3 = 5
There are 5 attendants in all.

2 jet airplanes.
3 flight attendants in each.
How many in all?

Groups are being joined.
The addends are the same.
You can multiply.
2 × 3 = 6
There are 6 attendants in all.

Would you ADD or can you MULTIPLY?

1. 5 pilots.
   5 copilots.
   How many in all?

2. 5 jet airplanes.
   5 crew members in each.
   How many members in all?

3. 6 crews report to work.
   8 members in each crew
   How many members in all?

4. 6 planes leave one hour.
   8 planes leave the next hour.
   How many planes in all?

152

Solve the problem.

5. 6 jumbo jets.
   4 engines on each.
   How many engines in all?

6. The pilot studied for 4 years
   in high school. The pilot
   studied for 2 years in college.
   How many years was this in all?

7. The pilot spoke to the passengers
   3 times. Each time the pilot
   spoke for 2 minutes. How many
   minutes was this in all?

8. The copilot spoke to the control
   tower 2 times. Each time the
   copilot spoke for 9 minutes. How
   many minutes was this in all?

9. The pilot is 32 years old.
   The pilot may fly for 28 more
   years. How old will the pilot
   be then?

10. The plane has flown for 50
    minutes. It will land in 20
    minutes. How many minutes
    of flying time is this in all?

Test

Multiply.

1. $8 \times 5 =$? (p. 132)

2. $4 \times 2 =$? (p. 132)

3. $7 \times 3 =$? (p. 134)

4. $9 \times 4 =$? (p. 136)

5. $5 \times 5 =$? (p. 132)

6. $4 \times 8 =$? (p. 142)

7. $7 \times 9 =$? (p. 144)

8. $5 \times 7 =$? (p. 140)

9. $6 \times 5 =$? (p. 132)

10. $\begin{array}{r} 6 \\ \times 8 \\ \hline \end{array}$ (p. 138)

11. $\begin{array}{r} 5 \\ \times 9 \\ \hline \end{array}$ (p. 132)

12. $\begin{array}{r} 0 \\ \times 4 \\ \hline \end{array}$ (p. 148)

13. $\begin{array}{r} 3 \\ \times 2 \\ \hline \end{array}$ (p. 134)

14. $\begin{array}{r} 4 \\ \times 7 \\ \hline \end{array}$ (p. 136)

15. $\begin{array}{r} 2 \\ \times 9 \\ \hline \end{array}$ (p. 132)

16. $\begin{array}{r} 1 \\ \times 3 \\ \hline \end{array}$ (p. 148)

17. $\begin{array}{r} 8 \\ \times 8 \\ \hline \end{array}$ (p. 142)

18. $\begin{array}{r} 5 \\ \times 4 \\ \hline \end{array}$ (p. 132)

19. $\begin{array}{r} 6 \\ \times 2 \\ \hline \end{array}$ (p. 138)

20. $\begin{array}{r} 9 \\ \times 0 \\ \hline \end{array}$ (p. 148)

21. $\begin{array}{r} 4 \\ \times 4 \\ \hline \end{array}$ (p. 136)

22. $\begin{array}{r} 7 \\ \times 6 \\ \hline \end{array}$ (p. 140)

23. $\begin{array}{r} 1 \\ \times 0 \\ \hline \end{array}$ (p. 148)

24. $\begin{array}{r} 9 \\ \times 9 \\ \hline \end{array}$ (p. 144)

25. $\begin{array}{r} 5 \\ \times 3 \\ \hline \end{array}$ (p. 132)

26. $\begin{array}{r} 4 \\ \times 8 \\ \hline \end{array}$ (p. 136)

27. $\begin{array}{r} 3 \\ \times 9 \\ \hline \end{array}$ (p. 134)

28. $\begin{array}{r} 5 \\ \times 1 \\ \hline \end{array}$ (p. 132)

29. $\begin{array}{r} 0 \\ \times 0 \\ \hline \end{array}$ (p. 148)

30. $\begin{array}{r} 8 \\ \times 2 \\ \hline \end{array}$ (p. 142)

31. $\begin{array}{r} 7 \\ \times 7 \\ \hline \end{array}$ (p. 140)

32. $\begin{array}{r} 7 \\ \times 2 \\ \hline \end{array}$ (p. 140)

33. $\begin{array}{r} 6 \\ \times 3 \\ \hline \end{array}$ (p. 138)

bonus

Solve the problem.

34. 7 jars.
    4 paint brushes in each.
    How many brushes in all?

    (p. 136)

35. A pencil costs 9¢.
    Buy 4.
    How much will they cost?

    (p. 146)

154

Keeping up

Write the numeral.

1. 486 thousand, 13 (p. 12)   **2.** 2 million, 604 thousand, 402 (p. 14)

In what place is the 3?

3. 7,423,259 (p. 14)   **4.** 5,314,952 (p. 14)

5. 3,647,295 (p. 14)   **6.** 9,635,001 (p. 14)

Complete.

7. ___?___ centimeters make 1 meter. (p. 50)   **8.** ___?___ meters make 1 kilometer. (p. 50)

9. The perimeter of this figure
is ___?___ centimeters. (p. 52)

10. The area of this figure
is ___?___ square centimeters. (p. 54)

Estimate the answer.   Use the nearest hundreds.

11. 325
     +457
        (p. 68)

12. 432
     +163
        (p. 68)

13. 792
     −439
        (p. 90)

14. 758
     −328
        (p. 90)

15. 860
     −307
        (p. 90)

Add.

16. 9474
     + 758
        (p. 82)

17. 8078
     +7959
        (p. 82)

18. 607
      708
     +893
        (p. 80)

19. 97
      385
     + 29
        (p. 80)

20. 149
       65
     +887
        (p. 80)

Subtract.

21. 783
     −259
        (p. 94)

22. 874
     −789
        (p. 100)

23. 600
     −257
        (p. 102)

24. 9876
     −3987
        (p. 106)

25. 617
     −439
        (p. 100)

155

Intersections

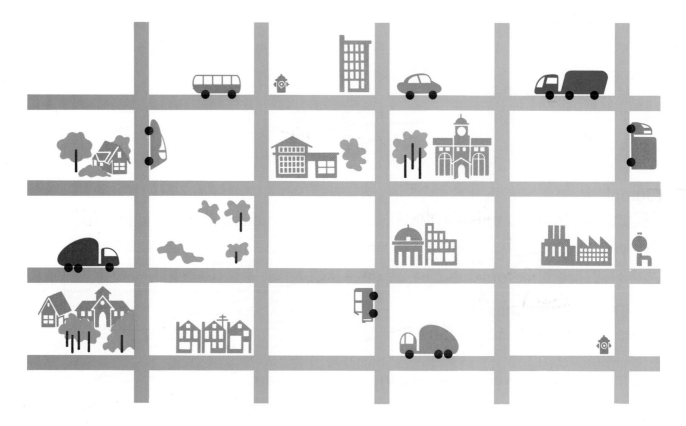

5 streets run north and south in Bedford Village.
4 streets run east and west.
They cross at 20 different points.

You can use multiplication to find the number of **intersections.**

$$5 \longleftarrow \text{north and south streets}$$
$$\underline{\times 4} \longleftarrow \text{east and west streets}$$
$$20 \longleftarrow \text{intersections}$$

Solve the problem.

1. Bedford Village builds more streets.

   They build 2 more that run north and south.

   They build 1 more that runs east and west.

   How many intersections do they have now?

2. Arborville wants a traffic light at each intersection.

   8 streets run north and south.

   7 streets run east and west.

   How many traffic lights should they buy?

3. Brunswick Village wants to place a tree

   at each intersection.

   3 streets run north and south.

   3 streets run east and west.

   How many trees do they need?

4. In Problem 3, you found the number of trees
   needed in Brunswick Village.

   6 floodlights are needed for each tree.

   How many floodlights should they order?

5. Millertown wants a litter basket on each corner.

   There are 4 corners at each intersection.

   2 streets run north and south.

   4 streets run east and west.

   How many litter baskets do they need?

8 Multiplying by Ones

Multiplying Tens

If you can count by tens, then you can multiply tens.

10	10	10	10	10	10	10	10	10
×1	×2	×3	×4	×5	×6	×7	×8	×9
10	20	30	40	50	60	70	80	90

If you can multiply ones, then you can multiply tens.

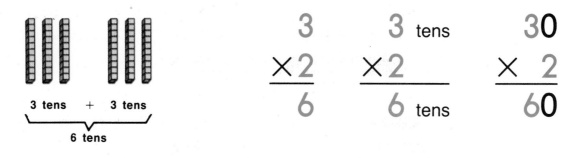

$$\begin{array}{r} 3 \\ \times 2 \\ \hline 6 \end{array} \qquad \begin{array}{r} 3 \text{ tens} \\ \times 2 \\ \hline 6 \text{ tens} \end{array} \qquad \begin{array}{r} 30 \\ \times \ 2 \\ \hline 60 \end{array}$$

3 tens + 3 tens

6 tens

If you can multiply 4 ones, then you can multiply 4 tens.

$$\begin{array}{r} 4 \\ \times 3 \\ \hline 12 \end{array} \qquad \begin{array}{r} 4 \text{ tens} \\ \times 3 \\ \hline 12 \text{ tens} \end{array} \qquad \begin{array}{r} 40 \\ \times \ 3 \\ \hline 120 \end{array}$$

4 tens + 4 tens + 4 tens

12 tens

Multiply.

1. 30 × 3	**2.** 50 × 5	**3.** 20 × 8	**4.** 30 × 4	**5.** 60 × 3	**6.** 90 × 5

now do these

Multiply.

7. 40 × 2	**8.** 30 × 5	**9.** 50 × 3	**10.** 50 × 4	**11.** 90 × 7	**12.** 70 × 9
13. 50 × 7	**14.** 70 × 6	**15.** 70 × 8	**16.** 60 × 5	**17.** 90 × 6	**18.** 60 × 6
19. 60 × 8	**20.** 70 × 4	**21.** 80 × 6	**22.** 80 × 9	**23.** 70 × 7	**24.** 50 × 8
25. 80 × 8	**26.** 60 × 9	**27.** 40 × 9	**28.** 90 × 8	**29.** 40 × 7	**30.** 90 × 9

CROSS THE BRIDGE

Cross the bridge 9 times.
The first time multiply each number by 1.
The second time multiply by 2.
The third time multiply by 3, and so on.
The last time, you will multiply by 9.

How fast can you cross?

159

Multiplying Hundreds

If you can count by hundreds, then you can multiply hundreds.

100	100	100	100	100	100	100	100	100
× 1	× 2	× 3	× 4	× 5	× 6	× 7	× 8	× 9
100	200	300	400	500	600	700	800	900

If you know the answer for 2 × 3 = _?_,
then you can give the answer for 2 × 300 = _?_.

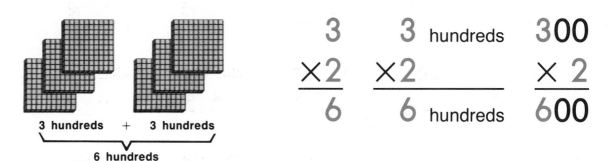

3 hundreds + 3 hundreds
6 hundreds

$$\begin{array}{r} 3 \\ \times 2 \\ \hline 6 \end{array} \qquad \begin{array}{r} 3 \text{ hundreds} \\ \times 2 \\ \hline 6 \text{ hundreds} \end{array} \qquad \begin{array}{r} 300 \\ \times\ 2 \\ \hline 600 \end{array}$$

What is the product for 3 × 4?
Then, what is the product for 3 × 400?

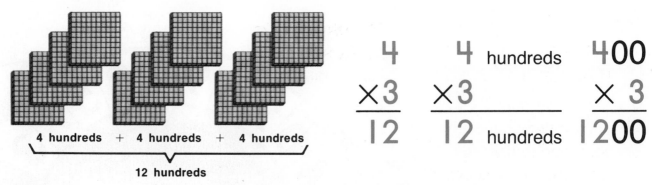

4 hundreds + 4 hundreds + 4 hundreds
12 hundreds

$$\begin{array}{r} 4 \\ \times 3 \\ \hline 12 \end{array} \qquad \begin{array}{r} 4 \text{ hundreds} \\ \times 3 \\ \hline 12 \text{ hundreds} \end{array} \qquad \begin{array}{r} 400 \\ \times\ 3 \\ \hline 1200 \end{array}$$

160

try these

Multiply.

1. 300
   × 4

2. 500
   × 5

3. 300
   × 3

4. 200
   × 8

5. 800
   × 5

6. 500
   × 9

now do these

Multiply.

7. 400
   × 2

8. 700
   × 2

9. 500
   × 4

10. 300
    × 5

11. 900
    × 7

12. 700
    × 6

13. 500
    × 7

14. 700
    × 9

15. 600
    × 5

16. 900
    × 6

17. 700
    × 8

18. 600
    × 6

19. 700
    × 4

20. 800
    × 6

21. 800
    × 9

22. 600
    × 8

23. 500
    × 8

24. 700
    × 7

25. 600
    × 9

26. 800
    × 8

27. 900
    × 8

28. 400
    × 9

29. 900
    × 9

30. 400
    × 7

Solve the problem.

31. 300 cheeseburgers
    sold each day.
    How many in 5 days?

32. 400 big burgers
    sold each day.
    How many in 3 days?

33. 700 shakes
    sold each day.
    How many in 4 days?

161

Add to Find the Product

Here is a way to find the product for 3 × 45.
Multiply the ones.   Multiply the tens.   Add your answers.

$$3 \times 45 = (3 \times 5) + (3 \times 40)$$

Step 1

```
  45
×  3
────
  15
```

Multiply the ones.

Step 2

```
  45
×  3
────
  15
 120
```

Multiply the tens.

Step 3

```
  45
×  3
────
  15
 120
────
 135
```

Add the answers.

Here is a way to find the product for 4 × 368.
Multiply the ones, the tens, and the hundreds.   Add your answers.

$$4 \times 368 = (4 \times 8) + (4 \times 60) + (4 \times 300)$$

Step 1

```
 368
×   4
─────
  32
```

Multiply the ones.

Step 2

```
 368
×   4
─────
  32
 240
```

Multiply the tens.

Step 3

```
 368
×   4
─────
  32
 240
1200
```

Multiply the hundreds.

Step 4

```
 368
×   4
─────
  32
 240
1200
─────
1472
```

Add the answers.

162

Copy and complete.

1. 56	2. 68	3. 79	4. 357	5. 468	6. 759
× 7	× 9	× 6	× 9	× 6	× 8
42	72	54	63	48	72
350	540	420	450	360	400
			2700	2400	5600

Multiply.

7. 45	8. 72	9. 35	10. 642	11. 116	12. 503
× 8	× 5	× 4	× 7	× 8	× 6

Multiply.

13. 85	14. 67	15. 74	16. 89	17. 26	18. 28
× 4	× 7	× 5	× 6	× 5	× 7

19. 92	20. 84	21. 96	22. 36	23. 74	24. 66
× 9	× 7	× 6	× 9	× 9	× 6

25. 789	26. 654	27. 978	28. 546	29. 970	30. 930
× 3	× 6	× 4	× 5	× 2	× 7

31. 805	32. 964	33. 425	34. 324	35. 405	36. 888
× 9	× 5	× 8	× 6	× 9	× 8

Multiplying Tens and Ones

Here is a shorter way to show multiplication.

Step 1

$$\begin{array}{r} \overset{3}{78} \\ \times\ 4 \\ \hline 2 \end{array}$$

Multiply the ones.
$4 \times 8 = 32$
Write the 2 ones.
Remember the 3 tens.

Step 2

$$\begin{array}{r} \overset{3}{78} \\ \times\ 4 \\ \hline 312 \end{array}$$

Multiply the tens.
$4 \times 7 = 28$
Add the 3 tens.
$28 + 3 = 31$
Write 31 tens.

try these

Copy and complete.

1. $\begin{array}{r} \overset{3}{29} \\ \times\ 4 \\ \hline 6 \end{array}$

2. $\begin{array}{r} \overset{2}{53} \\ \times\ 8 \\ \hline 4 \end{array}$

3. $\begin{array}{r} \overset{2}{94} \\ \times\ 7 \\ \hline 8 \end{array}$

4. $\begin{array}{r} \overset{2}{68} \\ \times\ 3 \\ \hline 4 \end{array}$

5. $\begin{array}{r} \overset{3}{47} \\ \times\ 5 \\ \hline 5 \end{array}$

6. $\begin{array}{r} \overset{2}{37} \\ \times\ 4 \\ \hline 8 \end{array}$

Multiply.

7. $\begin{array}{r} 69 \\ \times\ 2 \\ \hline \end{array}$

8. $\begin{array}{r} 40 \\ \times\ 6 \\ \hline \end{array}$

9. $\begin{array}{r} 86 \\ \times\ 9 \\ \hline \end{array}$

10. $\begin{array}{r} 84 \\ \times\ 7 \\ \hline \end{array}$

11. $\begin{array}{r} 46 \\ \times\ 8 \\ \hline \end{array}$

12. $\begin{array}{r} 66 \\ \times\ 6 \\ \hline \end{array}$

164

now do these

Multiply.

13. 39
× 3

14. 37
× 7

15. 28
× 5

16. 46
× 9

17. 60
× 2

18. 76
× 6

19. 59
× 4

20. 36
× 8

21. 48
× 6

22. 27
× 3

23. 92
× 8

24. 94
× 5

25. 82
× 7

26. 45
× 2

27. 70
× 5

28. 52
× 9

29. 47
× 8

30. 68
× 9

31. 53
× 6

32. 56
× 3

33. 65
× 5

34. 47
× 4

35. 69
× 7

36. 48
× 3

37. 58
× 8

38. 38
× 4

39. 29
× 6

40. 54
× 7

41. 70
× 9

42. 89
× 6

quick check

Multiply.

1. 60
× 7

2. 80
× 9

3. 300
× 7

4. 800
× 6

5. 75
× 3

6. 69
× 7

7. 46
× 9

8. 934
× 8

9. 842
× 4

10. 630
× 6

Multiplying Hundreds, Tens, and Ones

Step 1

$$\begin{array}{r} \overset{4}{346} \\ \times\ 7 \\ \hline 2 \end{array}$$

Multiply the ones.
$7 \times 6 = 42$
Write the 2 ones.
Remember the 4 tens

Step 2

$$\begin{array}{r} \overset{3\ 4}{346} \\ \times\ 7 \\ \hline 22 \end{array}$$

Multiply the tens.
$7 \times 4 = 28$
Add the 4 tens.
$28 + 4 = 32$
Write the 2 tens.
Remember the 3 hundreds.

Step 3

$$\begin{array}{r} \overset{3\ 4}{346} \\ \times\ 7 \\ \hline 2422 \end{array}$$

Multiply the hundreds.
$7 \times 3 = 21$
Add the 3 hundreds.
$21 + 3 = 24$
Write 24 hundreds.

try these

Copy and complete.

1. $\begin{array}{r} \overset{1\ 1}{923} \\ \times\ 6 \\ \hline 38 \end{array}$

2. $\begin{array}{r} \overset{4\ 1}{893} \\ \times\ 5 \\ \hline 65 \end{array}$

3. $\begin{array}{r} \overset{1\ 2}{724} \\ \times\ 7 \\ \hline 68 \end{array}$

4. $\begin{array}{r} \overset{1}{240} \\ \times\ 4 \\ \hline 60 \end{array}$

5. $\begin{array}{r} \overset{1\ 2}{823} \\ \times\ 8 \\ \hline 4 \end{array}$

6. $\begin{array}{r} \overset{1}{603} \\ \times\ 6 \\ \hline 8 \end{array}$

Multiply.

7. $\begin{array}{r} 195 \\ \times\ 3 \\ \hline \end{array}$

8. $\begin{array}{r} 369 \\ \times\ 2 \\ \hline \end{array}$

9. $\begin{array}{r} 135 \\ \times\ 9 \\ \hline \end{array}$

10. $\begin{array}{r} 820 \\ \times\ 6 \\ \hline \end{array}$

11. $\begin{array}{r} 235 \\ \times\ 8 \\ \hline \end{array}$

12. $\begin{array}{r} 503 \\ \times\ 5 \\ \hline \end{array}$

now do these

Multiply.

13. 276
  × 5

14. 365
  × 7

15. 150
  × 4

16. 726
  × 9
  6534

17. 248
  × 2
  496

18. 179
  × 6
  1134

19. 456
  × 8
  3644

20. 204
  × 3
  612

21. 389
  × 4
  1556

22. 179
  × 8
  1382

23. 189
  × 7
  1323

24. 498
  × 9
  4482

25. 145
  × 5
  722

26. 758
  × 6
  4598

27. 984
  × 9
  8856

28. 157
  × 2
  314

29. 376
  × 3
  1128

30. 640
  × 8
  5120

31. 420
  × 4
  1680

32. 247
  × 7
  1729

33. 938
  × 5
  4690

34. 607
  × 6
  3642

35. 513
  × 9
  4617

36. 398
  × 3
  1194

37. 456
  × 3
  1368

38. 308
  × 8
  2464

39. 284
  × 2
  568

40. 635
  × 7
  4245

41. 726
  × 5
  3630

42. 306
  × 2
  612

Solve the problem.

There are 168 hours in a week.
How many hours are in

43. 2 weeks?

44. 4 weeks?

45. 8 weeks?

Multiplying Amounts of Money

Multiply amounts of money as if you were multiplying whole numbers. Remember to write the dollar sign and the cents point in the answer.

Step 1	Step 2	Step 3
$\overset{5}{}$ $5.98 × 7 ——— 6	$\overset{6\ 5}{}$ $5.98 × 7 ——— 86	$\overset{6\ 5}{}$ $5.98 × 7 ——— $41.86

try these

Copy and complete.

1. $\overset{4\ 3}{}$ $3.65
   × 7
   ———
   55

2. $\overset{5}{}$ $7.06
   × 9
   ———
   54

3. $\overset{3}{}$ $.89
   × 4
   ———
   56

4. $\overset{4\ 4}{}$ $4.56
   × 8
   ———
   8

5. $\overset{1}{}$ $.84
   × 3
   ———
   2

Multiply.

6. $4.56
   × 3
   ———

7. $2.84
   × 2
   ———

8. $3.08
   × 8
   ———

9. $.26
   × 5
   ———

10. $1.35
    × 7
    ———

Multiply.

11. $8.39 × 4	**12.** $.97 × 8	**13.** $4.68 × 6	**14.** $2.76 × 9	**15.** $1.09 × 7
16. $1.79 × 6	**17.** $3.98 × 3	**18.** $6.45 × 8	**19.** $3.96 × 2	**20.** $4.98 × 9
21. $4.06 × 3	**22.** $3.28 × 8	**23.** $2.04 × 7	**24.** $6.37 × 2	**25.** $7.26 × 5
26. $1.45 × 5	**27.** $7.58 × 6	**28.** $9.84 × 9	**29.** $7.57 × 2	**30.** $3.76 × 3
31. $2.35 × 8	**32.** $1.95 × 3	**33.** $3.09 × 2	**34.** $1.35 × 9	**35.** $.84 × 6

Solve the problem.

36. Carol spent $.98 for a record. Meg spent 4 times that much for a record album. How much did Meg spend?

37. Carl spent $4.05 for a tape. Tim spent 5 times that much for a tape player. How much did Tim spend?

169

Going Shopping

$3.95

You buy 5.
How much will they cost?

$$\overset{\overset{4}{}\ \overset{2}{}}{\$3.95} \times 5 = \$19.75$$

---

try these

How much will they cost?

1. $1.45	2. $.39	3. $.37	4. $.28
Buy 3.	Buy 3.	Buy 4.	Buy 5.
5. $1.56	6. $2.36	7. $1.48	8. $1.27
Buy 4.	Buy 8.	Buy 6.	Buy 3.

How much will they cost?

9. $.92 Buy 8.	10. $.68 Buy 9.	11. $.48 Buy 3.	12. $.76 KIWI BROWN Buy 6.
13. $1.94 Buy 5.	14. $2.58 Buy 8.	15. $1.69 Buy 7.	16. $1.29 LISTERINE Buy 6.
17. $2.54 To sheen for the NATURAL Buy 7.	18. $.73 Buy 9.	19. $.38 SOLO RUBBER TIPPED BOB PINS Buy 4.	20. $4.07 Boldool Buy 4.
21. $.65 Buy 5.	22. $1.56 WashnDri Buy 3.	23. $3.53 Buy 6.	24. $1.47 Deep Magic Buy 8.

171

too much information

Ron Rogers is a reporter for *The Daily Record*.
He is writing a story about a recycling center.
There are many facts in his notes. Which facts
would you use to answer this question:

How many cans did the students collect?

The recycling center is at 385 Hanover Street.

24 people brought in over 500 cans today.

3 students collected aluminum cans.

The students filled 5 bags with cans.

Each bag had 9 cans in it.

The numbers you need are 5 bags with 9 cans in each.
They collected 5 × 9, or 45 cans.

Which numbers would you need to answer the question?

1. How many people helped Diego?

Diego's 3 cats were up in a tree. 15 neighbors tried
to get them down. 5 fire fighters also helped.
They used a ladder to get the cats down.
It took them 3 hours.

2. How many people voted in all?

An election was held in District 5. 15 people arrived
at 9 A.M. 22 more arrived during the next hour.
After that only 17 more people came. The polls
were open from 9 A.M. to 8 P.M.

Solve the problem. Use only the facts you need.

3. How many fire fighters in all?

A 10-story building caught fire.
2 alarms were sounded.
4 fire trucks answered the alarms.
Each truck carried 6 fire fighters.

4. How many people attended the meeting?

The town council met for 4 hours.
There were 6 council members present.
24 citizens also attended.
8 questions were raised.

5. How many bicycles were sold opening day?

A new bicycle shop opened in town.
98 people visited the shop on opening day.
7 bicycles were sold in the morning.
8 were sold in the afternoon.
The shop is open from 8 A.M. to 5 P.M.
It is open 6 days a week.

6. How many crossing guards in all?

1480 students attend school in town.
1232 of them walk to school.
They cross a highway at 7 different places.
2 crossing guards will be assigned to each place.
Each guard will be there 4 hours a day.

Problem-solving Help 173

Test

Multiply.

1. 60
$\times\ 7$
(p. 158)

2. 40
$\times\ 3$
(p. 158)

3. 80
$\times\ 2$
(p. 158)

4. 50
$\times\ 5$
(p. 158)

5. 300
$\times\ \ 7$
(p. 160)

6. 700
$\times\ \ 5$
(p. 160)

7. 900
$\times\ \ 9$
(p. 160)

8. 200
$\times\ \ 6$
(p. 160)

9. 87
$\times\ 4$
(p. 162, 164)

10. 26
$\times\ 5$
(p. 162, 164)

11. 13
$\times\ 9$
(p. 162, 164)

12. 58
$\times\ 7$
(p. 162, 164)

13. 137
$\times\ \ 6$
(p. 162, 166)

14. 482
$\times\ \ 9$
(p. 162, 166)

15. 526
$\times\ \ 7$
(p. 162, 166)

16. 888
$\times\ \ 3$
(p. 162, 166)

17. $8.06
$\times\ \ \ 5$
(p. 168)

18. $3.47
$\times\ \ \ 9$
(p. 168)

19. $2.24
$\times\ \ \ 6$
(p. 168)

20. $9.04
$\times\ \ \ 2$
(p. 168)

bonus

Solve the problem.

21. 300 newspapers are
sold each day.
How many are sold in 2 days?
(p. 160)

22. A tee shirt costs $2.00.
Buy 4.
How much will they cost?
(p. 170)

174

Keeping up

Write the numeral.

1. 37 thousand, 3 (p. 12)

2. 4 million, 7 thousand, 800 (p. 14)

Name

3. 100 more than 735,814. (p. 12)

4. 1000 more than 683,987. (p. 12)

5. 10,000 more than 814,001. (p. 12)

6. 100,000 more than 980,016. (p. 12)

Multiply.

7. 5
$\times$8
(p. 132)

8. 6
$\times$4
(p. 138)

9. 7
$\times$8
(p. 140)

10. 8
$\times$8
(p. 142)

11. 6
$\times$6
(p. 138)

12. 8
$\times$6
(p. 142)

13. 7
$\times$3
(p. 140)

14. 9
$\times$4
(p. 144)

15. 5
$\times$9
(p. 132)

16. 9
$\times$6
(p. 144)

17. 7
$\times$9
(p. 140)

18. 5
$\times$7
(p. 132)

19. 6
$\times$8
(p. 136)

20. 9
$\times$9
(p. 144)

21. 8
$\times$9
(p. 142)

Add.

22. $8.07
7.06
+ 3.98
(p. 84)

23. $1.94
.56
+ 8.78
(p. 84)

24. $ .65
4.09
+ 5.78
(p. 84)

25. $ 6.87
+ 97.76
(p. 84)

26. $68.07
+ 31.99
(p. 84)

Subtract.

27. $6.53
− 4.79
(p. 108)

28. $7.00
− 4.79
(p. 108)

29. $10.42
− 9.67
(p. 108)

30. $72.47
− 71.69
(p. 108)

31. $8.45
− 2.37
(p. 108)

175

Combinations

4   kinds of ice cream.
2   kinds of cones.

Use only one kind
of each at a time.
How many different
kinds of ice cream
cones can you make?

  4   kinds of ice cream
×2   kinds of cones
  8   kinds of ice cream cones

Remember: Use only one kind of each at a time.

1. 3 kinds of jelly.
   2 kinds of bread.
   How many different ways can
   you have bread and jelly?

2. 3 kinds of sandwich spread.
   3 kinds of bread.
   How many different kinds of
   sandwiches can you make?

3. 4 kinds of ice cream.
   3 kinds of cake.
   How many different ways can
   you have ice cream and cake?

4. 8 kinds of ice cream.
   4 kinds of topping.
   How many different kinds of
   ice cream sundaes can you make?

All, None, Some

Each of these sentences is true.

| **All** of the cats are inside the box. | **Some** of the cats are inside the box. | **None** of the cats is inside the box. |

Read the sentence. Then write TRUE or FALSE.

1. All of the puppies are lying down.

2. Some of the puppies are lying down.

3. None of the puppies is lying down.

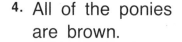   

4. All of the ponies are brown.

5. Some of the ponies are brown.

6. None of the ponies is brown.

9 Multiplying by Tens and Ones

Multiplying by Ten

Look for a pattern.

$$
\begin{array}{r} 3 \\ \times 10 \\ \hline 30 \end{array}
\qquad
\begin{array}{r} 7 \\ \times 10 \\ \hline 70 \end{array}
\qquad
\begin{array}{r} 12 \\ \times 10 \\ \hline 120 \end{array}
\qquad
\begin{array}{r} 46 \\ \times 10 \\ \hline 460 \end{array}
\qquad
\begin{array}{r} 138 \\ \times\ 10 \\ \hline 1380 \end{array}
$$

The red digits in the product are the same as the red digits in the factor.

Look at the products again.
Which digit is always in the ones place of the product?

Here is a fast way to multiply by 10.

Step 1	Step 2
$$\begin{array}{r} 421 \\ \times\ 10 \\ \hline 0 \end{array}$$	$$\begin{array}{r} 421 \\ \times\ 10 \\ \hline 4210 \end{array}$$
Write 0 in the ones place.	Multiply by 1.

178

try these

Copy and complete.

1. 5
    ×10
    ───
      0

2. 17
    ×10
    ───
      0

3. 58
    ×10
    ───
      0

4. 97
    ×10
    ───
      0

5. 249
    × 10
    ────
       0

6. 555
    × 10
    ────
       0

now do these

Multiply.

7. 7
    ×10
    ───

8. 2
    ×10
    ───

9. 9
    ×10
    ───

10. 6
     ×10
     ───

11. 3
     ×10
     ───

12. 8
     ×10
     ───

13. 4
     ×10
     ───

14. 5
     ×10
     ───

15. 53
     ×10
     ───

16. 86
     ×10
     ───

17. 20
     ×10
     ───

18. 71
     ×10
     ───

19. 342
     × 10
     ────

20. 510
     × 10
     ────

21. 187
     × 10
     ────

22. 734
     × 10
     ────

23. 621
     × 10
     ────

24. 279
     × 10
     ────

25. 800
     × 10
     ────

26. 463
     × 10
     ────

27. 382
     × 10
     ────

28. 640
     × 10
     ────

29. 900
     × 10
     ────

30. 970
     × 10
     ────

GOING SHOPPING

Buy 10.
How many cookies do you get?

A.
24 COOKIES

B.
16 COOKIES

C.
36 COOKIES

D.
48 COOKIES

179

Multiplying by Tens

Find the product: 30×42.

To find the product. $\longrightarrow$	30×42
Think of 30 as 3×10. $\longrightarrow$	$3 \times 10 \times 42$
Multiply by 10. $\longrightarrow$	3×420
Then multiply by 3. $\longrightarrow$	1260

Here is one way to show your work.

Step 1

$$\begin{array}{r} 42 \\ \times 30 \\ \hline \end{array}$$

Think of 30
as 3×10.

Step 2

$$\begin{array}{r} 42 \\ \times 30 \\ \hline 0 \end{array}$$

Write 0 in
the ones place.

Step 3

$$\begin{array}{r} 42 \\ \times\ 30 \\ \hline 1260 \end{array}$$

Multiply by 3.

Multiply: 40×128.

Step 1

$$\begin{array}{r} 128 \\ \times\ 40 \\ \hline \end{array}$$

Think of 40
as 4×10.

Step 2

$$\begin{array}{r} 128 \\ \times\ 40 \\ \hline 0 \end{array}$$

Write 0 in
the ones place.

Step 3 | 3

$$\begin{array}{r} 128 \\ \times\ 40 \\ \hline 5120 \end{array}$$

Multiply by 4.

try these

Copy and complete.

1. 43
    × 20
    ———
      0

2. 75
    × 40
    ———
      0

3. 84
    × 20
    ———
      0

4. 126
    × 30
    ———
      0

5. 189
    × 60
    ———
      0

6. 289
    × 30
    ———
      0

now do these

Multiply.

7. 16
    × 20
    ———

8. 85
    × 70
    ———

9. 38
    × 40
    ———

10. 90
    × 30
    ———

11. 71
    × 40
    ———

12. 27
    × 80
    ———

13. 60
    × 50
    ———

14. 49
    × 30
    ———

15. 50
    × 90
    ———

16. 93
    × 60
    ———

17. 72
    × 50
    ———

18. 66
    × 40
    ———

19. 156
    × 20
    ———

20. 207
    × 50
    ———

21. 310
    × 70
    ———

22. 641
    × 30
    ———

23. 860
    × 40
    ———

24. 538
    × 20
    ———

25. 409
    × 60
    ———

26. 274
    × 40
    ———

27. 482
    × 30
    ———

28. 903
    × 80
    ———

29. 320
    × 90
    ———

30. 756
    × 50
    ———

GOING SHOPPING

How many cookies?

24 COOKIES

36 COOKIES

48 COOKIES

60 COOKIES

A. Buy 20 boxes.

B. Buy 30 cans.

C. Buy 40 bags.

D. Buy 50 boxes.

Multiplying by Tens and Ones

Multiply: 23 × 68.

Step 1	Step 2	Step 3
$$\begin{array}{r} 68 \\ \times\, 23 \\ \hline 204 \end{array}$$	$$\begin{array}{r} 68 \\ \times\, 23 \\ \hline 204 \\ 1360 \end{array}$$	$$\begin{array}{r} 68 \\ \times\, 23 \\ \hline 204 \\ 1360 \\ \hline 1564 \end{array}$$
Think of 23 as 20 + 3. Multiply by 3.	Multiply by 20.	Add the products.

Multiply: 49 × 85.

Step 1	Step 2	Step 3
$$\begin{array}{r} 85 \\ \times\, 49 \\ \hline 765 \end{array}$$	$$\begin{array}{r} 85 \\ \times\, 49 \\ \hline 765 \\ 3400 \end{array}$$	$$\begin{array}{r} 85 \\ \times\, 49 \\ \hline 765 \\ 3400 \\ \hline 4165 \end{array}$$
Think of 49 as 40 + 9. Multiply by 9.	Multiply by 40.	Add the products.

Copy and complete.

1. 94	2. 64	3. 45	4. 95	5. 42	6. 60
×27	×48	×36	×54	×83	×34
658	512	270	380	126	240
1880	2560	1350	4750	3360	1800

Multiply.

7. 78	8. 89	9. 98	10. 36	11. 90	12. 20
×72	×61	×19	×92	×63	×75

Multiply.

13. 82	14. 64	15. 73	16. 46	17. 91	18. 80
×47	×28	×39	×71	×17	×14

19. 25	20. 57	21. 60	22. 39	23. 48	24. 43
×94	×63	×29	×82	×50	×33

25. 82	26. 47	27. 28	28. 17	29. 94	30. 70
×39	×73	×46	×92	×57	×77

31. 63	32. 94	33. 82	34. 29	35. 71	36. 50
×60	×39	×25	×48	×39	×75

Multiplying by Tens and Ones

Multiply: 42 × 237.

Step 1	Step 2	Step 3

Step 1

```
  237
×  42
  474
```

Multiply by 2.

Step 2

```
  237
×  42
  474
 9480
```

Multiply by 40.

Step 3

```
  237
×  42
  474
 9480
 9954
```

Add the products.

Multiply: 76 × 305.

Step 1

```
  305
×  76
 1830
```

Multiply by 6.

Step 2

```
  305
×  76
 1830
21350
```

Multiply by 70.

Step 3

```
   305
×   76
  1830
 21350
23,180
```

Add the products.

Copy and complete.

1. 248	2. 469	3. 605	4. 583	5. 374	6. 803
× 92	× 63	× 72	× 54	× 48	× 75
496	1407	1210	2332	2992	4015
22320	28140	42350	29150	14960	56210

Multiply.

7. 792	8. 926	9. 107	10. 238	11. 819	12. 902
× 27	× 61	× 83	× 94	× 19	× 34

Multiply.

13. 237	14. 345	15. 406	16. 174	17. 382	18. 308
× 73	× 52	× 64	× 93	× 47	× 38

19. 263	20. 438	21. 327	22. 409	23. 182	24. 777
× 26	× 84	× 62	× 93	× 17	× 32

25. 225	26. 384	27. 426	28. 539	29. 148	30. 607
× 62	× 94	× 53	× 74	× 46	× 18

31. 273	32. 146	33. 237	34. 329	35. 408	36. 909
× 82	× 60	× 28	× 92	× 76	× 99

Multiplying Amounts of Money

Multiply amounts of money as if you were multiplying whole numbers. Remember to write the dollar sign and the cents point in the answer.

Step 1	Step 2	Step 3
$$\begin{array}{r} \$.62 \\ \times\ 35 \\ \hline 310 \end{array}$$	$$\begin{array}{r} \$.62 \\ \times\ 35 \\ \hline 310 \\ 1860 \end{array}$$	$$\begin{array}{r} \$.62 \\ \times\ 35 \\ \hline 310 \\ 1860 \\ \hline \$21.70 \end{array}$$
Multiply by 5.	Multiply by 30.	Add the products.

Remember to write the dollar sign and the cents point in the answer.

Step 1	Step 2	Step 3
$$\begin{array}{r} \$3.98 \\ \times\ 24 \\ \hline 1592 \end{array}$$	$$\begin{array}{r} \$3.98 \\ \times\ 24 \\ \hline 1592 \\ 7960 \end{array}$$	$$\begin{array}{r} \$3.98 \\ \times\ 24 \\ \hline 1592 \\ 7960 \\ \hline \$95.52 \end{array}$$
Multiply by 4.	Multiply by 20.	Add the products.

186

try these

Copy and complete.

1. $.89
   × 36
   ‾‾‾‾
   534
   2670

2. $1.07
   × 38
   ‾‾‾‾
   856
   3210

3. $.36
   × 29
   ‾‾‾‾
   324
   720

4. $2.38
   × 49
   ‾‾‾‾
   2142
   9520

5. $.95
   × 45
   ‾‾‾‾
   475
   3800

Multiply.

6. $.78
   × 27
   ‾‾‾‾

7. $7.92
   × 72
   ‾‾‾‾

8. $.45
   × 63
   ‾‾‾‾

9. $6.55
   × 27
   ‾‾‾‾

10. $2.09
    × 27
    ‾‾‾‾

now do these

Multiply.

11. $.36
    × 60
    ‾‾‾‾

12. $2.73
    × 28
    ‾‾‾‾

13. $.94
    × 93
    ‾‾‾‾

14. $1.46
    × 70
    ‾‾‾‾

15. $.82
    × 52
    ‾‾‾‾

16. $3.29
    × 67
    ‾‾‾‾

17. $.29
    × 84
    ‾‾‾‾

18. $4.06
    × 67
    ‾‾‾‾

19. $.39
    × 28
    ‾‾‾‾

20. $1.48
    × 64
    ‾‾‾‾

21. $.47
    × 37
    ‾‾‾‾

22. $5.39
    × 47
    ‾‾‾‾

23. $.28
    × 64
    ‾‾‾‾

24. $4.26
    × 53
    ‾‾‾‾

25. $.17
    × 29
    ‾‾‾‾

26. $3.04
    × 94
    ‾‾‾‾

27. $.94
    × 57
    ‾‾‾‾

28. $2.25
    × 26
    ‾‾‾‾

29. $.25
    × 49
    ‾‾‾‾

30. $1.82
    × 77
    ‾‾‾‾

187

Going Shopping

$4.98

You buy 36.
How much will they cost?

$$
\begin{array}{r}
\$4.98 \\
\times \quad 36 \\
\hline
2988 \\
14940 \\
\hline
\$179.28
\end{array}
$$

---

try these

How much will they cost?

1. $1.25	2. $.25	3. $1.63	4. $2.07
WELCOME			
Buy 12.	Buy 49.	Buy 26.	Buy 36.
5. $.57	6. $4.38	7. $.60	8. $3.50
Buy 16.	Buy 28.	Buy 39.	Buy 15.

How much will they cost?

9. $.82	10. $4.38	11. $.64	12. $3.27
Buy 16.	Buy 48.	Buy 28.	Buy 26.

13. $.73	14. $3.09	15. $.48	16. $1.82
Buy 39.	Buy 13.	Buy 50.	Buy 17.

17. $.46	18. $3.82	19. $.90	20. $2.65
Buy 63.	Buy 47.	Buy 20.	Buy 32.

21. $.92	22. $1.74	23. $.98	24. $3.45
Buy 36.	Buy 27.	Buy 18.	Buy 70.

Test

Multiply.

1. 26
×10
<small>(p. 178)</small>

2. 39
×10
<small>(p. 178)</small>

3. 403
× 10
<small>(p. 178)</small>

4. 600
× 10
<small>(p. 178)</small>

5. 85
×40
<small>(p. 180)</small>

6. 73
×60
<small>(p. 180)</small>

7. 803
× 90
<small>(p. 180)</small>

8. 411
× 20
<small>(p. 180)</small>

9. 81
×63
<small>(p. 182)</small>

10. 74
×21
<small>(p. 182)</small>

11. 38
×83
<small>(p. 182)</small>

12. 14
×66
<small>(p. 182)</small>

13. 832
× 26
<small>(p. 184)</small>

14. 337
× 53
<small>(p. 184)</small>

15. 732
× 62
<small>(p. 184)</small>

16. 623
× 49
<small>(p. 184)</small>

17. $1.63
× 14
<small>(p. 186)</small>

18. $7.87
× 45
<small>(p. 186)</small>

19. $6.29
× 37
<small>(p. 186)</small>

20. $9.05
× 51
<small>(p. 186)</small>

bonus

Solve the problem.

21. There are 24 hours in a day. How many hours are there in 30 days?

<small>(p. 180)</small>

22. A pair of socks costs $1.19. Buy 10 pairs. How much will they cost?

<small>(p. 188)</small>

Keeping up

Name

1. 1000 more than 80,462. (p. 12)
2. 10,000 more than 795,001. (p. 12)
3. 100,000 more than 4,373,065 (p. 14)
4. 1,000,000 more than 3,006,100. (p. 14)

Choose the correct unit.

5. Ann's room is about 3 (centimeters, meters) wide. (p. 50)
6. Carla is 150 (centimeters, meters) tall. (p. 50)
7. Jeff's dog weighs 4 (grams, kilograms). (p. 56)
8. Sam drinks 4 (cups, liters) of milk a day. (p. 58)

Add.

9.
```
   67
  986
+  28
```
(p. 80)

10.
```
  237
   89
 +763
```
(p. 80)

11.
```
  506
  708
 +897
```
(p. 80)

12.
```
   659
 +9876
```
(p. 82)

13.
```
  7809
 +7687
```
(p. 82)

Subtract.

14.
```
 7547
-3899
```
(p. 106)

15.
```
  700
 -398
```
(p. 102)

16.
```
 1774
- 689
```
(p. 106)

17.
```
  713
 -497
```
(p. 100)

18.
```
  652
 -567
```
(p. 100)

Multiply.

19.
```
  89
×  7
```
(p. 164)

20.
```
  65
×  8
```
(p. 164)

21.
```
  90
×  8
```
(p. 158)

22.
```
  94
×  6
```
(p. 164)

23.
```
  87
×  9
```
(p. 164)

24.
```
 $1.59
×    5
```
(p. 168)

25.
```
 $1.97
×    3
```
(p. 168)

26.
```
 $2.45
×    9
```
(p. 168)

27.
```
 $3.67
×    7
```
(p. 168)

28.
```
 $4.06
×    6
```
(p. 168)

THREE FACTORS

There are 4 trucks.
There are 3 cartons in each truck.
There are 2 toys in each carton.
How many toys in all?

You multiply to solve.
Does it matter which numbers you multiply first?

Complete to find out.

$4 \times 3 \times 2$
$12 \times 2 = \underline{?}$

$4 \times 3 \times 2$
$4 \times 6 = \underline{?}$

$4 \times 3 \times 2$
$3 \times 8 = \underline{?}$

Find the product.

1. $3 \times 4 \times 7$

2. $5 \times 3 \times 6$

3. $9 \times 6 \times 7$

4. $8 \times 9 \times 7$

5. $6 \times 7 \times 9$

6. $3 \times 7 \times 9$

7. $4 \times 6 \times 20$

8. $7 \times 4 \times 30$

9. $6 \times 80 \times 7$

10. $5 \times 60 \times 8$

11. $4 \times 8 \times 70$

12. $5 \times 7 \times 90$

13. $6 \times 30 \times 25$

14. $8 \times 15 \times 40$

15. $7 \times 13 \times 30$

16. $6 \times 18 \times 50$

17. $8 \times 14 \times 60$

18. $8 \times 20 \times 30$

10 Division Facts

Separating Groups

How many twos in 8?

$4 \times 2 = 8$

Copy and complete the sentence.

1.

$\underline{\text{?}} \times 2 = 10$

2.

$\underline{\text{?}} \times 5 = 10$

3.

$\underline{\text{?}} \times 2 = 16$

4.

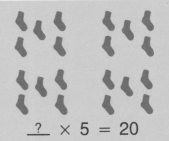

$\underline{\text{?}} \times 5 = 20$

5.

$\underline{\text{?}} \times 2 = 6$

6.

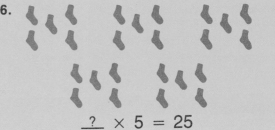

$\underline{\text{?}} \times 5 = 25$

Missing Factors

How many twos in 12?
Find the missing factor: $\underline{?} \times 2 = 12$.

The frog starts at 0. It hops by twos.
It makes 6 hops to reach 12.

$$6 \times 2 = 12$$

Find the missing factor: $\underline{?} \times 5 = 30$.

This frog hops by fives.
It makes 6 hops to reach 30.

$$6 \times 5 = 30$$

194

Find the missing factor.

1. _?_ × 2 = 10

2. _?_ × 2 = 14

3. _?_ × 2 = 8

4. _?_ × 5 = 15

5. _?_ × 5 = 40

6. _?_ × 5 = 25

now do these

Find the missing factor.

7. _?_ × 2 = 2

8. _?_ × 5 = 45

9. _?_ × 2 = 16

10. _?_ × 5 = 30

11. _?_ × 2 = 18

12. _?_ × 5 = 35

13. _?_ × 2 = 6

14. _?_ × 5 = 20

15. _?_ × 2 = 12

16. _?_ × 5 = 10

17. _?_ × 5 = 5

18. _?_ × 2 = 4

19. _?_ × 2 = 14

20. _?_ × 5 = 15

21. _?_ × 5 = 30

22. _?_ × 5 = 45

23. _?_ × 2 = 8

24. _?_ × 2 = 10

25. _?_ × 2 = 2

26. _?_ × 5 = 40

27. _?_ × 5 = 25

THINK ABOUT IT

You can see 80 fingers.
How many people are
standing behind the fence?

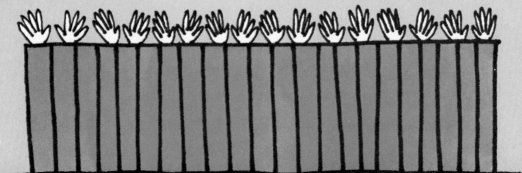

195

Division

Find the missing factor: _?_ × 3 = 18.
You can divide to find the missing factor.

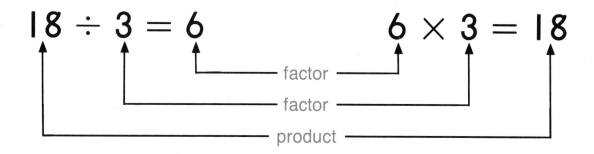

$$18 \div 3 = 6 \qquad\qquad 6 \times 3 = 18$$

factor

factor

product

The answer in division is called the **quotient.**

Find the quotient: 18 ÷ 3 = _?_.

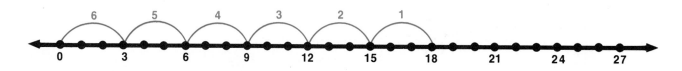

Begin at 18. Subtract threes until you reach 0.
How many threes did you subtract?

$$18 \div 3 = 6$$

Find the quotient.

1. $9 \div 3 = \underline{?}$

2. $15 \div 3 = \underline{?}$

3. $3 \div 3 = \underline{?}$

4. $12 \div 3 = \underline{?}$

5. $6 \div 3 = \underline{?}$

6. $18 \div 3 = \underline{?}$

— now do these —

Find the quotient.

7. $27 \div 3 = \underline{?}$

8. $21 \div 3 = \underline{?}$

9. $24 \div 3 = \underline{?}$

10. $6 \div 3 = \underline{?}$

11. $15 \div 3 = \underline{?}$

12. $12 \div 3 = \underline{?}$

13. $21 \div 3 = \underline{?}$

14. $9 \div 3 = \underline{?}$

15. $3 \div 3 = \underline{?}$

16. $18 \div 3 = \underline{?}$

17. $24 \div 3 = \underline{?}$

18. $27 \div 3 = \underline{?}$

19. $14 \div 2 = \underline{?}$

20. $40 \div 5 = \underline{?}$

21. $18 \div 2 = \underline{?}$

22. $35 \div 5 = \underline{?}$

23. $16 \div 2 = \underline{?}$

24. $45 \div 5 = \underline{?}$

25. $10 \div 2 = \underline{?}$

26. $30 \div 5 = \underline{?}$

27. $25 \div 5 = \underline{?}$

ALL IN THE FAMILY

The numbers 2, 3, and 6 belong to the same family.
One fact about the family leads you to other facts.

$2 \times 3 = 6$ —— so ——→ $3 \times 2 = 6$

so

so

$6 \div 3 = 2$

$6 \div 2 = 3$

Write the other facts about the family.

A. $4 \times 3 = 12$

B. $3 \times 6 = 18$

C. $9 \times 3 = 27$

197

Another Way to Show Division

Division can be shown in two ways.

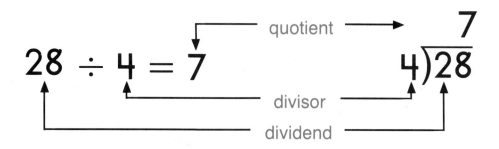

Three ways to find the quotient for 4)28.

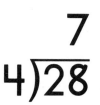

1. Begin at 0. Add fours until you reach 28.
   How many fours did you add?

2. Begin at 28. Subtract fours
   until you reach 0.
   How many fours did you subtract?

3. Think of a multiplication fact:
   What number times 4 is 28?

---

try these

Find the quotient.

1. 4)16
2. 4)28
3. 4)32
4. 4)24
5. 4)12
6. 4)20

7. 4)4
8. 4)36
9. 4)8
10. 4)20
11. 4)28
12. 4)32

now do these

Find the quotient.

13. $4\overline{)4}$ 14. $4\overline{)32}$ 15. $4\overline{)16}$ 16. $4\overline{)36}$ 17. $4\overline{)8}$ 18. $4\overline{)20}$

19. $4\overline{)28}$ 20. $4\overline{)12}$ 21. $4\overline{)20}$ 22. $4\overline{)32}$ 23. $4\overline{)24}$ 24. $4\overline{)16}$

25. $3\overline{)27}$ 26. $2\overline{)16}$ 27. $5\overline{)25}$ 28. $5\overline{)30}$ 29. $3\overline{)24}$ 30. $2\overline{)2}$

31. $2\overline{)18}$ 32. $3\overline{)18}$ 33. $5\overline{)45}$ 34. $2\overline{)14}$ 35. $2\overline{)12}$ 36. $5\overline{)10}$

37. $3\overline{)21}$ 38. $5\overline{)40}$ 39. $3\overline{)15}$ 40. $2\overline{)10}$ 41. $3\overline{)3}$ 42. $2\overline{)4}$

43. $2\overline{)6}$ 44. $5\overline{)20}$ 45. $3\overline{)9}$ 46. $5\overline{)15}$ 47. $2\overline{)8}$ 48. $5\overline{)5}$

HIGH HURDLES

A. Divide by 2 as you jump over each number.

 | 6 | 10 | 14 | 4 | 18 | 8 | 12 | 16 | 2 |

B. Divide by 3 as you jump over each number.

 | 12 | 24 | 6 | 15 | 27 | 3 | 18 | 9 | 21 | FINISH

C. Divide by 4 as you jump over each number.

 | 16 | 28 | 8 | 36 | 4 | 20 | 32 | 24 | 12 |

D. Divide by 5 as you jump over each number.

 | 10 | 25 | 35 | 45 | 15 | 30 | 5 | 20 | 40 | FINISH 199

Practicing With 6 and 7

The quotients are shown in red.
Use a piece of paper to hide them.
See how fast you can name them.

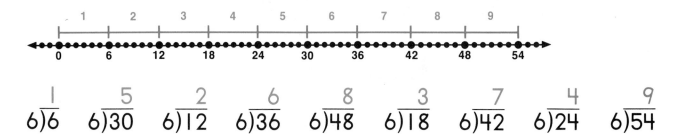

$$\overset{1}{6)6} \quad \overset{5}{6)30} \quad \overset{2}{6)12} \quad \overset{6}{6)36} \quad \overset{8}{6)48} \quad \overset{3}{6)18} \quad \overset{7}{6)42} \quad \overset{4}{6)24} \quad \overset{9}{6)54}$$

The quotients are shown in red.
Use a piece of paper to hide them.
See how fast you can name them.

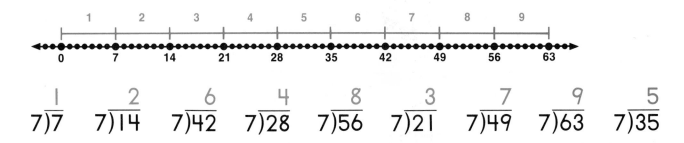

$$\overset{1}{7)7} \quad \overset{2}{7)14} \quad \overset{6}{7)42} \quad \overset{4}{7)28} \quad \overset{8}{7)56} \quad \overset{3}{7)21} \quad \overset{7}{7)49} \quad \overset{9}{7)63} \quad \overset{5}{7)35}$$

try these

Divide.

1. $6)\overline{48}$ 2. $6)\overline{36}$ 3. $6)\overline{54}$ 4. $6)\overline{42}$ 5. $6)\overline{24}$ 6. $6)\overline{6}$

7. $7)\overline{49}$ 8. $7)\overline{63}$ 9. $7)\overline{56}$ 10. $7)\overline{42}$ 11. $7)\overline{28}$ 12. $7)\overline{7}$

200

— **now do these** —

Divide.

13. 6)‾4‾2‾   14. 6)‾1‾8‾   15. 7)‾2‾1‾   16. 7)‾7‾   17. 6)‾1‾2‾   18. 6)‾3‾0‾

19. 7)‾1‾4‾   20. 6)‾6‾   21. 7)‾3‾5‾   22. 6)‾5‾4‾   23. 7)‾2‾8‾   24. 7)‾4‾2‾

25. 6)‾3‾6‾   26. 7)‾5‾6‾   27. 6)‾4‾8‾   28. 7)‾4‾9‾   29. 6)‾3‾0‾   30. 7)‾7‾

31. 7)‾6‾3‾   32. 6)‾2‾4‾   33. 7)‾4‾2‾   34. 6)‾1‾8‾   35. 7)‾3‾5‾   36. 6)‾4‾8‾

37. 4)‾3‾6‾   38. 3)‾2‾4‾   39. 5)‾4‾0‾   40. 4)‾3‾2‾   41. 3)‾2‾1‾   42. 4)‾2‾0‾

43. 6)‾6‾   44. 3)‾2‾7‾   45. 7)‾1‾4‾   46. 7)‾3‾5‾   47. 5)‾4‾5‾   48. 5)‾3‾0‾

49. 4)‾2‾4‾   50. 7)‾2‾1‾   51. 5)‾3‾5‾   52. 6)‾1‾2‾   53. 5)‾3‾0‾   54. 3)‾1‾8‾

HIGH HURDLES

A. Divide by 6 as you jump over each number.

 24 54 42 12 6 30 48 18 36

B. Divide by 7 as you jump over each number.

 28 49 14 7 35 63 21 56 42

FINISH

201

Practicing With 8 and 9

The quotients are shown in red.
Use a piece of paper to hide them.
See how fast you can name them.

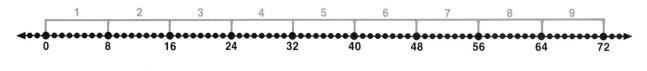

$$\overset{1}{8\overline{)8}} \quad \overset{5}{8\overline{)40}} \quad \overset{2}{8\overline{)16}} \quad \overset{8}{8\overline{)64}} \quad \overset{3}{8\overline{)24}} \quad \overset{7}{8\overline{)56}} \quad \overset{9}{8\overline{)72}} \quad \overset{6}{8\overline{)48}} \quad \overset{4}{8\overline{)32}}$$

The quotients are shown in red.
Use a piece of paper to hide them.
See how fast you can name them.

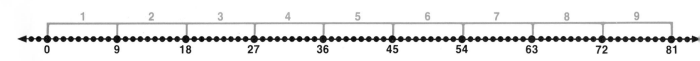

$$\overset{1}{9\overline{)9}} \quad \overset{2}{9\overline{)18}} \quad \overset{8}{9\overline{)72}} \quad \overset{4}{9\overline{)36}} \quad \overset{7}{9\overline{)63}} \quad \overset{3}{9\overline{)27}} \quad \overset{6}{9\overline{)54}} \quad \overset{9}{9\overline{)81}} \quad \overset{5}{9\overline{)45}}$$

---

try these

Divide.

1. $8\overline{)64}$ 2. $8\overline{)48}$ 3. $8\overline{)72}$ 4. $8\overline{)56}$ 5. $8\overline{)32}$ 6. $9\overline{)9}$

7. $9\overline{)81}$ 8. $9\overline{)63}$ 9. $9\overline{)54}$ 10. $9\overline{)72}$ 11. $9\overline{)45}$ 12. $8\overline{)8}$

202

Divide.

13. 8)‾56‾ 14. 8)‾24‾ 15. 9)‾27‾ 16. 9)‾9‾ 17. 8)‾16‾ 18. 8)‾32‾

19. 8)‾8‾ 20. 9)‾18‾ 21. 9)‾45‾ 22. 8)‾40‾ 23. 9)‾36‾ 24. 9)‾9‾

25. 9)‾81‾ 26. 8)‾64‾ 27. 9)‾63‾ 28. 8)‾48‾ 29. 9)‾72‾ 30. 9)‾54‾

31. 8)‾72‾ 32. 9)‾36‾ 33. 8)‾32‾ 34. 9)‾54‾ 35. 9)‾27‾ 36. 8)‾8‾

37. 8)‾24‾ 38. 6)‾42‾ 39. 7)‾21‾ 40. 7)‾35‾ 41. 6)‾54‾ 42. 7)‾42‾

43. 9)‾18‾ 44. 7)‾28‾ 45. 8)‾16‾ 46. 6)‾36‾ 47. 7)‾56‾ 48. 4)‾28‾

49. 6)‾48‾ 50. 7)‾49‾ 51. 6)‾30‾ 52. 8)‾40‾ 53. 7)‾63‾ 54. 3)‾24‾

HIGH HURDLES

A. Divide by 8 as you jump over each number.

| 16 | 40 | 64 | 8 | 24 | 72 | 56 | 32 | 48 |

B. Divide by 9 as you jump over each number.

| 27 | 9 | 81 | 54 | 18 | 72 | 45 | 63 | 36 |

FINISH

203

The Mean

Andrea threw 5 balls.
These are her scores.

8, 3, 2, 7, 10

Find the **mean,** or
average, of the scores.

To find the mean:

1 Find the sum of the scores.

$8 + 3 + 2 + 7 + 10 = 30$

2 Divide the sum by the number of scores.

$$5 \overline{)30} \quad \text{(quotient } 6\text{)}$$

The mean is 6.

Find the mean of these scores: 7, 2, 5, 6, 1, 3.

$$\text{NUMBER OF SCORES} \rightarrow 6 \overline{)24} \leftarrow \text{SUM OF SCORES}$$
$$4 \leftarrow \text{MEAN}$$

204

Find the mean.

1. 5, 9, 4   2. 12, 8, 3, 5   3. 9, 7, 8, 1, 5

now do these

Find the mean.

4. 8, 9, 7   5. 6, 5, 7   6. 12, 0, 6

7. 10, 7, 1   8. 5, 8, 2   9. 4, 10, 7

10. 8, 0, 10   11. 9, 9, 6   12. 7, 1, 4

13. 6, 9, 7, 6   14. 9, 8, 0, 3   15. 9, 8, 7, 4

16. 7, 0, 8, 9   17. 7, 4, 8, 5   18. 6, 0, 5, 9

19. 10, 3, 7, 8   20. 6, 6, 6, 10   21. 8, 9, 4, 11

22. 7, 8, 9, 5, 6   23. 1, 2, 3, 4, 5   24. 7, 6, 5, 8, 9

25. 8, 3, 9, 4, 7, 5   26. 6, 8, 7, 5, 4, 6   27. 7, 5, 8, 7, 6, 9

quick check

Divide.

1. $2\overline{)16}$ 2. $5\overline{)45}$ 3. $6\overline{)36}$ 4. $7\overline{)63}$ 5. $9\overline{)36}$

6. $6\overline{)48}$ 7. $8\overline{)72}$ 8. $9\overline{)81}$ 9. $7\overline{)49}$ 10. $5\overline{)30}$

205

Quotients With Some Left Over

There are 23 marbles.
Four people want to share them.
How many should each get?

The question: How many fours in 23?

$$4\overline{)23}$$

Think:

1 x 4 = 4	Since 6 fours is greater than 23,
2 x 4 = 8	there must be 5 fours in 23.
3 x 4 = 12	The quotient is 5.
4 x 4 = 16	
(5 x 4 = 20)	Each person gets 5.
6 x 4 = 24	There will be some left over.

Find the quotient for $7\overline{)18}$.

Think:

1 x 7 = 7	3 × 7 is greater than 18.
(2 x 7 = 14)	So, the quotient is 2.
3 x 7 ≐ 21	There are some left over.

Find the quotient.

1. 4)33   2. 6)43   3. 5)37   4. 3)29   5. 7)29   6. 2)19

Find the quotient.

7. 3)25   8. 5)27   9. 4)29   10. 3)23   11. 5)33   12. 6)38

13. 8)57   14. 7)65   15. 9)55   16. 8)43   17. 9)38   18. 4)37

19. 6)49   20. 8)74   21. 7)50   22. 8)34   23. 9)46   24. 3)19

25. 4)26   26. 6)56   27. 8)49   28. 5)44   29. 7)38   30. 3)17

31. 5)48   32. 4)23   33. 6)35   34. 7)59   35. 8)67   36. 9)75

Solve the problem.

37. 65 fish.
    9 in a school.
    About how many schools?

38. 85 baboons.
    9 groups.
    About how many in a group?

39. 45 wolves.
    7 in a pack.
    About how many packs?

40. 67 ducks.
    8 flocks.
    About how many in a flock?

207

Quotients and Remainders

Sometimes when you divide, you have some left over.
The number left over is the **remainder.**
Find the quotient and the remainder: $6\overline{)27}$.

Step 1	Step 2	Step 3
$\begin{array}{r} 4 \\ 6\overline{)27} \end{array}$	$\begin{array}{r} 4 \\ 6\overline{)27} \\ 24 \end{array}$	$\begin{array}{r} 4 \ \text{r}3 \\ 6\overline{)27} \\ \underline{24} \\ 3 \end{array}$
Find the quotient. $1 \times 6 = 6$ $2 \times 6 = 12$ $3 \times 6 = 18$ $\boxed{4 \times 6 = 24}$ $5 \times 6 = 30$	Multiply: $4 \times 6 = 24$. Write the product under 27.	Subtract to find the remainder. Show the remainder in the answer.

Here is a way to check your answer.

$\begin{array}{r} 4 \ \text{r}3 \\ 6\overline{)27} \\ \underline{24} \\ 3 \end{array}$

1. Multiply the divisor by the quotient.
$4 \times 6 = 24$

2. Add the remainder.
$24 + 3 = 27$

3. The result should equal the dividend.

208

Copy and complete.

5	3	7	6	4	4
1. 2)11	2. 6)21	3. 4)30	4. 5)34	5. 7)30	6. 6)29
10	18	28	30	28	24

6	4	9	3	7	3
7. 3)19	8. 8)35	9. 2)19	10. 4)15	11. 9)65	12. 7)25

Find the quotient and the remainder.

13. 9)29　　14. 8)73　　15. 4)37　　16. 8)26　　17. 6)23　　18. 3)16

19. 5)27　　20. 4)23　　21. 7)45　　22. 9)47　　23. 3)28　　24. 2)15

25. 3)25　　26. 7)17　　27. 4)34　　28. 2)17　　29. 5)38　　30. 8)43

31. 3)22　　32. 4)17　　33. 8)15　　34. 6)39　　35. 3)11　　36. 8)49

37. 7)58　　38. 4)33　　39. 6)45　　40. 7)51　　41. 9)77　　42. 6)57

Division Practice

You have 15 gumdrops.
You want to give 2 to
each friend.
How many friends will
get 2 gumdrops?

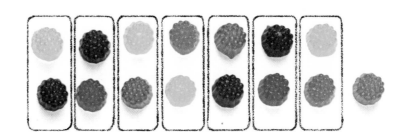

To solve, think:
How many twos in 15?

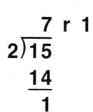

$$\begin{array}{r} 7 \text{ r } 1 \\ 2\overline{)15} \\ 14 \\ \hline 1 \end{array}$$

You can give 2 gumdrops to 7 friends.
You will have 1 gumdrop left over.

You have 15 gumdrops.
You want to give them
to 2 friends in a fair way.
How many will each get?

To solve, think:
15 separated into 2 fair shares.

$$\begin{array}{r} 7 \text{ r } 1 \\ 2\overline{)15} \\ 14 \\ \hline 1 \end{array}$$

You can give each friend 7 gumdrops.
You will have 1 gumdrop left over.

210

try these

Find the quotient and the remainder.

1. $3\overline{)23}$ 2. $5\overline{)19}$ 3. $7\overline{)26}$ 4. $6\overline{)33}$ 5. $8\overline{)44}$ 6. $7\overline{)47}$

now do these

Find the quotient and the remainder.

7. $8\overline{)52}$ 8. $4\overline{)27}$ 9. $9\overline{)30}$ 10. $6\overline{)49}$ 11. $8\overline{)29}$ 12. $6\overline{)19}$

13. $9\overline{)50}$ 14. $7\overline{)20}$ 15. $5\overline{)39}$ 16. $5\overline{)33}$ 17. $9\overline{)33}$ 18. $8\overline{)60}$

19. $6\overline{)20}$ 20. $7\overline{)60}$ 21. $8\overline{)23}$ 22. $4\overline{)11}$ 23. $5\overline{)28}$ 24. $7\overline{)52}$

25. $4\overline{)35}$ 26. $6\overline{)51}$ 27. $5\overline{)41}$ 28. $8\overline{)70}$ 29. $9\overline{)71}$ 30. $6\overline{)41}$

31. $4\overline{)39}$ 32. $6\overline{)58}$ 33. $5\overline{)42}$ 34. $9\overline{)40}$ 35. $7\overline{)59}$ 36. $5\overline{)24}$

THINK ABOUT IT

You want to fill cups with candy.
Each cup will hold 9 pieces.

How many cups can you fill with

A. 85 cherry candies?
B. 48 lemon candies?
C. 59 lime candies?

multiply or divide?

Doris makes plant hangers with string and beads. She has 21 meters of string. She cuts it into pieces 3 meters long. How many pieces will she get?

Think: How many threes in 21?
You should divide.

$$3\overline{)21}^{7}$$

She will get 7 pieces.

Dave has 7 packages of beads. There are 5 beads in each package. How many beads are there in all?

Think: How many is 7 fives?
You should multiply.

$$\begin{array}{r} 5 \\ \times 7 \\ \hline 35 \end{array}$$

There are 35 beads in all.

Would you MULTIPLY or DIVIDE?

1. Doris has 8 pieces of string. Each is 4 meters long. How many meters of string does she have in all?

2. Dave has 32 pieces of string. Each plant hanger takes 8 pieces. How many plant hangers can he make?

3. Dave made 5 plant hangers. It took him 15 hours. How long did it take him to make each hanger?

4. Doris has 5 boxes of string. There are 5 balls of string in each box. How many balls of string has she in all?

Solve the problem.

5. Dave sells the plant hangers for $6.95 each. Yesterday, he sold 7. How much did he earn?

6. Dave has 72 beads. He needs 9 for one plant hanger. How many plant hangers can he make?

7. A plant hanger takes 3 hours to make. Doris has 18 hours to work. How many plant hangers can she make?

8. There are 12 balls of string on the counter. There are 50 meters of string on each ball. How many meters of string is this in all?

9. There are 5 balls of string in each box. Each ball costs $.90. How much does the whole box cost?

10. There are 50 meters of string on a ball. Doris needs pieces 9 meters long. How many pieces this length can she get from one ball?

Problem-solving Help   213

Test

Find the missing factor.

1. $\underline{}\times 5 = 10$ (p. 194) **2.** $\underline{}\times 2 = 16$ (p. 194) **3.** $\underline{}\times 5 = 45$ (p. 194)

Divide.

4. $24 \div 3 = \underline{}$ (p. 196) **5.** $18 \div 2 = \underline{}$ (p. 196) **6.** $35 \div 5 = \underline{}$ (p. 196)

(p. 202) (p. 200) (p. 202) (p. 198) (p. 200) (p. 202)

7. $8\overline{)64}$ **8.** $7\overline{)28}$ **9.** $9\overline{)72}$ **10.** $4\overline{)24}$ **11.** $6\overline{)42}$ **12.** $8\overline{)56}$

(p. 198) (p. 202) (p. 200) (p. 200) (p. 198) (p. 202)

13. $4\overline{)12}$ **14.** $9\overline{)63}$ **15.** $6\overline{)36}$ **16.** $7\overline{)49}$ **17.** $5\overline{)40}$ **18.** $9\overline{)81}$

(p. 208) (p. 208) (p. 208) (p. 208) (p. 208) (p. 208)

19. $7\overline{)57}$ **20.** $5\overline{)39}$ **21.** $8\overline{)66}$ **22.** $3\overline{)23}$ **23.** $9\overline{)56}$ **24.** $4\overline{)22}$

(p. 208) (p. 208) (p. 208) (p. 208) (p. 208) (p. 208)

25. $9\overline{)85}$ **26.** $6\overline{)57}$ **27.** $5\overline{)28}$ **28.** $3\overline{)17}$ **29.** $4\overline{)19}$ **30.** $8\overline{)46}$

Find the mean.

31. 6, 8, 7 (p. 204) **32.** 3, 5, 6, 2 (p. 204) **33.** 1, 0, 6, 4, 9 (p. 204)

bonus

Solve the problem.

34. You have 19 cupcakes.
You want to give 3 to each friend.
How many friends will get 3 cupcakes?
How many cupcakes will be left over? (p. 210)

214

Keeping up

Add.

1. $ .30	2. $3.17	3. $43.72	4. $16.13	5. $ .18
7.62	.02	8.10	4.63	3.70
+ .48	+ 9.99	+ 20.89	+ .79	+ 27.22
(p. 84)	(p. 84)	(p. 84)	(p. 84)	(p. 84)

Subtract.

6. $3.64	7. $4.32	8. $83.00	9. $63.20	10. $90.01
− .98	− 1.57	− 17.49	− 7.64	− 89.78
(p. 108)	(p. 108)	(p. 108)	(p. 108)	(p. 108)

11. The perimeter of this figure is _?_ centimeters. (p. 52)

12. The area of the figure is _?_ square centimeters. (p. 54)

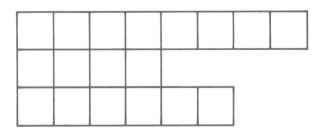

Multiply.

13. 7	14. 8	15. 5	16. 8	17. 9
×6	×9	×7	×6	×9
(p. 140)	(p. 142)	(p. 132)	(p. 142)	(p. 144)

18. $6.87	19. $4.03	20. $.83	21. $4.00	22. $6.97
× 5	× 9	× 6	× 8	× 8
(p. 168)	(p. 168)	(p. 168)	(p. 168)	(p. 168)

23. $.38	24. $8.42	25. $.73	26. $6.56	27. $8.88
× 20	× 40	× 52	× 75	× 88
(p. 186)	(p. 186)	(p. 186)	(p. 186)	(p. 186)

215

The Median

Rosa is captain of a
Little League team.
They have played 7 games.

Games	1	2	3	4	5	6	7
Scores	3	2	0	5	5	4	2

Rosa arranged the scores
in order.

0, 2, 2, 3, 4, 5, 5

↑
median

The middle score, 3, is
called the **median.**

Find the mean.
Does the mean equal
the median?

$$3 \leftarrow \text{mean}$$
$$7\overline{)21}$$
$$\underline{21}$$
$$0$$

Alfred's team earned
these scores.

11, 7, 2, 6, 14

He arranged the
scores in order.
What is the median?

2, 6, 7, 11, 14

He added the scores and
divided to find the mean.
Does the mean equal
the median this time?

$$8$$
$$5\overline{)40}$$

1. What is the mean number of puppies purchased in April?

2. What is the median?

3. What is the mean number of puppies purchased in May?

4. What is the median?

POPULAR PUPPIES PURCHASED

	APRIL	MAY
Beagles	3	2
Doberman pinschers	5	5
Irish setters	6	8
Poodles	14	20
German shepherds	7	10

5. What is the mean score for Pax?

6. What is the median score?

7. What is the mean score for Max?

8. What is the median score?

BARKERVILLE DOG SHOW

	PAX	MAX
Color	7	8
Posture	8	6
Body	6	5
Coat and teeth	5	4
Feet	4	2

Dividing Tens

If you can divide ones, then you can divide tens.

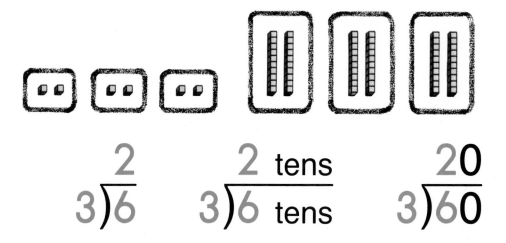

$$3\overline{)6} = 2$$ $$3\overline{)6 \text{ tens}} = 2 \text{ tens}$$ $$3\overline{)60} = 20$$

If you can divide 12 ones, then you can divide 12 tens.

$$2\overline{)12} = 6$$ $$2\overline{)12 \text{ tens}} = 6 \text{ tens}$$ $$2\overline{)120} = 60$$

Divide.

1. $7\overline{)140}$ 2. $3\overline{)90}$ 3. $5\overline{)350}$ 4. $4\overline{)80}$ 5. $6\overline{)240}$

Divide.

6. $2\overline{)80}$ 7. $3\overline{)240}$ 8. $6\overline{)120}$ 9. $2\overline{)60}$ 10. $4\overline{)200}$

11. $3\overline{)180}$ 12. $6\overline{)480}$ 13. $5\overline{)450}$ 14. $2\overline{)100}$ 15. $4\overline{)40}$

16. $4\overline{)280}$ 17. $9\overline{)270}$ 18. $3\overline{)60}$ 19. $8\overline{)320}$ 20. $7\overline{)280}$

21. $5\overline{)350}$ 22. $7\overline{)210}$ 23. $9\overline{)360}$ 24. $4\overline{)240}$ 25. $6\overline{)420}$

26. $4\overline{)320}$ 27. $8\overline{)480}$ 28. $3\overline{)270}$ 29. $5\overline{)200}$ 30. $2\overline{)40}$

31. $2\overline{)20}$ 32. $7\overline{)350}$ 33. $4\overline{)360}$ 34. $6\overline{)300}$ 35. $8\overline{)240}$

36. $8\overline{)720}$ 37. $6\overline{)360}$ 38. $7\overline{)560}$ 39. $9\overline{)630}$ 40. $6\overline{)540}$

41. $5\overline{)450}$ 42. $7\overline{)490}$ 43. $6\overline{)180}$ 44. $8\overline{)400}$ 45. $9\overline{)720}$

Dividing Tens and Ones

Here is a way to think about $3\overline{)246}$.
Think of 246 as 240 + 6.

Divide 240 by 3.	Divide 6 by 3.	Add the quotients.
$\begin{array}{r} 80 \\ 3\overline{)240} \end{array}$	$\begin{array}{r} 2 \\ 3\overline{)6} \end{array}$	$80 + 2 = 82$

Here is a way to show your work.

Step 1

$$\begin{array}{r} 80 \\ 3\overline{)246} \\ \underline{240} \\ 6 \end{array}$$

Think: $3\overline{)24}$ is 8, so $3\overline{)246}$ is about 80.
Multiply: $80 \times 3 = 240$.
Subtract to find what is left to divide.

Step 2

$$\begin{array}{r} 2 \\ 80 \\ 3\overline{)246} \\ \underline{240} \\ 6 \\ \underline{6} \\ 0 \end{array}$$

Think: $3\overline{)6}$ is 2.
Multiply: $2 \times 3 = 6$.
Subtract to find the remainder.

Step 3

$$\begin{array}{r} 82 \\ 2 \\ 80 \\ 3\overline{)246} \\ \underline{240} \\ 6 \\ \underline{6} \\ 0 \end{array}$$

Add to find the quotient.

Copy and complete.

70	30	20	20	40
1. 5)355	2. 3)96	3. 7)147	4. 4)84	5. 4)168
350	90	140	80	
5	6			

Divide.

6. 3)156   7. 4)88   8. 2)128   9. 3)63   10. 5)305

Divide.

11. 3)129   12. 5)155   13. 4)244   14. 2)46   15. 3)279

16. 2)82   17. 6)126   18. 4)48   19. 5)105   20. 6)426

21. 5)255   22. 2)108   23. 3)39   24. 6)66   25. 4)284

26. 4)328   27. 5)405   28. 4)208   29. 6)366   30. 3)186

31. 2)86   32. 5)200   33. 3)216   34. 4)124   35. 6)246

36. 3)246   37. 4)324   38. 6)306   39. 3)99   40. 6)486

221

Tens in the Quotient

Sometimes there are tens in the quotient.

There are more than 10 fives in 486.
There are fewer than 100 fives.

$$1 \times 5 = 5$$
$$10 \times 5 = 50$$
$$100 \times 5 = 500 \quad \leftarrow 486$$

There are tens in the quotient.

$$5\overline{)486}$$

Now, find how many tens are in the quotient.

Think: $5\overline{)48}$ is about 9, so
$5\overline{)486}$ is about 90.
Write 90 in the quotient.

$$5\overline{)486} \quad 90$$

try these

Are there tens in the quotient? Write YES or NO.

1. $4\overline{)17}$
2. $4\overline{)178}$
3. $9\overline{)75}$
4. $9\overline{)756}$
5. $8\overline{)572}$

Find the tens in the quotient.

6. $4\overline{)176}$
7. $9\overline{)756}$
8. $3\overline{)192}$
9. $5\overline{)235}$
10. $7\overline{)322}$

now do these

Find the tens in the quotient.

11. $4\overline{)132}$
12. $5\overline{)435}$
13. $5\overline{)85}$
14. $6\overline{)72}$
15. $3\overline{)144}$

16. $3\overline{)165}$
17. $4\overline{)316}$
18. $2\overline{)132}$
19. $6\overline{)144}$
20. $2\overline{)196}$

21. $5\overline{)220}$
22. $6\overline{)426}$
23. $2\overline{)174}$
24. $4\overline{)268}$
25. $4\overline{)276}$

26. $6\overline{)396}$
27. $3\overline{)249}$
28. $6\overline{)96}$
29. $2\overline{)78}$
30. $3\overline{)111}$

31. $5\overline{)245}$
32. $3\overline{)231}$
33. $6\overline{)264}$
34. $5\overline{)375}$
35. $4\overline{)336}$

36. $8\overline{)592}$
37. $6\overline{)576}$
38. $7\overline{)385}$
39. $4\overline{)356}$
40. $8\overline{)504}$

41. $7\overline{)658}$
42. $8\overline{)648}$
43. $6\overline{)372}$
44. $5\overline{)463}$
45. $9\overline{)874}$

223

Dividing Tens and Ones

Find the quotient: $4\overline{)296}$. Are there tens in the quotient?

Step 1

$$
\begin{array}{r}
70 \\
4\overline{)296} \\
280 \\
\hline
16
\end{array}
$$

Find the tens.
Think: $4\overline{)29}$ is about 7, so
$4\overline{)296}$ is about 70.
Multiply: $70 \times 4 = 280$.
Subtract.

Step 2

$$
\begin{array}{r}
4 \\
70 \\
4\overline{)296} \\
280 \\
\hline
16 \\
16 \\
\hline
0
\end{array}
$$

Find the ones.
Think: $4\overline{)16}$ is 4.
Multiply: $4 \times 4 = 16$.
Subtract.

Step 3

$$
\begin{array}{r}
74 \\
4 \\
70 \\
4\overline{)296} \\
280 \\
\hline
16 \\
16 \\
\hline
0
\end{array}
$$

Add to find the quotient.

try these

Copy and complete.

1.
$$
\begin{array}{r}
70 \\
4\overline{)304} \\
280 \\
\hline
24
\end{array}
$$

2.
$$
\begin{array}{r}
60 \\
8\overline{)512} \\
480 \\
\hline
32
\end{array}
$$

3.
$$
\begin{array}{r}
80 \\
7\overline{)609} \\
560 \\
\hline
\end{array}
$$

4.
$$
\begin{array}{r}
60 \\
9\overline{)576} \\
540 \\
\hline
\end{array}
$$

5.
$$
\begin{array}{r}
70 \\
6\overline{)474}
\end{array}
$$

Divide.

6. $3\overline{)171}$

7. $4\overline{)392}$

8. $5\overline{)445}$

9. $6\overline{)582}$

10. $7\overline{)546}$

224

Divide.

11. 3)192   12. 4)292   13. 5)75   14. 6)90   15. 3)132

16. 5)210   17. 6)414   18. 2)172   19. 4)272   20. 3)102

21. 6)396   22. 3)249   23. 6)72   24. 2)98   25. 4)252

26. 5)235   27. 3)222   28. 6)252   29. 5)365   30. 4)344

31. 8)744   32. 6)498   33. 7)441   34. 4)388   35. 9)306

36. 7)658   37. 8)656   38. 6)384   39. 5)475   40. 9)864

41. 4)192   42. 5)65   43. 7)483   44. 8)96   45. 9)495

quick check

Divide.

1. 3)60   2. 8)640   3. 2)80   4. 3)270   5. 9)360

6. 7)497   7. 3)69   8. 6)426   9. 5)65   10. 8)352

Remainders Other Than 0

Find the quotient and the remainder: $3\overline{)257}$.

Step 1

$$
\begin{array}{r}
80 \\
3\overline{)257} \\
240 \\
\hline
17
\end{array}
$$

Find the tens.
Think: $3\overline{)25}$ is about 8, so
$3\overline{)257}$ is about 80.
Multiply: $80 \times 3 = 240$.
Subtract.

Step 2

$$
\begin{array}{r}
5 \\
80 \\
3\overline{)257} \\
240 \\
\hline
17 \\
15 \\
\hline
2
\end{array}
$$

Find the ones.
Think: $3\overline{)17}$ is about 5.
Multiply: $5 \times 3 = 15$.
Subtract.

Step 3

$$
\begin{array}{r}
85\ r2 \\
5 \\
80 \\
3\overline{)257} \\
240 \\
\hline
17 \\
15 \\
\hline
2
\end{array}
$$

Add to find
the quotient.
Show the remainder
in the answer.

try these

Copy and complete.

1.
$$
\begin{array}{r}
30 \\
5\overline{)193} \\
150 \\
\hline
43
\end{array}
$$

2.
$$
\begin{array}{r}
80 \\
2\overline{)179} \\
160 \\
\hline
19
\end{array}
$$

3.
$$
\begin{array}{r}
90 \\
3\overline{)278} \\
270 \\
\hline
8
\end{array}
$$

4.
$$
\begin{array}{r}
40 \\
6\overline{)253} \\
240 \\
\hline
\end{array}
$$

5.
$$
\begin{array}{r}
70 \\
4\overline{)295}
\end{array}
$$

Divide.

6. $6\overline{)157}$

7. $5\overline{)393}$

8. $4\overline{)274}$

9. $5\overline{)186}$

10. $2\overline{)195}$

now do these

Divide.

11. 4)299   12. 6)443   13. 2)133   14. 3)97   15. 5)89

16. 5)408   17. 4)186   18. 6)397   19. 4)234   20. 3)148

21. 2)97   22. 6)218   23. 3)202   24. 6)350   25. 5)479

26. 4)169   27. 5)437   28. 2)151   29. 6)297   30. 3)265

31. 7)383   32. 4)358   33. 8)595   34. 6)583   35. 8)514

36. 6)505   37. 8)747   38. 7)485   39. 4)359   40. 9)605

41. 4)74   42. 6)319   43. 8)97   44. 5)308   45. 9)428

A RIDDLE

Each quotient stands for a letter.
Find the quotients. Then solve the riddle.

S	**L**	**A**	**B**
5)205	3)126	6)306	8)488

M	**U**	**R**	**E**
2)128	7)497	4)248	9)279

What are raised in Brazil during the rainy season?

71 — 64 — 61 — 62 — 31 — 42 — 42 — 51 — 41

227

Hundreds in the Quotient

Sometimes there are hundreds in the quotient.

There are more than 100 fours in 2128.
There are fewer than 1000 fours.

$$1 \times 4 = 4$$
$$10 \times 4 = 40$$
$$100 \times 4 = 400$$
$$1000 \times 4 = 4000 \quad \longleftarrow 2128$$

$$4)\overline{2128}$$

There are hundreds in the quotient.

Now, find how many hundreds are in the quotient.

Think: $4)\overline{21}$ is about 5, so
$4)\overline{2128}$ is about 500.
Write 500 in the quotient.

$$\begin{array}{r} 500 \\ 4)\overline{2128} \end{array}$$

Are there hundreds in the quotient? Write YES or NO.

1. 6)187 2. 8)5719 3. 3)1627 4. 9)89 5. 8)49

Find the hundreds in the quotient.

6. 9)7354 7. 2)1313 8. 7)3566 9. 5)4344 10. 8)5035

now do these

Find the hundreds in the quotient.

11. 2)1962 12. 4)2750 13. 3)1125 14. 4)3156 15. 8)5012

16. 6)700 17. 4)2628 18. 6)1407 19. 2)785 20. 5)3740

21. 7)3829 22. 6)3750 23. 7)4456 24. 6)2628 · 25. 2)1745

26. 3)1825 27. 5)2200 28. 6)3964 29. 5)2459 30. 7)843

A RIDDLE

Each quotient stands for a letter.
Find the quotients. Then solve the riddle.

Q	U	E	P	Y
7)350	4)120	8)560	9)180	2)20

T	H	A	C	K
5)300	9)810	1)100	3)120	6)480

What happens to ducks when they fly upside-down?

60 — 90 — 70 — 10   50 — 30 — 100 — 40 — 80   30 — 20

Dividing Hundreds, Tens, and Ones

Find the quotient and the remainder: $3\overline{)1492}$.

Step 1

$$
\begin{array}{r}
400 \\
3\overline{)1492} \\
1200 \\
\hline
292
\end{array}
$$

Find the hundreds.
Think:
$3\overline{)14}$ is about 4, so
$3\overline{)1492}$ is about 400.
Multiply:
$400 \times 3 = 1200$.
Subtract.

Step 2

$$
\begin{array}{r}
90 \\
400 \\
3\overline{)1492} \\
1200 \\
\hline
292 \\
270 \\
\hline
22
\end{array}
$$

Find the tens.
Think:
$3\overline{)29}$ is about 9, so
$3\overline{)292}$ is about 90.
Multiply:
$90 \times 3 = 270$.
Subtract.

Step 3

$$
\begin{array}{r}
7 \\
90 \\
400 \\
3\overline{)1492} \\
1200 \\
\hline
292 \\
270 \\
\hline
22 \\
21 \\
\hline
1
\end{array}
$$

Find the ones.
Think:
$3\overline{)22}$ is about 7.
Multiply:
$7 \times 3 = 21$.
Subtract.

Step 4

$$
\begin{array}{r}
497 \text{ r } 1 \\
7 \\
90 \\
400 \\
3\overline{)1492} \\
1200 \\
\hline
292 \\
270 \\
\hline
22 \\
21 \\
\hline
1
\end{array}
$$

Add to find
the quotient.
Show the
remainder in
the answer.

Copy and complete.

```
       3              6
      20             60            10
     500            600           800          700           800
1. 7)3665      2. 2)1332     3. 9)7345     4. 8)5936     5. 5)4443
   3500           1200          7200          5600
   ────           ────          ────
    165            132           145
    140            120            90
   ────           ────          ───
     25             12
     21             12
    ───            ───
      4
```

Divide.

6. 8)5609   7. 3)1572   8. 5)3124   9. 4)1935   10. 6)5075

Divide.

11. 5)3565   12. 9)7587   13. 7)5063   14. 5)4812   15. 9)1539

16. 6)2725   17. 4)1632   18. 6)2126   19. 2)1410   20. 8)3512

21. 9)3999   22. 6)5053   23. 8)6496   24. 8)5683   25. 7)4350

26. 8)4008   27. 3)2096   28. 3)1719   29. 2)998   30. 5)1304

31. 5)2271   32. 6)3864   33. 8)5947   34. 3)1925   35. 6)5729

A Shorter Way

Find the quotient and the remainder: $3\overline{)1492}$.

Step 1

$$
\begin{array}{r}
4 \\
3\overline{)1492} \\
1200 \\
\hline
292
\end{array}
$$

Find the hundreds.
$3\overline{)14}$ is about 4, so
$3\overline{)1492}$ is about 400.
Write 4 in the hundreds
place in the quotient.
Multiply: $400 \times 3 = 1200$.
Subtract.

Step 2

$$
\begin{array}{r}
49 \\
3\overline{)1492} \\
1200 \\
\hline
292 \\
270 \\
\hline
22
\end{array}
$$

Find the tens.
$3\overline{)29}$ is about 9, so
$3\overline{)292}$ is about 90.
Write 9 in the tens
place in the quotient.
Multiply: $90 \times 3 = 270$.
Subtract.

Step 3

$$
\begin{array}{r}
497 \text{ r}1 \\
3\overline{)1492} \\
1200 \\
\hline
292 \\
270 \\
\hline
22 \\
21 \\
\hline
1
\end{array}
$$

Find the ones.
$3\overline{)22}$ is about 7.
Write 7 in the ones
place of the quotient.
Multiply: $7 \times 3 = 21$.
Subtract.
Show the remainder
in the answer.

Copy and complete.

1.
```
   127
 5)637
   500
   137
   100
    37
```

2.
```
    32
 3)973
   900
    73
    60
```

3.
```
    24
 8)1984
   1600
    384
```

4.
```
     4
 6)2475
   2400
     75
```

5.
```
     3
 7)2280
```

Divide.

6. 2)693

7. 5)638

8. 7)1020

9. 3)734

10. 4)1005

Divide.

11. 6)739

12. 3)1245

13. 8)1715

14. 9)1145

15. 4)890

16. 5)1117

17. 2)1692

18. 9)1935

19. 7)865

20. 3)1630

21. 8)1776

22. 4)930

23. 6)1998

24. 2)1830

25. 7)3195

26. 3)2664

27. 5)2775

28. 2)643

29. 6)1478

30. 8)3650

31. 9)1000

32. 4)1285

33. 6)2666

34. 8)2666

35. 5)2280

36. 2)913

37. 7)2415

38. 4)1285

39. 3)406

40. 9)5679

233

dividing with money

8 party hats cost $1.92.
What is the cost **per** hat?

To find the answer, divide the
cost by the number of hats.

$$8\overline{)\$1.92}$$

Divide amounts of money as if you were dividing whole numbers.
Remember to write the dollar sign and the cents point in the answer.

longer way	shorter way
$.24	
4	
20	$ .24
8)$1.92	8)$1.92
1 60	1 60
32	32
32	32
0	0

Each hat costs $.24.
Unit price is the cost for one item or one unit.
So, the unit price of the hat is $.24.

Divide to find the unit price.

1. 9 candleholders for $.27.

2. 6 noisemakers for $.96.

3. 2 tablecloths for $1.58.

4. 6 spoons for $.48.

5. 8 plates for $.72.

6. 6 party favors for $3.12.

7. 6 cupcakes for $1.32.

8. 8 balloons for $.96.

9. 4 liters of ice cream for $5.16.

10. 3 rolls of film for $8.25.

235

Test

Divide.

1. (p. 218) 9)810

2. (p. 218) 2)60

3. (p. 218) 4)240

4. (p. 220) 3)96

5. (p. 220) 2)168

6. (p. 220) 6)246

7. (p. 224) 3)192

8. (p. 224) 9)297

9. (p. 224) 5)280

10. (p. 224) 7)245

11. (p. 226) 9)607

12. (p. 226) 2)77

13. (p. 226) 4)338

14. (p. 230, 232) 8)1743

15. (p. 230, 232) 3)1376

16. (p. 230, 232) 6)700

17. (p. 230, 232) 7)3630

18. (p. 230, 232) 2)1735

19. (p. 230, 232) 4)517

20. (p. 230, 232) 5)4931

bonus

Solve the problem.

21. There are 369 balloons.
8 friends will share them.
How many balloons should each get?
How many will be left over? (p. 226)

Keeping up

Write the numeral.

1. 18 thousand, 34 (p. 12)

2. 400 thousand, 3 (p. 12)

3. 3 million, 6 thousand, 15 (p. 14)

4. 9 million, 8 thousand (p. 14)

Name

5. 1000 more than 9653. (p. 12)

6. 10,000 more than 96,043. (p. 12)

7. 100,000 more than 915,001. (p. 14)

8. 1,000,000 more than 786,477. (p. 14)

Multiply.

9.
$$\begin{array}{r} 6 \\ \times 8 \\ \hline \end{array}$$
(p. 138)

10.
$$\begin{array}{r} 7 \\ \times 5 \\ \hline \end{array}$$
(p. 140)

11.
$$\begin{array}{r} 8 \\ \times 7 \\ \hline \end{array}$$
(p. 142)

12.
$$\begin{array}{r} 9 \\ \times 6 \\ \hline \end{array}$$
(p. 144)

13.
$$\begin{array}{r} 8 \\ \times 9 \\ \hline \end{array}$$
(p. 142)

14.
$$\begin{array}{r} 90 \\ \times 6 \\ \hline \end{array}$$
(p. 158)

15.
$$\begin{array}{r} 700 \\ \times 7 \\ \hline \end{array}$$
(p. 160)

16.
$$\begin{array}{r} 83 \\ \times 9 \\ \hline \end{array}$$
(p. 164)

17.
$$\begin{array}{r} 587 \\ \times 5 \\ \hline \end{array}$$
(p. 166)

18.
$$\begin{array}{r} 888 \\ \times 8 \\ \hline \end{array}$$
(p. 166)

19.
$$\begin{array}{r} 784 \\ \times 10 \\ \hline \end{array}$$
(p. 178)

20.
$$\begin{array}{r} 932 \\ \times 40 \\ \hline \end{array}$$
(p. 180)

21.
$$\begin{array}{r} 75 \\ \times 39 \\ \hline \end{array}$$
(p. 182)

22.
$$\begin{array}{r} 437 \\ \times 58 \\ \hline \end{array}$$
(p. 184)

23.
$$\begin{array}{r} 802 \\ \times 77 \\ \hline \end{array}$$
(p. 184)

Divide.

24. (p. 198) $4\overline{)36}$

25. (p. 200) $6\overline{)36}$

26. (p. 202) $8\overline{)32}$

27. (p. 200) $7\overline{)63}$

28. (p. 202) $9\overline{)45}$

29. (p. 200) $7\overline{)56}$

30. (p. 202) $9\overline{)81}$

31. (p. 202) $9\overline{)45}$

32. (p. 200) $6\overline{)48}$

33. (p. 202) $8\overline{)72}$

34. (p. 208) $3\overline{)20}$

35. (p. 208) $9\overline{)78}$

36. (p. 208) $6\overline{)41}$

37. (p. 208) $7\overline{)66}$

38. (p. 208) $8\overline{)39}$

237

Time, Rate, and Distance

Barry has a bicycle.
He can ride at a **rate**
of 15 kilometers per hour.
(Each hour he can go a
distance of 15 kilometers.)
How far can he ride
in 3 hours?

You can make a table.

hours	kilometers
1	15
2	30
3	45

You can also multiply.

$$\begin{array}{r} 15 \\ \times 3 \\ \hline 45 \end{array}$$

Barry can ride 45 kilometers
in 3 hours.

Suppose Barry can keep up
this rate for 5 hours.
How far can he ride?

Becky can walk 1 kilometer in 12 minutes. At this rate, how many kilometers can she walk in 60 minutes?

You can make a table.

minutes	kilometers
12	1
24	2
36	3
48	4
60	5

You can also think: How many 12's in 60?

$$\begin{array}{r} 5 \\ 12\overline{)60} \\ 60 \\ \hline 0 \end{array}$$

Becky can walk 5 kilometers in 60 minutes.

At this rate, how many kilometers can Becky walk in 2 hours?

Dividing by Tens

$$1\overline{)2}\quad\text{quotient }2$$

How many ones in 2?
Think: $\underline{\ ?\ } \times 1 = 2$.
The quotient is 2.

$$10\overline{)20}\quad\text{quotient }2$$

How many tens in 20?
Think: $\underline{\ ?\ } \times 10 = 20$.
The quotient is 2.

$$2\overline{)8}\quad\text{quotient }4$$

How many twos in 8?
Think: $\underline{\ ?\ } \times 2 = 8$.
The quotient is 4.

$$20\overline{)80}\quad\text{quotient }4$$

How many twenties in 80?
Think: $\underline{\ ?\ } \times 20 = 80$.
The quotient is 4.

$$7\overline{)21}\quad\text{quotient }3$$

How many sevens in 21?
Think: $\underline{\ ?\ } \times 7 = 21$.
The quotient is 3.

$$70\overline{)210}\quad\text{quotient }3$$

How many seventies in 210?
Think: $\underline{\ ?\ } \times 70 = 210$.
The quotient is 3.

try these

Use the completed example to find the quotient.

1. $4\overline{)24}$ = 6
2. $5\overline{)35}$ = 7
3. $8\overline{)48}$ = 6
4. $6\overline{)30}$ = 5
5. $9\overline{)72}$ = 8

$40\overline{)240}$ $50\overline{)350}$ $80\overline{)480}$ $60\overline{)300}$ $90\overline{)720}$

Divide.

6. $70\overline{)280}$
7. $30\overline{)90}$
8. $90\overline{)450}$
9. $20\overline{)180}$
10. $50\overline{)400}$

240

now do these

Divide.

11. $40 \overline{)320}$
12. $60 \overline{)360}$
13. $50 \overline{)450}$
14. $70 \overline{)350}$
15. $30 \overline{)210}$

16. $90 \overline{)630}$
17. $70 \overline{)560}$
18. $70 \overline{)140}$
19. $40 \overline{)200}$
20. $80 \overline{)400}$

21. $30 \overline{)270}$
22. $50 \overline{)300}$
23. $50 \overline{)100}$
24. $20 \overline{)80}$
25. $60 \overline{)240}$

26. $80 \overline{)640}$
27. $90 \overline{)540}$
28. $70 \overline{)490}$
29. $80 \overline{)320}$
30. $90 \overline{)270}$

31. $40 \overline{)280}$
32. $50 \overline{)250}$
33. $30 \overline{)180}$
34. $60 \overline{)480}$
35. $20 \overline{)140}$

36. $90 \overline{)360}$
37. $70 \overline{)420}$
38. $90 \overline{)810}$
39. $80 \overline{)240}$
40. $70 \overline{)630}$

41. $40 \overline{)80}$
42. $60 \overline{)420}$
43. $90 \overline{)180}$
44. $50 \overline{)150}$
45. $30 \overline{)240}$

Solve the problem.

46. 300 birds.
    60 birds in a cage.
    How many cages?

47. 160 balloons.
    Each person sells 40.
    How many people sell balloons?

48. 120 peanuts.
    Each person buys 20.
    How many people buy peanuts?

241

What the Remainder Means

Each bus can carry 40 people.
There are 228 people.
How many buses can be filled?
How many people will be left over?

Step 1

$$5 \overline{\smash{\big)}\,} \; 40)\overline{228}$$

Find the ones.
Think: $4)\overline{22}$ is about 5,
so $40)\overline{228}$ is about 5.

Step 2

$$5 \\ 40)\overline{228} \\ 200$$

Multiply.

Step 3

$$5 \, r28 \\ 40)\overline{228} \\ \underline{200} \\ 28$$

Subtract.
Show the remainder
in the answer.

You can fill 5 buses.
There will be 28 people left over.

Here is a way to check the answer.

$$\begin{array}{r} 5 \; r28 \\ 40)\overline{228} \\ \underline{200} \\ 28 \end{array}$$

1. Multiply the divisor by the quotient.
   $5 \times 40 = 200$

2. Add the remainder.
   $200 + 28 = 228$

3. The result should equal the dividend.

242

Copy and complete.

1. $\begin{array}{r} 5 \\ 50\overline{)278} \\ 250 \\ \hline 28 \end{array}$

2. $\begin{array}{r} 7 \\ 70\overline{)509} \\ 490 \\ \hline \end{array}$

3. $\begin{array}{r} 8 \\ 40\overline{)347} \\ 320 \\ \hline \end{array}$

4. $\begin{array}{r} 6 \\ 90\overline{)575} \end{array}$

5. $\begin{array}{r} 6 \\ 80\overline{)519} \end{array}$

Divide.

6. $80\overline{)739}$

7. $60\overline{)540}$

8. $50\overline{)488}$

9. $70\overline{)329}$

10. $60\overline{)475}$

now do these

Divide.

11. $20\overline{)105}$

12. $80\overline{)267}$

13. $90\overline{)323}$

14. $70\overline{)425}$

15. $90\overline{)810}$

16. $30\overline{)214}$

17. $30\overline{)190}$

18. $80\overline{)663}$

19. $60\overline{)497}$

20. $70\overline{)378}$

21. $50\overline{)307}$

22. $20\overline{)180}$

23. $40\overline{)276}$

24. $80\overline{)477}$

25. $60\overline{)459}$

26. $40\overline{)240}$

27. $50\overline{)480}$

28. $70\overline{)576}$

29. $70\overline{)319}$

30. $80\overline{)495}$

31. $60\overline{)375}$

32. $90\overline{)381}$

33. $50\overline{)447}$

34. $90\overline{)540}$

35. $30\overline{)294}$

36. $20\overline{)165}$

37. $60\overline{)270}$

38. $40\overline{)177}$

39. $30\overline{)261}$

40. $90\overline{)788}$

41. $50\overline{)392}$

42. $80\overline{)339}$

43. $70\overline{)477}$

44. $60\overline{)190}$

45. $90\overline{)496}$

Dividing by Tens and Ones

Find the quotient and the remainder: $52\overline{)374}$.

Step 1

$$\begin{array}{r} 7 \\ 52\overline{)374} \end{array}$$

Estimate the quotient.
Think: 52 is near 50.
$5\overline{)37}$ is about 7, so
$50\overline{)374}$ is about 7.
Try 7.

Step 2

$$\begin{array}{r} 7 \\ 52\overline{)374} \\ 364 \end{array}$$

Multiply.

Step 3

$$\begin{array}{r} 7 \text{ r} 10 \\ 52\overline{)374} \\ \underline{364} \\ 10 \end{array}$$

Subtract.
Show the remainder
in the answer.

try these

Copy and complete.

1. $\begin{array}{r} 9 \\ 82\overline{)740} \\ \underline{738} \\ 2 \end{array}$

2. $\begin{array}{r} 3 \\ 63\overline{)221} \\ \underline{189} \end{array}$

3. $\begin{array}{r} 6 \\ 51\overline{)324} \\ \underline{306} \end{array}$

4. $\begin{array}{r} 6 \\ 42\overline{)264} \end{array}$

5. $\begin{array}{r} 3 \\ 91\overline{)289} \end{array}$

Divide.

6. $62\overline{)391}$

7. $30\overline{)145}$

8. $42\overline{)179}$

9. $21\overline{)126}$

10. $72\overline{)157}$

Divide.

11. 84)695   12. 83)340   13. 91)197   14. 63)275   15. 74)381

16. 50)323   17. 61)211   18. 82)495   19. 31)265   20. 83)352

21. 73)523   22. 52)281   23. 94)659   24. 54)384   25. 54)444

26. 60)445   27. 81)435   28. 73)596   29. 83)593   30. 62)350

31. 71)200   32. 72)224   33. 62)505   34. 72)235   35. 73)322

36. 54)243   37. 61)257   38. 43)394   39. 92)747   40. 44)275

41. 33)267   42. 63)201   43. 41)268   44. 81)650   45. 52)493

quick check

Divide.

1. 20)60   2. 60)420   3. 50)400   4. 80)560   5. 30)284

6. 40)345   7. 90)767   8. 22)179   9. 64)385   10. 83)456

Too Much

Sometimes your first estimate
is too much.

Estimate the quotient.
Think: 80)564 .
Since 8)56 is 7,
you should try 7.

But 7 is too much.
So, try 6.

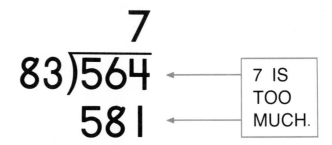

$$7$$
$$83)\overline{564} \longleftarrow$$
$$581 \longleftarrow$$

7 IS
TOO
MUCH.

Step 1	Step 2	Step 3
$$6$$ $$83)\overline{564}$$ $$498$$	$$6$$ $$83)\overline{564}$$ $$\underline{498}$$ $$66$$	$$6\ r66$$ $$83)\overline{564}$$ $$\underline{498}$$ $$66$$
Find the quotient. Multiply.	Subtract.	Show the remainder.

Is the first estimate too much?   Write YES or NO.

1. $\overset{6}{64\overline{)362}}$ 2. $\overset{3}{82\overline{)257}}$ 3. $\overset{9}{93\overline{)825}}$ 4. $\overset{9}{74\overline{)675}}$ 5. $\overset{7}{44\overline{)306}}$

Divide.

6. $94\overline{)747}$ 7. $63\overline{)503}$ 8. $84\overline{)435}$ 9. $74\overline{)508}$ 10. $53\overline{)467}$

now do these

Divide.

11. $84\overline{)664}$ 12. $73\overline{)507}$ 13. $94\overline{)186}$ 14. $74\overline{)361}$ 15. $54\overline{)424}$

16. $63\overline{)187}$ 17. $84\overline{)413}$ 18. $93\overline{)649}$ 19. $84\overline{)495}$ 20. $72\overline{)141}$

21. $94\overline{)654}$ 22. $63\overline{)430}$ 23. $73\overline{)573}$ 24. $54\overline{)423}$ 25. $74\overline{)219}$

26. $83\overline{)579}$ 27. $74\overline{)218}$ 28. $64\overline{)503}$ 29. $83\overline{)324}$ 30. $52\overline{)152}$

31. $72\overline{)286}$ 32. $84\overline{)415}$ 33. $43\overline{)385}$ 34. $62\overline{)361}$ 35. $72\overline{)637}$

36. $44\overline{)295}$ 37. $83\overline{)331}$ 38. $64\overline{)249}$ 39. $73\overline{)352}$ 40. $44\overline{)296}$

41. $92\overline{)726}$ 42. $54\overline{)265}$ 43. $34\overline{)294}$ 44. $44\overline{)255}$ 45. $34\overline{)295}$

Dividing by Tens and Ones

Find the quotient and the remainder: $28\overline{)247}$.

Step 1

$$\begin{array}{r} 8 \\ 28\overline{)247} \end{array}$$

Estimate.
Think: 28 is near 30.
$3\overline{)24}$ is 8, so
$30\overline{)247}$ is about 8.
Try 8.

Step 2

$$\begin{array}{r} 8 \\ 28\overline{)247} \\ 224 \end{array}$$

Multiply.

Step 3

$$\begin{array}{r} 8 \text{ r}23 \\ 28\overline{)247} \\ \underline{224} \\ 23 \end{array}$$

Subtract.
Show the remainder.

try these

Copy and complete.

1. $\begin{array}{r} 6 \\ 57\overline{)363} \\ \underline{342} \\ 21 \end{array}$

2. $\begin{array}{r} 7 \\ 86\overline{)685} \\ \underline{602} \end{array}$

3. $\begin{array}{r} 8 \\ 68\overline{)565} \\ \underline{544} \end{array}$

4. $\begin{array}{r} 9 \\ 37\overline{)363} \end{array}$

5. $\begin{array}{r} 7 \\ 76\overline{)564} \end{array}$

Divide.

6. $46\overline{)352}$

7. $75\overline{)568}$

8. $67\overline{)569}$

9. $78\overline{)489}$

10. $59\overline{)434}$

now do these

Divide.

11. 67)365   12. 59)433   13. 85)720   14. 57)372   15. 68)632

16. 47)219   17. 35)240   18. 69)507   19. 75)640   20. 86)457

21. 77)494   22. 58)484   23. 45)157   24. 69)367   25. 76)562

26. 88)377   27. 75)489   28. 69)583   29. 86)642   30. 67)654

31. 65)563   32. 76)258   33. 58)315   34. 77)579   35. 38)253

36. 49)216   37. 37)255   38. 49)267   39. 37)365   40. 68)509

41. 35)207   42. 86)813   43. 57)423   44. 78)643   45. 49)201

MAGIC BEANS

There are 168 magic beans.
Find how many handfuls each can take.
Then find how many beans will be left over.

A. Jack takes 37 beans
in each handful.

B. Jack's mother takes 45 beans
in each handful.

C. The giant takes 77 beans
in each handful.

249

Not Enough

Sometimes your first estimate is not enough.

Estimate the quotient.
Think: 70)624.
Since 7)62 is about 8, you should try 8.

$$\begin{array}{r} 8 \\ 67\overline{)624} \\ 536 \\ \hline 88 \end{array}$$

8 IS NOT ENOUGH.

But when you multiply and subtract, you have more than 67 left over.
So, try 9.

Step 1

$$\begin{array}{r} 9 \\ 67\overline{)624} \\ 603 \end{array}$$

Find the quotient.
Multiply.

Step 2

$$\begin{array}{r} 9 \\ 67\overline{)624} \\ 603 \\ \hline 21 \end{array}$$

Subtract.

Step 3

$$\begin{array}{r} 9\ r21 \\ 67\overline{)624} \\ 603 \\ \hline 21 \end{array}$$

Show the remainder.

250

Is the first estimate enough?   Write YES or NO.

1. $\overset{8}{67)\overline{607}}$ 2. $\overset{7}{55)\overline{427}}$ 3. $\overset{7}{75)\overline{600}}$ 4. $\overset{7}{86)\overline{672}}$ 5. $\overset{4}{47)\overline{247}}$

Divide.

6. $55)\overline{495}$ 7. $69)\overline{485}$ 8. $77)\overline{475}$ 9. $85)\overline{356}$ 10. $46)\overline{379}$

now do these

Divide.

11. $67)\overline{469}$ 12. $49)\overline{249}$ 13. $58)\overline{409}$ 14. $37)\overline{115}$ 15. $78)\overline{398}$

16. $46)\overline{276}$ 17. $69)\overline{208}$ 18. $25)\overline{191}$ 19. $47)\overline{290}$ 20. $68)\overline{343}$

21. $85)\overline{348}$ 22. $56)\overline{463}$ 23. $39)\overline{237}$ 24. $75)\overline{153}$ 25. $68)\overline{206}$

26. $29)\overline{147}$ 27. $67)\overline{405}$ 28. $48)\overline{96}$ 29. $39)\overline{159}$ 30. $28)\overline{114}$

31. $57)\overline{297}$ 32. $77)\overline{310}$ 33. $77)\overline{385}$ 34. $86)\overline{774}$ 35. $48)\overline{344}$

36. $35)\overline{246}$ 37. $65)\overline{325}$ 38. $29)\overline{175}$ 39. $69)\overline{559}$ 40. $77)\overline{620}$

41. $69)\overline{553}$ 42. $58)\overline{464}$ 43. $67)\overline{337}$ 44. $59)\overline{413}$ 45. $45)\overline{185}$

do an easier problem first

Dr. Gleason is a dentist.
She treated 120 patients this week.
55 were children.
How many were not children?

Would you add or subtract?

Think of an easier problem first.

12 patients.	12
5 children.	-5
? were not children.	7

Then solve the first problem
the same way.

$$\begin{array}{r} 120 \\ -55 \\ \hline 65 \end{array}$$

You subtract to solve.
65 patients were not children.

Would you ADD or SUBTRACT?
If you cannot decide, solve the easier problem first.

1. 96 patients came for dental checkups.
   24 came for gum treatments.
   How many came in all?

   10 checkups.
   2 gum treatments.
   ? in all.

2. Dr. Gleason sent dental reminders
   to 270 patients.
   75 made appointments.
   How many did not?

   27 people were sent reminders.
   8 made appointments.
   ? did not make appointments.

Solve the problem.
You may want to solve the easier problem first.

3. 1000 children visited Dr. Gleason.   10 children.
   850 had tooth decay.   8 with tooth decay.
   How many did not?   ? without tooth decay.

4. 800 adults visited Dr. Gleason.   8 adults.
   32 did not have tooth decay.   3 without tooth decay.
   How many did have tooth decay?   ? with tooth decay.

5. One week, Dr. Gleason gave away   3 toothbrushes.
   137 toothbrushes.   6 toothbrushes.
   The next week, she gave away 163.   ? in all.
   How many did she give away in all?

6. Preparing a tooth for a filling   5 seconds for step one.
   takes 50 seconds.   18 seconds for step two.
   Preparing the filling takes 180 seconds. ? seconds for both steps.
   How many seconds to prepare in all?

7. Dr. Gleason studied 40 months in college.   4 months of study.
   She studied 40 months in dental school.   4 more months.
   How many months did she study in all?   ? months in all.

253

Test

Divide.

1. $50\overline{)350}$ (p. 240)

2. $90\overline{)810}$ (p. 240)

3. $30\overline{)150}$ (p. 240)

4. $70\overline{)560}$ (p. 240)

5. $20\overline{)100}$ (p. 240)

6. $80\overline{)572}$ (p. 242)

7. $60\overline{)443}$ (p. 242)

8. $40\overline{)306}$ (p. 242)

9. $30\overline{)195}$ (p. 242)

10. $70\overline{)666}$ (p. 242)

11. $24\overline{)104}$ (p. 246)

12. $57\overline{)353}$ (p. 250)

13. $91\overline{)472}$ (p. 244)

14. $46\overline{)121}$ (p. 248)

15. $78\overline{)579}$ (p. 248)

16. $38\overline{)241}$ (p. 248)

17. $66\overline{)554}$ (p. 250)

18. $82\overline{)248}$ (p. 244)

19. $27\overline{)257}$ (p. 250)

20. $73\overline{)280}$ (p. 246)

bonus

Solve the problem.

21. Each boat can carry 25 people.
There are 211 people.
How many boats can be filled?
How many people will be left over? (p. 250)

254

Keeping up

In what place is the 6?

1. 7,650,403 (p. 14)

2. 8,236,981 (p. 14)

3. 4,001,867 (p. 14)

4. 6,302,009 (p. 14)

Which unit would you use to measure?
Write CENTIMETER, GRAM, CUP, or DEGREE CELSIUS.

5. Height of a bottle. (p. 46)

6. Amount of water in a bottle. (p. 58)

7. Weight of a bottle. (p. 56)

8. Temperature of the water. (p. 64)

Multiply.

9. 75
× 6 (p. 164)

10. 83
× 9 (p. 164)

11. 465
× 5 (p. 166)

12. 809
× 7 (p. 166)

13. 666
× 6 (p. 166)

14. 32
×45 (p. 182)

15. 18
×57 (p. 182)

16. 713
× 28 (p. 184)

17. 302
× 29 (p. 184)

18. 789
× 16 (p. 184)

19. $8.30
× 6 (p. 168)

20. $.98
× 9 (p. 168)

21. $.65
× 45 (p. 186)

22. $8.34
× 78 (p. 186)

23. $7.06
× 53 (p. 186)

Divide.

24. 3)29 (p. 208)

25. 7)53 (p. 208)

26. 6)58 (p. 208)

27. 8)63 (p. 208)

28. 9)78 (p. 208)

29. 7)490 (p. 218)

30. 9)630 (p. 218)

31. 6)366 (p. 220)

32. 2)188 (p. 220)

33. 8)672 (p. 224)

34. 7)294 (p. 224)

35. 5)189 (p. 226)

36. 9)502 (p. 226)

37. 4)1574 (p. 230)

38. 9)7489 (p. 230)

255

Pancakes

DIRECTIONS FOR MAKING PANCAKES

3 cups of pancake mix.
2 cups of milk.
Makes about 24 pancakes.

Roberto and Maryanne
want to make 48 pancakes.

48 is twice as many as 24.
They should use twice as many cups of mix.
How many cups is that?
They should use twice as many cups of milk.
How many cups is that?

Suppose they want to make 72 pancakes.
How many cups of mix should they use?
How many cups of milk?

Suppose they have a pancake party.
They want to make 96 pancakes.
How many cups of mix should they use?
How many cups of milk?

13 Fractions

Fair Shares

Anna, Hal, and Ruth want to share a candy bar.
Which shows fair shares?

The pieces are the same size.
These are fair shares.

The pieces are different sizes.
These are not fair shares.

Do these show fair shares?   Write YES or NO.

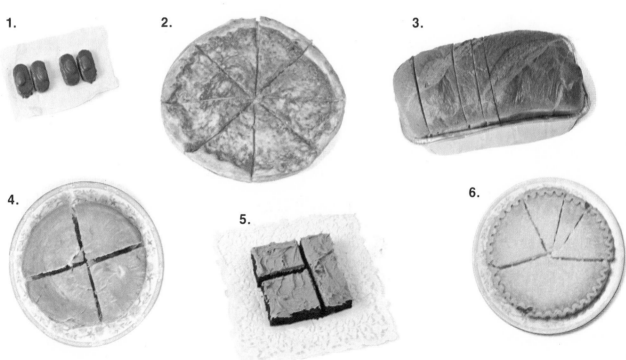

1.

2.

3.

4.

5.

6.

257

Fractions

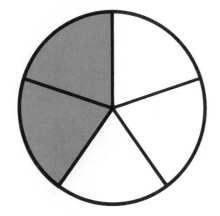

Two red shares.
Five fair shares in all.
Two fifths is red.

$\dfrac{2}{5}$ ←numerator

←denominator

---

try these

Write the fraction.

1.

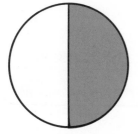

One half is red.

2.

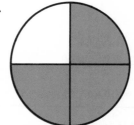

Three fourths is red.

3.

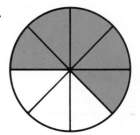

Five eighths is red.

4.

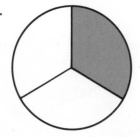

One third is red.

5.

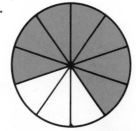

Seven tenths is red.

6.

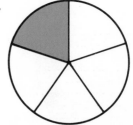

One fifth is red.

now do these

What part is red? Write the fraction.

7.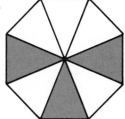

8.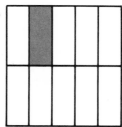

9.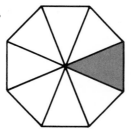

10.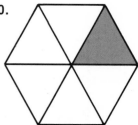

11.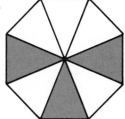

12.

13.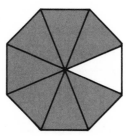

14.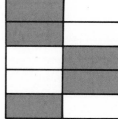

15.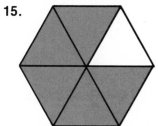

16.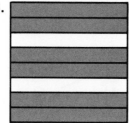

17.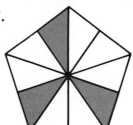

18.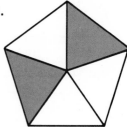

19.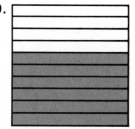

20.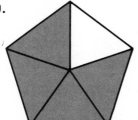

21.

22.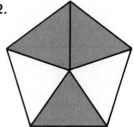

259

Comparing Fractions

When the denominators are the same, compare the numerators.

Which is less? Which is greater?

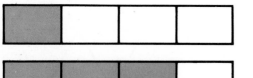

$\frac{1}{4}$

$\frac{3}{4}$

$\frac{1}{4} < \frac{3}{4}$ $\frac{3}{4} > \frac{1}{4}$

$\frac{2}{5}$

$\frac{4}{5}$

$\frac{2}{5} < \frac{4}{5}$ $\frac{4}{5} > \frac{2}{5}$

When the numerators are the same, compare the denominators.

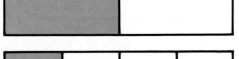

$\frac{1}{2}$

$\frac{1}{4}$

$\frac{1}{4} < \frac{1}{2}$ $\frac{1}{2} > \frac{1}{4}$

$\frac{2}{3}$

$\frac{2}{5}$

$\frac{2}{5} < \frac{2}{3}$ $\frac{2}{3} > \frac{2}{5}$

try these

Write > or <.

1.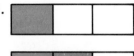

$$\frac{1}{3} \quad \bigcirc \quad \frac{2}{3}$$

2.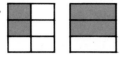

$$\frac{2}{6} \quad \bigcirc \quad \frac{2}{3}$$

3.

$$\frac{3}{4} \quad \bigcirc \quad \frac{2}{4}$$

4.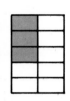

$$\frac{3}{5} \quad \bigcirc \quad \frac{3}{10}$$

now do these

Write > or <.

5.

$$\frac{1}{4} \quad \bigcirc \quad \frac{1}{8}$$

6.

$$\frac{2}{5} \quad \bigcirc \quad \frac{3}{5}$$

7.

$$\frac{1}{3} \quad \bigcirc \quad \frac{1}{6}$$

8.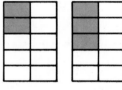

$$\frac{2}{10} \quad \bigcirc \quad \frac{3}{10}$$

9.

$$\frac{4}{5} \quad \bigcirc \quad \frac{4}{10}$$

10.

$$\frac{2}{6} \quad \bigcirc \quad \frac{2}{8}$$

11.

$$\frac{3}{8} \quad \bigcirc \quad \frac{5}{8}$$

12.

$$\frac{1}{2} \quad \bigcirc \quad \frac{1}{4}$$

13.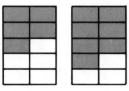

$$\frac{5}{10} \quad \bigcirc \quad \frac{7}{10}$$

14.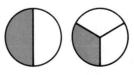

$$\frac{1}{2} \quad \bigcirc \quad \frac{1}{3}$$

15.

$$\frac{3}{4} \quad \bigcirc \quad \frac{3}{8}$$

16.

$$\frac{3}{6} \quad \bigcirc \quad \frac{4}{6}$$

261

Fractions and Groups

What part of the group of kittens has bows?

$\dfrac{2}{5}$ ← kittens with bows

← kittens in all

The puppies are in 4 pairs.
What part of the group has bows?

$\dfrac{1}{4}$ ← pairs with bows

← pairs in all

try these

Write the fraction.

1. What part is brown?	2. What part is brown?	3. What part has bows?
 $\dfrac{?}{5}$	$\dfrac{?}{2}$	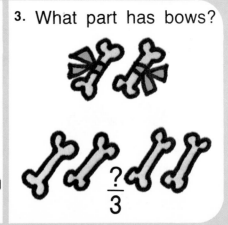 $\dfrac{?}{3}$

Write the fraction.

4. What part is gray?

5. What part is spotted?

6. What part has worms?

7. What part is new?

8. What part is green?

9. What part is jumping?

10. What part is flying?

11. What part has leaves?

12. What part is brownies?

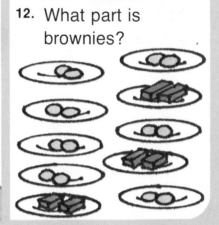

263

Finding Part of a Group

There are 6 kittens.
$\frac{1}{3}$ of them belong to Dave.
How many kittens belong
to Dave?

1. Make 3 groups with the same number in each.
2. Count the number in 1 group.
3. Write the sentence.

$$\frac{1}{3} \text{ of } 6 = 2$$

There are 12 puppies.
$\frac{1}{4}$ of them belong to Marge.
How many puppies belong
to Marge?

1. Make 4 groups with the same number in each.
2. Count the number in 1 group.
3. Write the sentence.

$$\frac{1}{4} \text{ of } 12 = 3$$

Complete the sentence.

1.
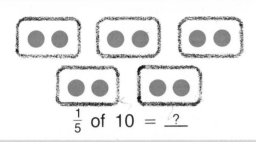
$\frac{1}{5}$ of 10 = ___?___

2.

$\frac{1}{3}$ of 9 = ___?___

now do these

Complete the sentence.

3.

$\frac{1}{2}$ of 6 = ___?___

4.

$\frac{1}{8}$ of 16 = ___?___

5.

$\frac{1}{3}$ of 12 = ___?___

6.
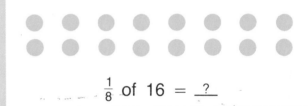
$\frac{1}{4}$ of 16 = ___?___

7.

$\frac{1}{5}$ of 15 = ___?___

8.
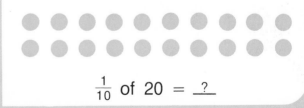
$\frac{1}{10}$ of 20 = ___?___

Finding Parts of Groups

There are 12 cookies.
$\frac{2}{3}$ of them are for Susan.
How many cookies are
for Susan?

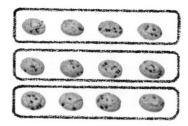

1. Make 3 groups with
   the same number in each.
2. Count the number in 1 group.
3. Multiply by the number of
   groups that are for Susan.
4. Write the sentence.

$$\frac{2}{3} \text{ of } 12 = 8$$

There are 10 cupcakes.
$\frac{3}{5}$ of them are for Ben.
How many cupcakes are
for Ben?

1. Make 5 groups with
   the same number in each.
2. Count the number in 1 group.
3. Multiply by 3.
4. Write the sentence.

$$\frac{3}{5} \text{ of } 10 = 6$$

Complete the sentence.

1.

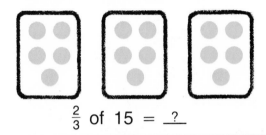

$\frac{2}{3}$ of 15 = ___?___

2.

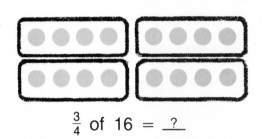

$\frac{3}{4}$ of 16 = ___?___

Complete the sentence.

3.

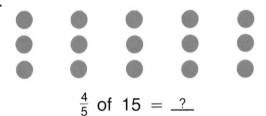

$\frac{4}{5}$ of 15 = ___?___

4.

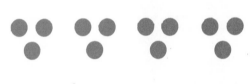

$\frac{3}{4}$ of 12 = ___?___

5.

$\frac{3}{8}$ of 16 = ___?___

6.

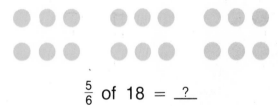

$\frac{5}{6}$ of 18 = ___?___

7.

$\frac{4}{5}$ of 20 = ___?___

8.

$\frac{7}{10}$ of 20 = ___?___

Equivalent Fractions

Fold a paper in half.
Color one half red.

$$\frac{1}{2} \text{ is red.}$$

Fold the paper again.
$\frac{2}{4}$ is red.

$$\frac{1}{2} = \frac{2}{4}$$

Fold it again.
$\frac{4}{8}$ is red.

$$\frac{2}{4} = \frac{4}{8}$$

$\frac{1}{2}$, $\frac{2}{4}$, and $\frac{4}{8}$ name the same numbers.

$\frac{1}{2}$, $\frac{2}{4}$, and $\frac{4}{8}$ are **equivalent fractions.**

Copy and complete the sentence.

1.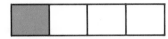

$$\frac{1}{4} = \frac{?}{8}$$

2.

$$\frac{4}{5} = \frac{?}{10}$$

3.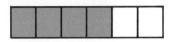

$$\frac{2}{3} = \frac{?}{6}$$

now do these

Copy and complete the sentence.

4.

$$\frac{1}{2} = \frac{?}{10}$$

5.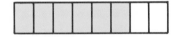

$$\frac{3}{4} = \frac{?}{8}$$

6.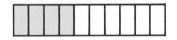

$$\frac{2}{5} = \frac{?}{10}$$

7.

$$\frac{6}{10} = \frac{?}{5}$$

8.

$$\frac{8}{10} = \frac{?}{5}$$

9.

$$\frac{2}{6} = \frac{?}{3}$$

10.

$$\frac{2}{2} = \frac{?}{3}$$

11.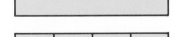

$$1 = \frac{?}{4}$$

12.

$$1 = \frac{?}{5}$$

269

Mixed Numerals

How much is there?

one   one   one fourth

2 crackers and $\frac{1}{4}$ cracker

$$2 \quad + \quad \frac{1}{4}$$

Mixed numeral $\longrightarrow$ $2\frac{1}{4}$

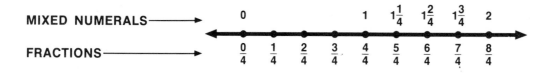

MIXED NUMERALS $\longrightarrow$

FRACTIONS $\longrightarrow$

$\frac{4}{4}$ is a fraction for 1.

What is a fraction for $1\frac{1}{4}$?

What is the mixed numeral for $\frac{7}{4}$?

---

try these

How much is red? Write a mixed numeral.

1.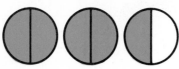

2.

3.

270

How much is red? Write a mixed numeral.

4.

5.

6.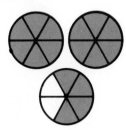

7.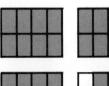

Write a mixed numeral.

8. 1 and $\frac{4}{5}$ **9.** 3 and $\frac{1}{2}$ **10.** 2 and $\frac{2}{3}$ **11.** 5 and $\frac{1}{4}$

12. 4 and $\frac{2}{5}$ **13.** 8 and $\frac{9}{10}$ **14.** 9 and $\frac{3}{8}$ **15.** 7 and $\frac{3}{4}$

16. 10 and $\frac{1}{3}$ **17.** 6 and $\frac{1}{5}$ **18.** 12 and $\frac{7}{8}$ **19.** 20 and $\frac{7}{10}$

20. $2 + \frac{1}{2}$ **21.** $4 + \frac{2}{3}$ **22.** $6 + \frac{1}{5}$ **23.** $5 + \frac{5}{8}$

24. $1 + \frac{3}{4}$ **25.** $10 + \frac{1}{8}$ **26.** $8 + \frac{3}{10}$ **27.** $7 + \frac{1}{10}$

28. $19 + \frac{3}{5}$ **29.** $15 + \frac{3}{10}$ **30.** $23 + \frac{2}{5}$ **31.** $50 + \frac{9}{10}$

quick check

Complete the sentence.

1. 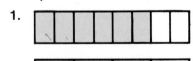 $\frac{6}{8} = \frac{?}{4}$

2. 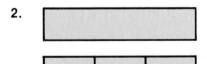 $1 = \frac{?}{3}$

3.  $\frac{1}{3}$ of 6 = __?__

4.  $\frac{3}{4}$ of 8 = __?__

Addition With Fractions

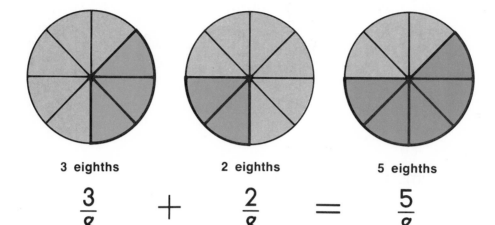

3 eighths   2 eighths   5 eighths

$$\frac{3}{8} \quad + \quad \frac{2}{8} \quad = \quad \frac{5}{8}$$

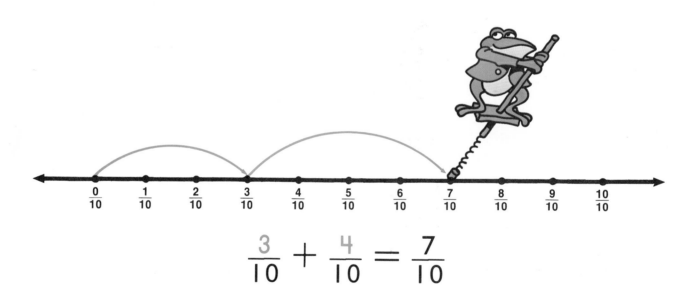

$$\frac{3}{10} + \frac{4}{10} = \frac{7}{10}$$

---

try these

Add.

1. $\frac{1}{8} + \frac{2}{8} = \frac{?}{8}$ **2.** $\frac{4}{8} + \frac{3}{8} = \underline{\ ?\ }$ **3.** $\frac{1}{8} + \frac{4}{8} = \underline{\ ?\ }$

4. $\frac{2}{10} + \frac{7}{10} = \frac{?}{10}$ **5.** $\frac{5}{10} + \frac{2}{10} = \underline{\ ?\ }$ **6.** $\frac{4}{10} + \frac{5}{10} = \underline{\ ?\ }$

— **now do these** —

Add.

7. $\frac{1}{3} + \frac{1}{3} = $ ___?___

8. $\frac{1}{4} + \frac{2}{4} = $ ___?___

9. $\frac{3}{6} + \frac{2}{6} = $ ___?___

10. $\frac{3}{8} + \frac{4}{8} = $ ___?___

11. $\frac{1}{5} + \frac{2}{5} = $ ___?___

12. $\frac{3}{8} + \frac{2}{8} = $ ___?___

13. $\frac{1}{8} + \frac{2}{8} = $ ___?___

14. $\frac{2}{10} + \frac{1}{10} = $ ___?___

15. $\frac{2}{5} + \frac{2}{5} = $ ___?___

16. $\frac{3}{10} + \frac{6}{10} = $ ___?___

17. $\frac{2}{8} + \frac{1}{8} = $ ___?___

18. $\frac{2}{5} + \frac{1}{5} = $ ___?___

19. $\frac{2}{4} + \frac{1}{4} = $ ___?___

20. $\frac{5}{8} + \frac{2}{8} = $ ___?___

21. $\frac{2}{6} + \frac{3}{6} = $ ___?___

22. $\frac{1}{6} + \frac{4}{6} = $ ___?___

23. $\frac{2}{10} + \frac{5}{10} = $ ___?___

24. $\frac{4}{8} + \frac{1}{8} = $ ___?___

SEE YOU LATER

The time is 3:00.
45 minutes later it will be 3:45.

Look at the clock.
What time will it be 45 minutes later?

A.

B.

C.

D.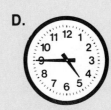

273

Subtraction With Fractions

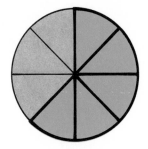

5 eights.

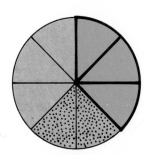

Take away 2 eights.
3 eights are left.

$$\frac{5}{8} - \frac{2}{8} = \frac{3}{8}$$

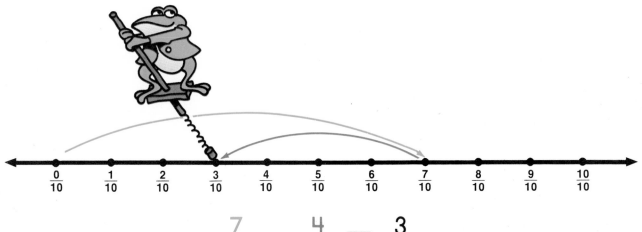

$$\frac{7}{10} - \frac{4}{10} = \frac{3}{10}$$

try these

Subtract.

1. $\frac{6}{8} - \frac{1}{8} = \frac{?}{8}$

2. $\frac{7}{8} - \frac{2}{8} = \underline{\ ?\ }$

3. $\frac{4}{8} - \frac{3}{8} = \underline{\ ?\ }$

4. $\frac{8}{10} - \frac{1}{10} = \frac{?}{10}$

5. $\frac{5}{10} - \frac{2}{10} = \underline{\ ?\ }$

6. $\frac{9}{10} - \frac{6}{1\cdot0} = \underline{\ ?\ }$

274

now do these

Subtract.

7. $\dfrac{5}{6} - \dfrac{4}{6} = $ ___?___

8. $\dfrac{3}{4} - \dfrac{2}{4} = $ ___?___

9. $\dfrac{2}{3} - \dfrac{1}{3} = $ ___?___

10. $\dfrac{4}{5} - \dfrac{3}{5} = $ ___?___

11. $\dfrac{6}{8} - \dfrac{3}{8} = $ ___?___

12. $\dfrac{3}{5} - \dfrac{2}{5} = $ ___?___

13. $\dfrac{3}{6} - \dfrac{2}{6} = $ ___?___

14. $\dfrac{7}{8} - \dfrac{4}{8} = $ ___?___

15. $\dfrac{4}{5} - \dfrac{2}{5} = $ ___?___

16. $\dfrac{5}{8} - \dfrac{2}{8} = $ ___?___

17. $\dfrac{4}{6} - \dfrac{3}{6} = $ ___?___

18. $\dfrac{5}{10} - \dfrac{4}{10} = $ ___?___

19. $\dfrac{5}{8} - \dfrac{4}{8} = $ ___?___

20. $\dfrac{4}{5} - \dfrac{1}{5} = $ ___?___

21. $\dfrac{9}{10} - \dfrac{2}{10} = $ ___?___

22. $\dfrac{7}{8} - \dfrac{2}{8} = $ ___?___

23. $\dfrac{10}{10} - \dfrac{3}{10} = $ ___?___

24. $\dfrac{8}{8} - \dfrac{5}{8} = $ ___?___

WHAT TIME WAS THAT?

The time is 3:00.
One-half hour ago it was 2:30.

Look at the clock.
What time was it one-half hour ago?

A.

B.

C.

D.

275

Addition With Mixed Numerals

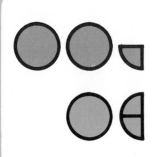 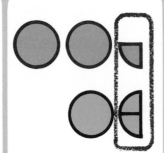 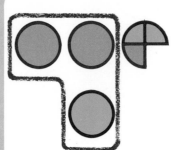 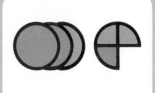

$2\frac{1}{4}$ pies. $1\frac{2}{4}$ pies. How many pies in all?

Join the parts.
$\frac{1}{4} + \frac{2}{4} = \frac{3}{4}$

Join the wholes.
$2 + 1 = 3$

$3\frac{3}{4}$ pies

Find the sum: $2\frac{1}{4} + 1\frac{2}{4}$.

Step 1

$$\begin{array}{r} 2\frac{1}{4} \\ +1\frac{2}{4} \\ \hline \frac{3}{4} \end{array}$$

Add: $\frac{1}{4} + \frac{2}{4}$.

Step 2

$$\begin{array}{r} 2\frac{1}{4} \\ +1\frac{2}{4} \\ \hline 3\frac{3}{4} \end{array}$$

Add: $2 + 1$.

276

Copy and complete.

1. $3\frac{1}{3}$
   $+4\frac{1}{3}$
   $\frac{}{\ \ \frac{2}{3}}$

2. $2\frac{1}{5}$
   $+1\frac{3}{5}$
   $\frac{}{\ \ \frac{4}{5}}$

3. $4\frac{2}{4}$
   $+2\frac{1}{4}$
   $\frac{}{6}$

4. $3\frac{2}{8}$
   $+3\frac{3}{8}$
   $\frac{}{6}$

5. $2\frac{4}{6}$
   $+5\frac{1}{6}$
   $\frac{}{7}$

Add.

6. $2\frac{1}{8}$
   $+3\frac{4}{8}$

7. $4\frac{4}{10}$
   $+4\frac{3}{10}$

8. $2\frac{2}{6}$
   $+4\frac{3}{6}$

9. $3\frac{2}{8}$
   $+4\frac{5}{8}$

10. $3\frac{2}{6}$
    $+5\frac{3}{6}$

Add.

11. $3\frac{1}{4}$
    $+2\frac{2}{4}$

12. $4\frac{2}{5}$
    $+3\frac{2}{5}$

13. $6\frac{2}{8}$
    $+1\frac{5}{8}$

14. $5\frac{2}{6}$
    $+3\frac{3}{6}$

15. $2\frac{3}{8}$
    $+4\frac{4}{8}$

16. $5\frac{7}{10}$
    $+4\frac{2}{10}$

17. $6\frac{4}{8}$
    $+2\frac{3}{8}$

18. $2\frac{4}{6}$
    $+5\frac{1}{6}$

19. $4\frac{4}{6}$
    $+4\frac{1}{6}$

20. $3\frac{2}{8}$
    $+5\frac{3}{8}$

21. $6\frac{3}{6}$
    $+\ \ \frac{2}{6}$

22. $3\frac{4}{8}$
    $+\ \ \frac{1}{8}$

23. $1\frac{2}{4}$
    $+\ \ \frac{1}{4}$

24. $7\frac{6}{8}$
    $+\ \ \frac{1}{8}$

25. $2\frac{3}{10}$
    $+\ \ \frac{6}{10}$

26. $2\frac{1}{6}$
    $+3\frac{4}{6}$

27. $7\frac{2}{10}$
    $+\ \ \frac{5}{10}$

28. $5\frac{2}{4}$
    $+1\frac{1}{4}$

29. $9\frac{5}{8}$
    $+\ \ \frac{2}{8}$

30. $4\frac{2}{5}$
    $+4\frac{1}{5}$

Subtraction With Mixed Numerals

Subtract: $7\frac{7}{8} - 2\frac{2}{8}$.

<table>
<tr><td>

Step 1

$$7\frac{7}{8}$$
$$-2\frac{2}{8}$$
$$\overline{\quad\frac{5}{8}}$$

Subtract: $\frac{7}{8} - \frac{2}{8}$.

</td><td>

Step 2

$$7\frac{7}{8}$$
$$-2\frac{2}{8}$$
$$\overline{5\frac{5}{8}}$$

Subtract: $7 - 2$.

</td></tr>
</table>

---

try these

Copy and complete.

1. $8\frac{3}{5}$ $-2\frac{1}{5}$ $\overline{\frac{2}{5}}$

2. $7\frac{5}{6}$ $-5\frac{4}{6}$ $\overline{\frac{1}{6}}$

3. $9\frac{5}{8}$ $-4\frac{4}{8}$ $\overline{5}$

4. $6\frac{2}{4}$ $-4\frac{1}{4}$ $\overline{2}$

5. $5\frac{2}{3}$ $-4\frac{1}{3}$ $\overline{1}$

Subtract.

6. $6\frac{3}{4}$ $-4\frac{2}{4}$

7. $8\frac{4}{5}$ $-7\frac{1}{5}$

8. $7\frac{9}{10}$ $-3\frac{6}{10}$

9. $9\frac{2}{6}$ $-6\frac{1}{6}$

10. $5\frac{7}{8}$ $-2\frac{2}{8}$

278

now do these

Subtract.

11. $6\frac{4}{5}$
$-3\frac{2}{5}$

12. $9\frac{7}{8}$
$-4\frac{4}{8}$

13. $7\frac{3}{6}$
$-5\frac{2}{6}$

14. $8\frac{5}{8}$
$-5\frac{2}{8}$

15. $5\frac{3}{10}$
$-2\frac{2}{10}$

16. $8\frac{6}{8}$
$-5\frac{1}{8}$

17. $7\frac{2}{5}$
$-3\frac{1}{5}$

18. $6\frac{7}{8}$
$-4\frac{6}{8}$

19. $4\frac{3}{5}$
$-3\frac{2}{5}$

20. $5\frac{3}{6}$
$-1\frac{2}{6}$

21. $7\frac{6}{8}$
$-2\frac{1}{8}$

22. $6\frac{6}{8}$
$-3\frac{3}{8}$

23. $8\frac{6}{8}$
$-5\frac{5}{8}$

24. $9\frac{4}{5}$
$-4\frac{3}{5}$

25. $5\frac{8}{10}$
$-3\frac{1}{10}$

26. $8\frac{4}{6}$
$-8\frac{3}{6}$

27. $9\frac{8}{10}$
$-\frac{5}{10}$

28. $5\frac{7}{8}$
$-\frac{2}{8}$

29. $7\frac{3}{6}$
$-\frac{2}{6}$

30. $5\frac{7}{8}$
$-\frac{4}{8}$

WHAT TIME WAS THAT?

The time is 3:00.
One-quarter hour ago is was 2:45.

Look at the clock.
What time was it one-quarter hour ago?

A.

B.

C.

D.

279

making and using tables

Charlie and Susan are chefs.
Charlie's chowder is delicious.
Some days he makes a few pots.
Some days he makes many pots.

Each pot has 35 clams. How many clams
does he need for 2 pots? 5 pots? 7 pots?

Charlie makes a table. It helps
him to find the answers quickly.

pots	1	2	3	4	5	6	7	8	9	10
clams	35	70	105	140	175	210	245	280	315	350

The table shows that there are 70 clams in 2 pots.
There are 175 clams in 5 pots, and 245 in 7 pots.

Susan's salad dressing is tasty.
She uses 2 parts of vinegar for
each 5 parts of oil. She makes
a lot of dressing. She wants to
use a table to help her.
Which table below should she use?

A.

vinegar	2	4	6	8	10	12	14	16
oil	5	10	15	20	25	30	35	40

B.

vinegar	5	10	15	20	25	30	35	40
oil	2	4	6	8	10	12	14	16

Solve the problem.

1. Susan makes a special spaghetti dish.
   She uses 1 kg of meat for each 2 kg of spaghetti.
   Complete the table to help Susan.

meat	1	2	3	4	5	6	7	8	9	10
spaghetti	2	4	6	?	?	?	?	?	?	?

2. Use the chart you completed for Susan. How much spaghetti should she use with 4 kg of meat?

3. How much spaghetti should she use with 7 kg of meat?

4. How much meat should she use with 10 kg of spaghetti?

5. How much meat should she use with 16 kg of spaghetti?

6. Charlie makes a charming cherry dessert. He uses 2 cups of cream for each 3 cups of cherries. Complete the table to help Charlie.

cups of cream	2	4	6	8	10	12	14	16
cups of cherries	3	6	9	?	?	?	?	?

7. Use the chart you completed for Charlie. How many cups of cherries should be used with 6 cups of cream?

8. How many cups of cherries with 10 cups of cream?

9. How many cups of cream with 18 cups of cherries?

10. How many cups of cream with 24 cups of cherries?

Test

What part is red?
Write the fraction.

1.

(p. 258)

2.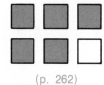

(p. 262)

Write > or <.

3.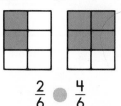

$$\frac{2}{6} \bullet \frac{4}{6}$$

(p. 260)

4.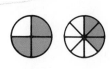

$$\frac{3}{4} \bullet \frac{3}{8}$$

(p. 260)

Complete the sentence.

5.

$$\frac{1}{3} \text{ of } 9 = \underline{\quad?\quad}$$

(p. 264)

6.

$$\frac{3}{5} \text{ of } 15 = \underline{\quad?\quad}$$

(p. 266)

7.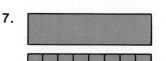

$$1 = \frac{?}{8}$$

(p. 268)

8.

$$\frac{2}{5} = \frac{?}{10}$$

(p. 268)

Add.

9. $\frac{6}{8} + \frac{1}{8} = \underline{\quad?\quad}$ (p. 272)

10. $\frac{3}{6} + \frac{2}{6} = \underline{\quad?\quad}$ (p. 272)

11. $5\frac{1}{4}$
$+ \ \frac{2}{4}$
(p. 276)

12. $6\frac{3}{8}$
$+2\frac{2}{8}$
(p. 276)

13. $7\frac{6}{10}$
$+1\frac{1}{10}$
(p. 276)

14. $2\frac{2}{4}$
$+4\frac{1}{4}$
(p. 276)

Subtract.

15. $\frac{7}{10} - \frac{6}{10} = \underline{\quad?\quad}$ (p. 274)

16. $\frac{3}{5} - \frac{1}{5} = \underline{\quad?\quad}$ (p. 274)

17. $4\frac{6}{8}$
$- \ \frac{5}{8}$
(p. 278)

18. $7\frac{4}{5}$
$-2\frac{1}{5}$
(p. 278)

19. $6\frac{5}{6}$
$-1\frac{4}{6}$
(p. 278)

20. $3\frac{9}{10}$
$-1\frac{6}{10}$
(p. 278)

Keeping up

Add.

1.	$ .45	**2.**	$9.00	**3.**	$63.35	**4.**	$19.99	**5.**	$ .16
	8.32		.35		2.75		5.23		5.75
	+ .03		+ 6.47		+ 70.10		+ .05		+ 72.98
	(p. 84)		(p. 84)		(p. 84)		(p. 84)		(p. 84)

Subtract.

6.	$6.87	**7.**	$8.23	**8.**	$45.00	**9.**	$40.30	**10.**	$50.07
	− .49		− 1.78		− 13.81		− 6.55		− 49.98
	(p. 108)		(p. 108)		(p. 108)		(p. 108)		(p. 108)

Which unit would you use to measure?
Write METER, KILOGRAM, LITER, or DEGREE CELSIUS.

11. Weight of water in a swimming pool.
(p. 56)
12. Length of a swimming pool.
(p. 50)
13. Amount of water in a pool.
(p. 58)
14. Temperature of the water.
(p. 64)

Multiply.

15.	$.37	**16.**	$.83	**17.**	$6.37	**18.**	$4.37	**19.**	$9.03
	× 42		× 75		× 55		× 64		× 68
	(p. 186)		(p. 186)		(p. 186)		(p. 186)		(p. 186)

Divide.

20. $8\overline{)640}$ (p. 218) **21.** $5\overline{)355}$ (p. 220) **22.** $7\overline{)504}$ (p. 224) **23.** $6\overline{)377}$ (p. 226) **24.** $9\overline{)307}$ (p. 226)

25. $40\overline{)120}$ (p. 240) **26.** $60\overline{)195}$ (p. 242) **27.** $30\overline{)126}$ (p. 242) **28.** $32\overline{)269}$ (p. 244) **29.** $63\overline{)580}$ (p. 244)

30. $42\overline{)368}$ (p. 246) **31.** $24\overline{)159}$ (p. 246) **32.** $65\overline{)397}$ (p. 250) **33.** $88\overline{)793}$ (p. 250) **34.** $57\overline{)495}$ (p. 250)

283

Probability

Put a red marble and a blue marble in a dish.
Without looking, draw out one marble.
Record its color. Put it back in the dish.

Suppose you do this 16 times.
What do you think will happen?

A. I will draw the red one more often.
B. I will draw the blue one more often.
C. I will draw both about the same
   number of times.

Guess. Then try it. Were you right?

Paul and Paula did the investigation in probability.
Each recorded the results. Then each wrote two fractions.
One fraction told what part of the draws was red.
The other fraction told what part of the draws was blue.

PAUL

	Record	Fraction
Red	JHT IIII	$\frac{9}{16}$
Blue	JHT II	$\frac{7}{16}$

PAULA

	Record	Fraction
Red	JHT II	$\frac{7}{16}$
Blue	JHT IIII	$\frac{9}{16}$

What part of Paul's draws was red?
What part of Paula's draws was red?
In your investigation, what part of your draws was red?
What part of your draws was blue?

In each investigation, draw a marble 20 times.
First make a prediction.

How many draws do you think will be red?
Write a fraction to tell what part will be red.

Then do the investigation.
Record the results.
Write a fraction to tell what part of the draws was red.
Compare the results with your prediction.

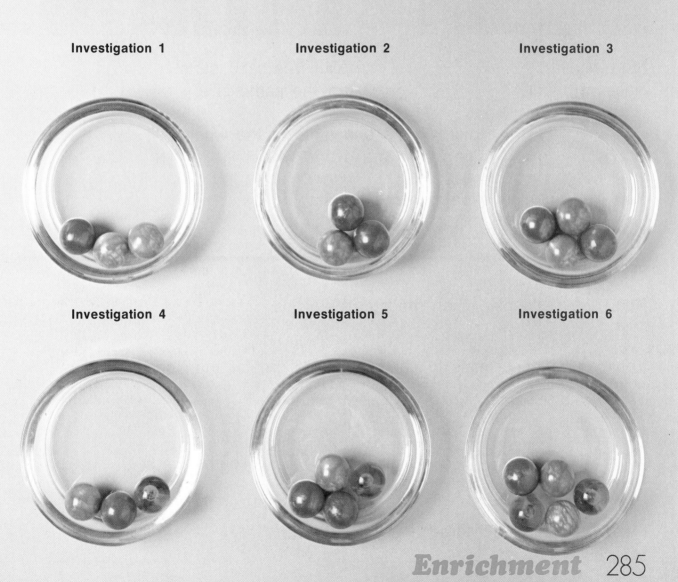

Investigation 1   **Investigation 2**   **Investigation 3**

Investigation 4   **Investigation 5**   **Investigation 6**

14 Decimals

Decimals

Start with a
piece of paper.

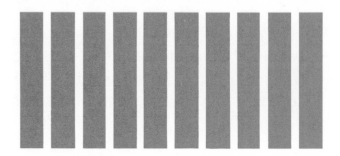

Cut it into 10 parts
of the same size.

Each part is one tenth of the whole.
Ten tenths make one whole.

You can write decimals to name tenths.

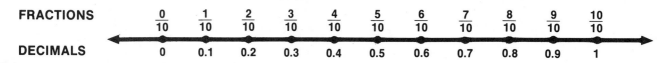

| FRACTIONS | $\frac{0}{10}$ | $\frac{1}{10}$ | $\frac{2}{10}$ | $\frac{3}{10}$ | $\frac{4}{10}$ | $\frac{5}{10}$ | $\frac{6}{10}$ | $\frac{7}{10}$ | $\frac{8}{10}$ | $\frac{9}{10}$ | $\frac{10}{10}$ |
| DECIMALS | 0 | 0.1 | 0.2 | 0.3 | 0.4 | 0.5 | 0.6 | 0.7 | 0.8 | 0.9 | 1 |

Read the fractions. Then read the decimals.

You can write decimals to name numbers greater than one.

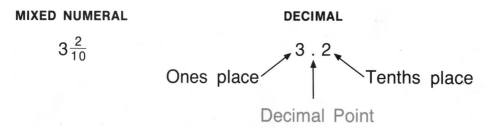

MIXED NUMERAL   DECIMAL

$3\frac{2}{10}$

3 . 2

Ones place   Tenths place

Decimal Point

Read both this way: three and two tenths.

286

Read the decimal.

1. 0.1   2. 0.4   3. 0.7   4. 2.3   5. 7.5   6. 9.8

Write the decimal.

7. $\frac{3}{10}$ 8. $\frac{5}{10}$ 9. $\frac{2}{10}$ 10. $1\frac{6}{10}$ 11. $4\frac{9}{10}$ 12. $8\frac{1}{10}$

13. Seven tenths   14. Five and four tenths

now do these

Read the decimal.

15. 0.3   16. 0.5   17. 0.8   18. 0.9   19. 9.9   20. 8.7

21. 6.6   22. 7.8   23. 9.5   24. 6.8   25. 7.2   26. 0.2

Write the decimal.

27. $5\frac{3}{10}$ 28. $6\frac{5}{10}$ 29. $9\frac{2}{10}$ 30. $8\frac{1}{10}$ 31. $1\frac{4}{10}$ 32. $2\frac{7}{10}$

33. $18\frac{6}{10}$ 34. $35\frac{9}{10}$ 35. $16\frac{8}{10}$ 36. $25\frac{7}{10}$ 37. $30\frac{3}{10}$ 38. $65\frac{5}{10}$

39. $122\frac{2}{10}$ 40. $111\frac{1}{10}$ 41. $128\frac{9}{10}$ 42. $176\frac{4}{10}$ 43. $182\frac{6}{10}$ 44. $198\frac{8}{10}$

45. Eight tenths   46. Seven and seven tenths

47. Nine and six tenths   48. Ten and one tenth

49. Four tenths   50. Thirteen and three tenths

Tenths

An odometer tells how far a car has gone. This odometer shows nine-tenths kilometer.

| 0 | 0 | 0 | 0 | 0 | 9 |

Read the numeral. ⟶ Nine tenths

Write. ⟶ 0.9

After nine tenths, what numeral will come up on the odometer?

This odometer is on another car.

| 0 | 0 | 0 | 2 | 7 | 3 |

Read the numeral. ⟶ Twenty-seven and three tenths

Write. ⟶ 27.3

288

Read the odometer.

1. | 0 | 0 | 0 | 0 | 0 | 4 |

2. | 0 | 0 | 0 | 0 | 9 | 9 |

3. | 0 | 0 | 0 | 1 | 0 | 3 |

4. | 0 | 0 | 0 | 6 | 5 | 3 |

5. | 0 | 0 | 4 | 5 | 6 | 3 |

6. | 0 | 0 | 6 | 5 | 4 | 1 |

now do these

Write the decimal.

7. | 0 | 0 | 0 | 0 | 3 | 4 |

8. | 0 | 0 | 0 | 0 | 7 | 2 |

9. | 0 | 0 | 0 | 0 | 8 | 8 |

10. | 0 | 0 | 0 | 1 | 0 | 0 |

11. | 0 | 0 | 0 | 1 | 0 | 2 |

12. | 0 | 0 | 0 | 1 | 2 | 2 |

13. | 0 | 0 | 0 | 3 | 0 | 3 |

14. | 0 | 0 | 0 | 4 | 0 | 0 |

15. | 0 | 0 | 0 | 6 | 1 | 0 |

16. | 0 | 0 | 2 | 3 | 5 | 5 |

17. | 0 | 0 | 3 | 2 | 6 | 4 |

18. | 0 | 0 | 6 | 4 | 5 | 3 |

19. | 0 | 0 | 2 | 0 | 0 | 2 |

20. | 0 | 0 | 4 | 1 | 1 | 1 |

21. | 0 | 0 | 3 | 0 | 0 | 0 |

THINK ABOUT IT

What will this odometer show after
the car has traveled 0.1 kilometer more?

| 0 | 0 | 9 | 9 | 9 | 9 |

Tenths in Measurement

A nickel is about 20 millimeters across.
A nickel is about 2 centimeters across.

Look at the ruler.
Each centimeter is marked into 10 parts.
Each part is 1 tenth centimeter.
Each part is 1 millimeter.

Some movie film is 35 millimeters wide.
That is 3 and 5 tenths centimeters.
Write: 3.5

Film for some pocket cameras
is 16 millimeters wide.
That is 1 and 6 tenths centimeters.
Write: 1.6

290

Complete. Use a decimal.

1.

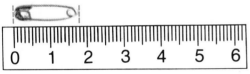

18 millimeters
_?_ centimeters

2.

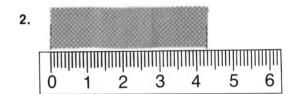

43 millimeters
_?_ centimeters

Write the decimal.

3.

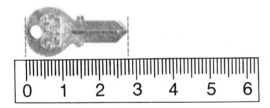

28 millimeters
_?_ centimeters

4.

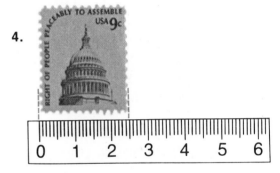

25 millimeters
_?_ centimeters

5.

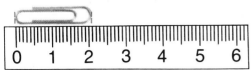

21 millimeters
_?_ centimeters

6.

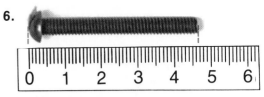

47 millimeters
_?_ centimeters

7. Some movie film is
70 millimeters wide.
How many centimeters
is that?

8. A quarter is 24 millimeters
across. How many
centimeters is that?

Hundredths

Start with a
piece of paper.

Cut it into tenths.

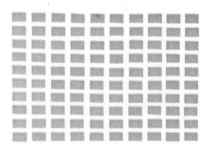

Cut each tenth
into 10 parts
of the same size.

Ten hundredths make one tenth.
Ten tenths make one whole.

You use place value to name tenths and hundredths.

You know about
the ones place.

3   three

One place to the right
is the tenths place.

0.3   three tenths

Two places to the right
is the hundredths place.

0.03   three hundredths

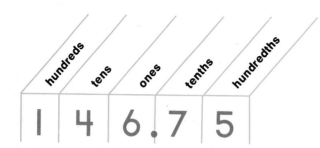

Read the numeral: One hundred forty-six and seventy-five hundredths.
In what place is the 5? In what place is the 7?

292

Read the decimal.

1. 0.06　　　　2. 0.75　　　　3. 1.42　　　　4. 34.85　　　　5. 215.38

Write the decimal.

6. Five hundredths

7. Seventy-two hundredths

8. Sixteen and sixty-one hundredths

9. One hundred twenty-five and thirty-seven hundredths

now do these

Read the decimal.

10. 0.03　　　　11. 0.54　　　　12. 1.02　　　　13. 10.03　　　　14. 16.73

15. 25.50　　　　16. 37.00　　　　17. 100.13　　　　18. 100.01　　　　19. 186.99

Write the decimal.

20. Two hundredths

21. Twenty-five hundredths

22. Three and five hundredths

23. Seven and fourteen hundredths

24. Twenty-five and seventy-five hundredths

25. Ten and one hundredth

26. One hundred twenty-eight and forty-five hundredths

27. Two hundred and two hundredths

28. One hundred thirty-seven and twenty hundredths

293

Adding Decimals

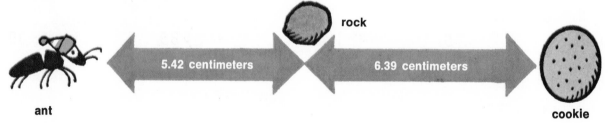

rock

5.42 centimeters   6.39 centimeters

ant

cookie

How far is it from the ant to the cookie?

Step 1	Step 2	Step 3
$$\begin{array}{r} \overset{1}{5.42} \\ +6.39 \\ \hline 1 \end{array}$$	$$\begin{array}{r} \overset{1}{5.42} \\ +6.39 \\ \hline 81 \end{array}$$	$$\begin{array}{r} \overset{1}{5.42} \\ +6.39 \\ \hline 11.81 \end{array}$$
Line up the decimal points. Add the hundredths.	Add the tenths.	Add the ones. Write the decimal point in the answer.

---

try these

Copy and complete.

1. $\begin{array}{r}\overset{1}{5.67}\\+8.17\\\hline .84\end{array}$	**2.** $\begin{array}{r}\overset{1}{7.09}\\+7.07\\\hline .16\end{array}$	**3.** $\begin{array}{r}\overset{1}{0.07}\\+0.18\\\hline 5\end{array}$	**4.** $\begin{array}{r}\overset{1}{10.35}\\+20.35\\\hline 0\end{array}$	**5.** $\begin{array}{r}\overset{1}{20.27}\\+\;9.58\\\hline 5\end{array}$

Add.

6. $\begin{array}{r}0.05\\+0.77\\\hline\end{array}$	**7.** $\begin{array}{r}7.05\\+0.98\\\hline\end{array}$	**8.** $\begin{array}{r}10.58\\+89.39\\\hline\end{array}$	**9.** $\begin{array}{r}4.08\\+7.06\\\hline\end{array}$	**10.** $\begin{array}{r}20.47\\+\;7.25\\\hline\end{array}$

294

now do these

Add.

11. 2.35 +9.47	**12.** 6.27 +8.69	**13.** 5.58 +6.29	**14.** 8.29 +4.36	**15.** 8.08 +4.06
16. 7.02 +5.04	**17.** 6.07 +0.08	**18.** 2.05 +0.06	**19.** 0.09 +0.15	**20.** 0.08 +0.46
21. 0.05 +0.39	**22.** 0.07 +0.36	**23.** 20.46 +30.44	**24.** 10.78 +10.17	**25.** 34.98 +43.06
26. 12.06 +27.04	**27.** 61.47 + 8.05	**28.** 20.13 + 9.48	**29.** 35.63 + 0.24	**30.** 45.62 + 4.28
31. 3.6 +4.6	**32.** 0.7 +0.8	**33.** 52.93 +35.90	**34.** 87.40 + 2.70	**35.** 0.79 +0.56

PATTERNS

Each number is five greater than the number named before it. What are the next two numbers?

7	12	17	?	?

What are the next two numbers in the pattern?

A.
3	11	19	?	?

B.
5	22	39	?	?

C.
4	52	100	?	?

D.
9	65	121	?	?

295

Subtracting Decimals

7.28 centimeters

13.54 centimeters

rock

cookie

How much farther must the ant go?

Step 1

    4 14
13.5̷4̷
− 7.28
        6

Line up the
decimal points.
Subtract the hundredths.

Step 2

    4 14
13.5̷4̷
− 7.28
      26

Subtract the tenths.

Step 3

    4 14
13.5̷4̷
− 7.28
    6.26

Subtract the ones.
Write the decimal point
in the answer.

---

try these

Copy and complete.

8 17	7 16	7 13	4 16	5 13
1. 8.9̷7̷	2. 9.8̷6̷	3. 9.8̷3̷	4. 19.5̷6̷	5. 17.6̷3̷
−3.39	−3.79	−0.69	−18.07	− 7.59
.58	.07	4	9	4

Subtract.

6. 8.74	7. 0.86	8. 48.35	9. 57.51	10. 86.93
−8.69	−0.28	−32.18	− 6.47	− 0.64

296

now do these

Subtract.

11. 4.52 − 1.28	**12.** 6.94 − 3.38	**13.** 3.84 − 3.36	**14.** 8.80 − 5.27	**15.** 0.52 − 0.37
16. 0.73 − 0.26	**17.** 0.21 − 0.08	**18.** 0.56 − 0.23	**19.** 6.93 − 0.25	**20.** 8.35 − 0.28
21. 4.82 − 0.63	**22.** 2.62 − 0.43	**23.** 34.65 − 12.37	**24.** 81.42 − 41.27	**25.** 69.42 − 13.08
26. 77.65 − 47.59	**27.** 25.30 − 3.15	**28.** 95.74 − 1.36	**29.** 40.40 − 0.28	**30.** 19.38 − 2.19
31. 8.2 − 4.7	**32.** 3.0 − 1.6	**33.** 92.8 − 40.9	**34.** 67.2 − 5.9	**35.** 6.18 − 4.35

PATTERNS

Each number is five less than the number named before it. What are the next two numbers?

27	22	17	?	?

What are the next two numbers in the pattern?

A.

36	28	20	?	?

B.

74	57	40	?	?

C.

201	153	105	?	?

D.

232	176	120	?	?

297

which answer is sensible?

Jane ran the 100-meter race in 17.3 seconds.
Charles took 0.8 seconds longer.
How long did Charles take?

Which answer is sensible?
    18.1 seconds or 181 seconds

Think: It took Jane about 17 seconds.
        Charles took less than one second more.
        The sensible answer is 18.1 seconds.

Choose the more sensible answer.

1. Donald swam 200 meters
   in 3.4 minutes. Sue did
   it in 0.5 minute less.
   What was Sue's time?

   29 minutes   2.9 minutes

2. In the high jump,
   Eileen jumped 143.7 centimeters.
   Alice jumped 157.8 centimeters.
   How much higher did Alice jump?

   14.1 centimeters   141 centimeters

Problem-solving Help

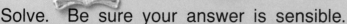

Solve. Be sure your answer is sensible.

3. Bobby earned these
   points for diving.
   First try — 7.1
   Second try — 6.3
   Third try — 8.0
   What was the total
   points he earned?

4. In the downhill ski race,
   Beth's time was 2.1 minutes.
   Danny's time was 1.7 minutes.
   How much faster was Danny?

5. In the 1500-meter
   skating race,
   Carmela's time was 3.1 minutes.
   Jill took 0.8 minute more.
   What was Jill's time?

6. In the bobsled race, the
   fastest time was 6.3 minutes.
   It took Jerry and Tim
   6.9 minutes.
   This was how much more
   than the fastest time?

7. In the slalom race,
   Mary's time was 4.7 minutes.
   Sue's time was 5.0 minutes.
   Nina's time was 3.9 minutes.
   John's time was 4.2 minutes.

   What was the difference
   between the fastest time
   and the slowest time?

8. Cross-Country Skiing Race

   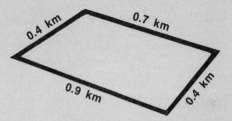

   What was the total length of
   the race course?

Test

Write the decimal.

1. $\frac{4}{10}$ (p. 286)

2. $\frac{7}{10}$ (p. 286)

3. $8\frac{3}{10}$ (p. 286)

4. $24\frac{1}{10}$ (p. 286)

5. Two tenths (p. 286)

6. Six and eight tenths (p. 286)

7. Fifty-three hundredths

(p. 292)

8. Eighty-five and one hundredth

(p. 292)

9.

0	0	0	6	2	0

(p. 288)

10.

0	0	5	3	0	6

(p. 288)

Tell how many centimeters.
Use a decimal.

11. 23 millimeters (p. 290)

12. 48 millimeters (p. 290)

Add.

13. 0.4
\+ 0.8
(p. 294)

14. 5.83
\+ 6.09
(p. 294)

15. 83.81
\+ 21.56
(p. 294)

16. 32.67
\+ 3.82
(p. 294)

Subtract.

17. 9.4
\- 6.7
(p. 296)

18. 8.39
\- 2.74
(p. 296)

19. 56.12
\- 43.08
(p. 296)

20. 96.96
\- 64.32
(p. 296)

Dimes and Pennies

10 dimes = 1 dollar   100 pennies = 1 dollar

A dime is worth one tenth of a dollar.
A penny is worth one hundredth of a dollar.

Complete the chart.

PART OF A DOLLAR	SYMBOL	PENNIES	DIMES AND PENNIES
5 hundredths	$.05	5 pennies	0 dimes 5 pennies
10 hundredths	$.10	10 pennies	1 dime 0 pennies
15 hundredths	$.15	15 pennies	1 dime 5 pennies
25 hundredths	$.25	25 pennies	2 dimes 5 pennies
30 hundredths	$.30	30 pennies	? dimes ? pennies
42 hundredths	$.42	? pennies	? dimes ? pennies
50 hundredths	$.50	? pennies	? dimes ? pennies
75 hundredths	$.75	? pennies	? dimes ? pennies

15 Geometry

Line Segments and Lines

Three pieces of yarn connect marble *A* and marble *B*.
Only one piece is straight. It is the shortest piece.
It is like a **line segment.**
Call it line segment *AB* or line segment *BA*.

Try to think of a straight piece of yarn that never ends.
That piece of yarn would be like a **line.**
A line is straight.
A line has no endpoints. It goes on forever.

The arrowheads show that a line has no endpoints.
Find line *AB* and line *CD.* They cross at a point.
Lines *AB* and *CD* are **intersecting lines.**

Line *PQ* and line *RS* do not cross. They can never cross.
Lines *PQ* and *RS* are **parallel lines.**

try these

Is it a line segment?   Write YES or NO.

1. M ● ～～～ ● Y

2. P ●━━━━━● B

3. J ● ～～～～ ● H

now do these

Name the line segment.

4. D ●———● T

5. X ●———● M

6. O ●———● Y

Name the line.

7. M ●———● G

8. L ●———● B

9. H ●———● K

Write INTERSECTING or PARALLEL.

10.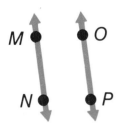
A C
B D

11.
F G H E

12.
K J I L

13.
M O N P

14.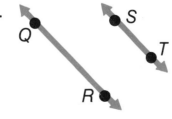
Q S T R

15.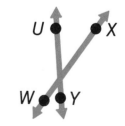
U X W Y

303

Rays and Angles

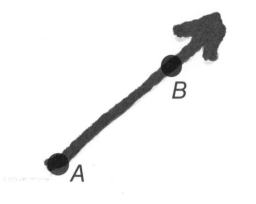

Try to think of a piece of yarn that never ends.
Pretend to cut it into two pieces.
Each piece now has one endpoint.
It goes on and on but only in one direction.
This piece of yarn is like a **ray.**

The picture shows ray *AB.*

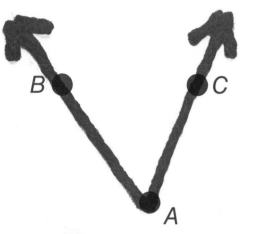

These two rays have the same endpoint.
These rays form an **angle.**

One name for the angle is angle *BAC.*
Another name is angle *CAB.*
In both names, the **vertex** of the
angle is named in the middle.

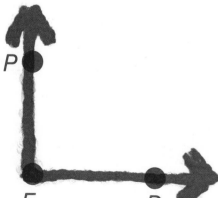

The corners of this page are
square corners.

Ray *ED* and ray *EP* form a
square corner.
Angle *PED* is a **right angle.**

Can you find other examples
of right angles?

Name the ray.

1.

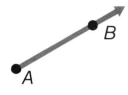

2.

3.

Name the angle.

4.

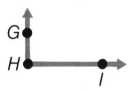

5.

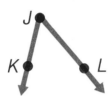

6.

now do these

Name the angle.

7.

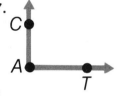

8.

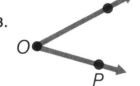

9.

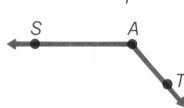

10.

11.

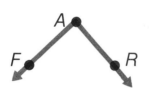

12.

MAKE A RIGHT ANGLE TESTER

Fold a piece of paper.

Fold it again.
Make the folded edges
match.

Test the angles above.
Which are right angles?

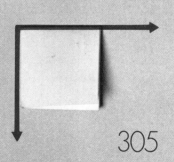

305

Polygons

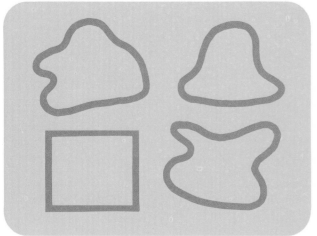

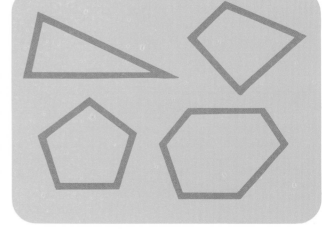

Each of these paths is a **simple closed path.**

The path does not cross over itself anywhere.

The path begins and ends at the same point.

Each of these simple closed paths is a **polygon.**

The sides are line segments.

The sides meet to form angles.

Some polygons have special names.

Triangle
Three sides

Quadrilateral
Four sides

Pentagon
Five sides

Octagon
Eight sides

Is it a polygon? Write YES or NO.

1.

2.

3.

4.

now do these

Name the polygon.

5.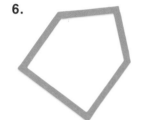

6.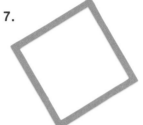

7.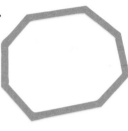

8.

9.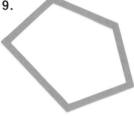

10.

11.

12.

CAN YOU FIND THEM ALL?

A. How many triangles?

B. How many quadrilaterals?

307

Polygons and Angles

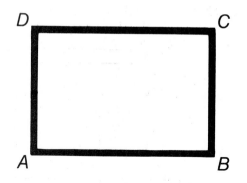

The sides of a polygon
meet at points.
You name the points with letters.

This polygon is a **rectangle.**
Call it rectangle *ABCD.*

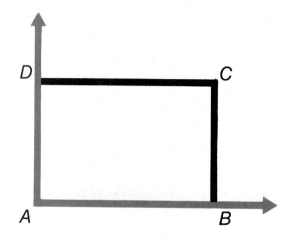

The sides of a polygon meet to
form angles.

One angle is marked in red on
the rectangle.

It is angle *DAB.*

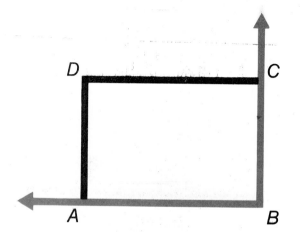

Another angle is marked
on the rectangle.

It is angle *ABC.*

There are two more angles in the
rectangle. What are their names?

try these

Name each angle in the triangle.   (There are three in each.)

1.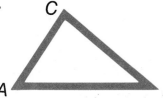

2.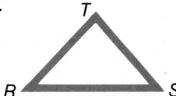

3.

now do these

Name each angle in the polygon.

4.

5.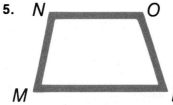

6.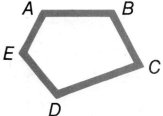

How many?

7.

_?_ sides
_?_ angles

8.

_?_ sides
_?_ angles

9.

_?_ sides
_?_ angles

10.

_?_ sides
_?_ angles

11.

_?_ sides
_?_ angles

12.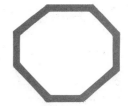

_?_ sides
_?_ angles

309

Congruent Segments and Polygons

Congruent line segments are the same length.
Are the red sides of this polygon congruent?

Here is how to find out.

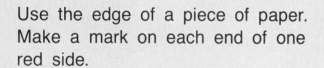

Use the edge of a piece of paper.
Make a mark on each end of one
red side.

Test the other red side.
If the endpoints match,
then the sides are congruent.

Congruent polygons are the same size and shape.

Are these polygons congruent?

Here is how to find out.

Trace both on paper.
Cut them out.

Put one on top of the other.
If they match exactly,
then they are congruent.

Are the red sides congruent? Write SIDES YES or SIDES NO.
Are the polygons congruent? Write POLYGONS YES or POLYGONS NO.

1.

2.

Are the red sides congruent? Write SIDES YES or SIDES NO.
Are the polygons congruent? Write POLYGONS YES or POLYGONS NO.

3.

4.

5.

6.

SPECIAL POLYGONS

A. A rectangle is a special
kind of quadrilateral.
Which sides are congruent?

B. A square is a special
kind of rectangle.
Which sides are congruent?

Circles

1. Trace around the bottom of a cup with a red crayon.

2. Cut out the shape.

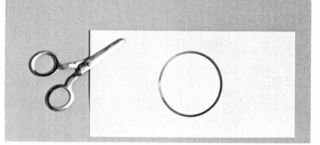

3. Fold in half so the parts match.

4. Fold in half again.

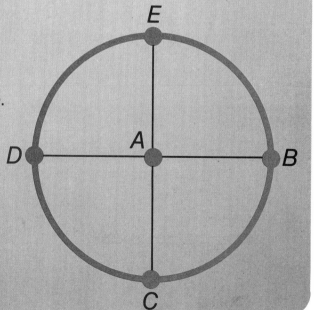

Unfold the shape.
The red path is a **circle.**
The fold lines cross at the **center.**
A **radius** is a line segment from the center to any point on the circle.
Line segment AB is a radius.
Name another radius.

A **diameter** is a line segment through the center with endpoints on the circle.
Line segment DB is a diameter.
Name another diameter.

1. Name the center of the circle.

2. Line segment *AB* is a diameter.
   Name another diameter.

3. Line segment *PC* is a radius.
   Name three more.

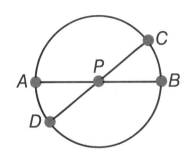

Trace this circle.

4. Draw a radius.
   Draw another radius.
   Are they congruent?

5. Draw two diameters.
   Are they congruent?

6. Compare the length of a radius
   with the length of a diameter.
   What do you discover?

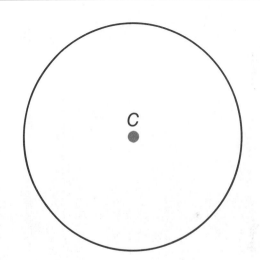

THE NEW POLYCAR

Figures 1 and 2 are not polygons. What are they?
The other figures are polygons.
What special names do they have?

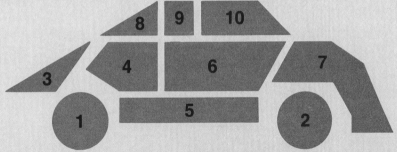

313

Three Dimensional Shapes

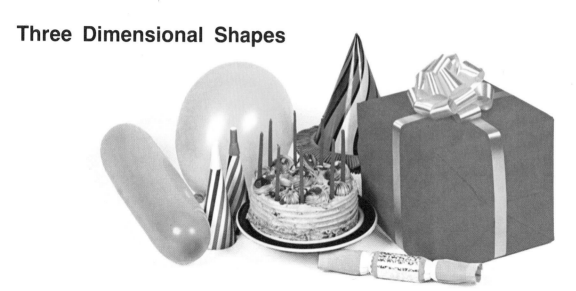

Find things in the picture that have these shapes.

Rectangular Prism

Cylinder

Cone

Sphere

---

try these

Name the shape.

1.

2.

3.

4.

5.

6.

314

How many?

7.

____?__ rectangular prisms
____?__ cylinders
____?__ cones
____?__ spheres

____?__ rectangular prisms
____?__ cylinders
____?__ cones
____?__ spheres

MAKING PRINTS

This block is dipped
in poster paint.

It can print a
rectangular shape.

What shape will the block print?

9. 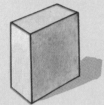 **10.**  **11.**  **12.**

13. Suppose you cut a
tennis ball in half.
You dip it in
poster paint and
make a print.
What shape does
the print have?

315

Test

Name the line segment.

1.

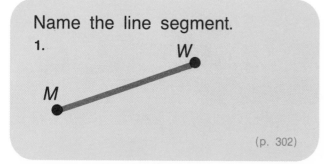

(p. 302)

Write INTERSECTING or PARALLEL.

2.

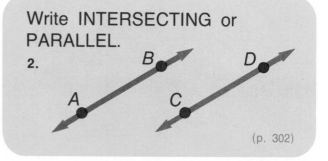

(p. 302)

Name the ray.

3.

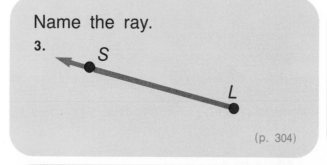

(p. 304)

Name the angle.

4.

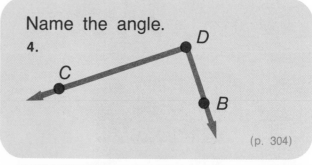

(p. 304)

Name each angle in the polygon.

5.

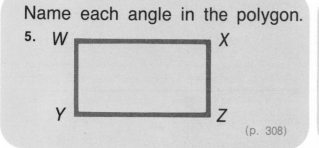

(p. 308)

Are the red sides congruent? Are the polygons congruent?

6.

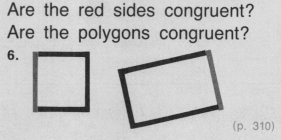

(p. 310)

Name the polygon.

7.

8.

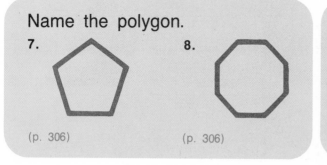

(p. 306)   (p. 306)

Name the shape.

9.

10.

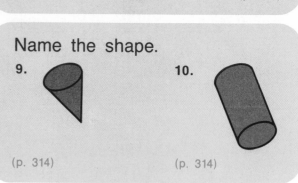

(p. 314)   (p. 314)

Keeping up

Add.

1. $\frac{6}{8} + \frac{1}{8} = \underline{}$ (p. 272)
2. $\frac{2}{10} + \frac{5}{10} = \underline{}$ (p. 272)
3. $\frac{1}{5} + \frac{2}{5} = \underline{}$ (p. 272)

Subtract.

4. $\frac{2}{3} - \frac{1}{3} = \underline{}$ (p. 274)
5. $\frac{3}{4} - \frac{2}{4} = \underline{}$ (p. 274)
6. $\frac{5}{6} - \frac{4}{6} = \underline{}$ (p. 274)

Write the decimal.

7. $\frac{3}{10}$ (p. 286)
8. $8\frac{4}{10}$ (p. 286)
9. $16\frac{1}{10}$ (p. 286)
10. $20\frac{7}{10}$ (p. 286)
11. $836\frac{6}{10}$ (p. 286)

12. Eight tenths (p. 286)
13. Fourteen and two tenths (p. 286)

14. Five hundredths (p. 292)
15. Two and twenty-five hundredths (p. 292)

16. Fifty and seven hundredths (p. 292)
17. Three hundred and forty hundredths (p. 292)

Add.

18. $\begin{array}{r} 8.3 \\ +4.7 \\ \hline \end{array}$ (p. 294)
19. $\begin{array}{r} 4.05 \\ +3.09 \\ \hline \end{array}$ (p. 294)
20. $\begin{array}{r} 0.42 \\ +0.86 \\ \hline \end{array}$ (p. 294)
21. $\begin{array}{r} 83.70 \\ +45.89 \\ \hline \end{array}$ (p. 294)
22. $\begin{array}{r} 30.93 \\ +\ 9.27 \\ \hline \end{array}$ (p. 294)

Subtract.

23. $\begin{array}{r} 6.81 \\ -2.49 \\ \hline \end{array}$ (p. 296)
24. $\begin{array}{r} 0.80 \\ -0.65 \\ \hline \end{array}$ (p. 296)
25. $\begin{array}{r} 1.47 \\ -0.08 \\ \hline \end{array}$ (p. 296)
26. $\begin{array}{r} 52.46 \\ -11.08 \\ \hline \end{array}$ (p. 296)
27. $\begin{array}{r} 99.10 \\ -\ 8.64 \\ \hline \end{array}$ (p. 296)

Divide.

28. (p. 240) $60\overline{)240}$
29. (p. 242) $40\overline{)272}$
30. (p. 242) $80\overline{)648}$
31. (p. 244) $52\overline{)307}$
32. (p. 244) $94\overline{)762}$

33. (p. 246) $73\overline{)498}$
34. (p. 246) $61\overline{)423}$
35. (p. 250) $35\overline{)189}$
36. (p. 250) $47\overline{)378}$
37. (p. 250) $87\overline{)703}$

317

Symmetry

1.

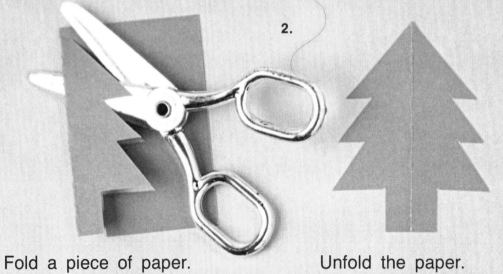

Fold a piece of paper.
Cut out a shape.

2.

Unfold the paper.
Describe the shape.

3.

Refold the shape.
Do the halves match?
If they do, then your
figure is **symmetric.**

4.

Unfold it again.
The line along the fold
is a **line of symmetry.**

Is the red line a line of symmetry?   Write YES or NO.

1.

2.

3.

4.

Trace the figure.   Draw a line of symmetry.

5.

6.

7.

8.

Trace the figure.   One line of symmetry is shown.   Draw another one.

9.

10.

11.

12.

How many lines of symmetry can you draw?

13.

14.

15.

16.

What is the Rule?

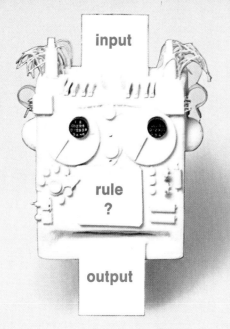

input

rule
?

output

Put in a number.
Amazo adds to the number
or subtracts from the number.
Out comes the answer.

Put in 7. Out comes 10.
What did Amazo do?
Amazo's rule was ADD 3.

Put in 7. Out comes 4.
What did Amazo do?
Amazo's rule was SUBTRACT 3.

What is Amazo's addition or subtraction rule?

1. Put in 4.
Out comes 9.

2. Put in 12.
Out comes 7.

3. Put in 8.
Out comes 18.

4. Put in 22.
Out comes 12.

5. Put in 39.
Out comes 9.

6. Put in 60.
Out comes 30.

7. Put in 27.
Out comes 35.

8. Put in 535.
Out comes 235.

9. Put in 250.
Out comes 500.

10. Put in 70.
Out comes 130.

11. Put in 257.
Out comes 100.

12. Put in 324.
Out comes 444.

13. Put in 75.
Out comes 225.

14. Put in 650.
Out comes 502.

15. Put in 630.
Out comes 787.

16. Put in 925.
Out comes 605.

17. Put in 490.
Out comes 700.

18. Put in 648.
Out comes 881.

19. Put in 360.
Out comes 6.

20. Put in 819.
Out comes 39.

Try These Answers

Unit 1
2. 1. 42 2. 63 3. 17 4. 73 5. 50 6. 39 7. 65 8. 94 9. 40
4. 1. 234 2. 628 3. 394 4. 230 5. 726 6. 804
7. 1. > 2. < 3. < 4. > 5. > 6. <
8. 1. 581 2. 273 3. 721 4. 403 5. 640 6. 808

7.   400   8.   700   9.   300   10.   700   11.   800   12.   300
      10   40   80   + 6   + 50   + 7
    + 7   + 5   + 9

10. 1. 4652 2. 8271 3. 4023 4. 7203
13. 1. 322,356 2. 45,700 3. 700,777 4. 203,083
15. 1. 1,437,800 2. 7,860,245 3. 9,054,388 4. 5,003,600
17. 1. Odd 2. Even 3. Odd 4. Even 5. Odd 6. Even 7. Odd 8. Even

Unit 2
21. 1. 16 2. 15 3. 12 4. 14 5. 13 6. 17 7. 15 8. 10 9. 10
22. 1. 7 2. 7 3. 10 4. 13 5. 12 6. 15
24. 1. 8 2. 18 3. 28 4. 14 5. 24 6. 34 7. 15 8. 25 9. 35 10. 45 11. 55 12. 65
27. 1. 17 2. 19 3. 24 4. 15 5. 19 6. 26
29. 1. 9576 2. 6833 3. $115.95 4. $69.45 5. $54.99
31. 1. 9 2. 7 3. 4 4. 8 5. 9 6. 9 7. 9 8. 9 9. 4

33. 1.   9   8 2.   8   5 3.   6   9 4.   7   8 5.   6   5 6.   3   8
       +8 +9   +5 +8   +9 +6   +8 +7   +5 +6   +8 +3
       17 17   13 13   15 15   15 15   11 11   11 11

7.   16   16 8.   11   11 9.   17   17 10.   15   15 11.   13   13 12.   10   10
   − 9 − 7   − 7 − 4   − 8 − 9   − 6 − 9   − 4 − 9   − 7 − 3
     7   9   4   7   9   8   9   6   9   4   3   7

37. 1. 4 2. 8 3. 8
39. 1. 3620 2. 1159 3. 190 4. 33 5. 1416 6. $36.20 7. $12.55 8. $1.10 9. $19.24
10. $41.43

Unit 3
45. 1. 5 paper clips
47. 1. 4 cm 2. 7 cm
49. 1. 137 mm 2. 113 mm
51. 1. Millimeter 2. Centimeter 3. Meter 4. Kilometer
53. 1. 13 cm 2. 12 cm
54. 1. 18 square centimeters 2. 10 square centimeters
56. 1. Less than 2. Less than 3. Greater than 4. Less than
58. 1. 1 liter 2. 5 cups 3. 2 liters

Unit 4

66. 1. $\begin{array}{r} 50 \\ +30 \\ \hline 80 \end{array}$ 2. $\begin{array}{r} 70 \\ +20 \\ \hline 90 \end{array}$ 3. $\begin{array}{r} 40 \\ +40 \\ \hline 80 \end{array}$ 4. $\begin{array}{r} 40 \\ 20 \\ +50 \\ \hline 110 \end{array}$ 5. $\begin{array}{r} 30 \\ 40 \\ +50 \\ \hline 120 \end{array}$ 6. $\begin{array}{r} 40 \\ 10 \\ +60 \\ \hline 110 \end{array}$

69. 1. 300 2. 200 3. $\begin{array}{r} 300 \\ +400 \\ \hline 700 \end{array}$ 4. $\begin{array}{r} 200 \\ +800 \\ \hline 1000 \end{array}$ 5. $\begin{array}{r} 200 \\ +600 \\ \hline 800 \end{array}$ 6. $\begin{array}{r} 400 \\ 100 \\ +200 \\ \hline 700 \end{array}$ 7. $\begin{array}{r} 400 \\ 600 \\ +300 \\ \hline 1300 \end{array}$ 8. $\begin{array}{r} 500 \\ 100 \\ +200 \\ \hline 800 \end{array}$

70. 1. 13 2. 24 3. 48

72. 1. 85 2. 32 3. 77 4. 161 5. 24 6. 58 7. 104 8. 63 9. 102 10. 45 11. 161 12. 120

74. 1. 158 2. 534

76. 1. 875 2. 1534 3. 1034 4. 707 5. 1000 6. 1029 7. 1007 8. 1356 9. 1026 10. 900 11. 1554 12. 1103

78. 1. 924 2. 1165 3. 1302 4. 862 5. 1053 6. 700 7. 1202 8. 1528 9. 971 10. 1015 11. 826 12. 1020

80. 1. 2032 2. 1737 3. 1500 4. 1552 5. 1828 6. 1412 7. 1363 8. 2208 9. 1022 10. 2624 11. 1720 12. 1605

82. 1. 6525 2. 10,640 3. 12,054 4. 8034 5. 5578 6. 13,003 7. 9041 8. 17,325 9. 7726 10. 10,110

85. 1. $137.68 2. $78.31 3. $119.73 4. $105.00 5. $150.63 6. $29.45 7. $50.60 8. $120.93 9. $23.00 10. $81.28

Unit 5

91. 1. $\begin{array}{r} 40 \\ -20 \\ \hline 20 \end{array}$ 2. $\begin{array}{r} 70 \\ -50 \\ \hline 20 \end{array}$ 3. $\begin{array}{r} 60 \\ -50 \\ \hline 10 \end{array}$ 4. $\begin{array}{r} 60 \\ -30 \\ \hline 30 \end{array}$ 5. $\begin{array}{r} 40 \\ -20 \\ \hline 20 \end{array}$ 6. $\begin{array}{r} 90 \\ -80 \\ \hline 10 \end{array}$ 7. $\begin{array}{r} 600 \\ -200 \\ \hline 400 \end{array}$ 8. $\begin{array}{r} 400 \\ -300 \\ \hline 100 \end{array}$ 9. $\begin{array}{r} 800 \\ -700 \\ \hline 100 \end{array}$ 10. $\begin{array}{r} 900 \\ -700 \\ \hline 200 \end{array}$

11. $\begin{array}{r} 500 \\ -200 \\ \hline 300 \end{array}$ 12. $\begin{array}{r} 400 \\ -200 \\ \hline 200 \end{array}$

92. 1. 36 2. 89 3. 60 4. 73 5. 26 6. 30 7. 94 8. 53 9. 20

94. 1. 36 2. 6 3. 516 4. 307 5. 11 6. 612 7. 7 8. 24 9. 5 10. 107 11. 407 12. 405

96. 1. 345 2. 456 3. 809 4. 373 5. 644 6. 425 7. 617 8. 904 9. 831

98. 1. 266 2. 480 3. 163 4. 75 5. 870 6. 320 7. 50 8. 86 9. 124 10. 570 11. 478 12. 661

101. 1. 366 2. 82 3. 793 4. 378 5. 656 6. 258 7. 99 8. 467 9. 83 10. 166 11. 578 12. 192

103. 1. 354 2. 167 3. 409 4. 763 5. 584 6. 7 7. 408 8. 747 9. 6 10. 396 11. 477 12. 35

104. 1. 5952 2. 1444 3. 1833 4. 771 5. 3811 6. 3721 7. 325 8. 733 9. 913 10. 3615

106. 1. 2535 2. 2826 3. 1407 4. 8265 5. 2765 6. 4889 7. 1208 8. 5756 9. 3066 10. 408

108. 1. $25.35 2. $28.77 3. $32.56 4. $5.18 5. $10.66 6. $57.89 7. $11.08 8. $27.65 9. $39.66 10. $8.57

Unit 6   115. 1. Friday 2. Wednesday 3. Thursday 4. Tuesday and Thursday

117. 1. Nickel 2. Paper clip 3. Pencil 4. Earring

119. 1. Hot dog stand 2. Hobby shop

121. 1. Orange 2. Grapefruit 3. Pear

123. 1. East 1, North 3 2. East 3, North 4 3. East 2, North 6

Unit 7   131. 1. $3 + 3 + 3 + 3 = 12$ 2. $5 + 5 = 10$ 3. $2 + 2 = 4$
$4 \times 3 = 12$ $2 \times 5 = 10$ $2 \times 2 = 4$

133. 1. 4 2. 15 3. 8 4. 25 5. 30 6. 16

135. 1. 21 2. 21 3. 12 4. 12 5. 27 6. 27

136. 1. 8, 4, 12 2. 20, 4, 24 3. 16, 16, 32 4. 16, 20, 36

138. 1. 36 2. 18 3. 42 4. 24 5. 48 6. 54 7. 48 8. 12 9. 54 10. 24 11. 30 12. 42

140. 1. 14 2. 42 3. 56 4. 28 5. 49 6. 21 7. 28 8. 63 9. 42 10. 35 11. 63 12. 56

142. 1. 48 2. 16 3. 64 4. 32 5. 56 6. 24 7. 32 8. 72 9. 48 10. 40 11. 72 12. 56

144. 1. 36 2. 81 3. 54 4. 27 5. 63 6. 45 7. 18 8. 72 9. 36 10. 54 11. 81 12. 63

146. 1. 16¢ 2. 30¢ 3. 36¢ 4. 18¢ 5. 16¢ 6. 27¢ 7. 49¢ 8. 20¢

148. 1. 0 2. 9 3. 8 4. 0 5. 7 6. 0 7. 0 8. 5 9. 0 10. 0 11. 6 12. 4

150. 1. 45 2. 28 3. 24 4. 42 5. 81 6. 48

Unit 8   159. 1. 90 2. 250 3. 160 4. 120 5. 180 6. 450

161. 1. 1200 2. 2500 3. 900 4. 1600 5. 4000 6. 4500

163. 1. 392 2. 612 3. 474 4. 3213 5. 2808 6. 6072 7. 360 8. 360 9. 140 10. 4494 11. 928
12. 3018

164. 1. 116 2. 424 3. 658 4. 204 5. 235 6. 148 7. 138 8. 240 9. 774 10. 588 11. 368
12. 396

166. 1. 5538 2. 4465 3. 5068 4. 960 5. 6584 6. 3618 7. 585 8. 738 9. 1215 10. 4920
11. 1880 12. 2515

168. 1. $25.55 2. $63.54 3. $3.56 4. $36.48 5. $2.52 6. $13.68 7. $5.68 8. $24.64
9. $1.30 10. $9.45

170. 1. $4.35 2. $1.17 3. $1.48 4. $1.40 5. $6.24 6. $18.88 7. $8.88 8. $3.81

Unit 9   179. 1. 50 2. 170 3. 580 4. 970 5. 2490 6. 5550

181. 1. 860 2. 3000 3. 1680 4. 3780 5. 11,340 6. 8670

183. 1. 2538 2. 3072 3. 1620 4. 5130 5. 3486 6. 2040 7. 5616 8. 5429 9. 1862 10. 3312
11. 5670 12. 1500

185. 1. 22,816 2. 29,547 3. 43,560 4. 31,482 5. 17,952 6. 60,225 7. 21,384 8. 56,486
9. 8881 10. 22,372 11. 15,561 12. 30,668

187. 1. $32.04 2. $40.66 3. $10.44 4. $116.62 5. $42.75 6. $21.06 7. $570.24 8. $28.35
9. $176.85 10. $56.43

188. 1. $15.00 2. $12.25 3. $42.38 4. $74.52 5. $9.12 6. $122.64 7. $23.40 8. $52.50

Unit 10 **195.** 1. 5 2. 7 3. 4 4. 3 5. 8 6. 5
197. 1. 3 2. 5 3. 1 4. 4 5. 2 6. 6
198. 1. 4 2. 7 3. 8 4. 6 5. 3 6. 5 7. 1 8. 9 9. 2 10. 5 11. 7 12. 8
200. 1. 8 2. 6 3. 9 4. 7 5. 4 6. 1 7. 7 8. 9 9. 8 10. 6 11. 4 12. 1
202. 1. 8 2. 6 3. 9 4. 7 5. 4 6. 1 7. 9 8. 7 9. 6 10. 8 11. 5 12. 1
205. 1. 6 2. 7 3. 6
207. 1. 8 2. 7 3. 7 4. 9 5. 4 6. 9
209. 1. 5 r1 2. 3 r3 3. 7 r2 4. 6 r4 5. 4 r2 6. 4 r5 7. 6 r1 8. 4 r3 9. 9 r1 10. 3 r3 11. 7 r2
12. 3 r4
211. 1. 7 r2 2. 3 r4 3. 3 r5 4. 5 r3 5. 5 r4 6. 6 r5

Unit 11 **219.** 1. 20 2. 30 3. 70 4. 20 5. 40
221. 1. 71 2. 32 3. 21 4. 21 5. 42 6. 52 7. 22 8. 64 9. 21 10. 61
223. 1. No 2. Yes 3. No 4. Yes 5. Yes 6. 40 7. 80 8. 60 9. 40 10. 40
224. 1. 76 2. 64 3. 87 4. 64 5. 79 6. 57 7. 98 8. 89 9. 97 10. 78
226. 1. 38 r3 2. 89 r1 3. 92 r2 4. 42 r1 5. 73 r3 6. 26 r1 7. 78 r3 8. 68 r2 9. 37 r1
10. 97 r1
229. 1. No 2. Yes 3. Yes 4. No 5. No 6. 800 7. 600 8. 500 9. 800 10. 600
231. 1. 523 r4 2. 666 3. 816 r1 4. 742 5. 888 r3 6. 701 r1 7. 524 8. 624 r4 9. 483 r3
10. 845 r5
233. 1. 127 r2 2. 324 r1 3. 248 4. 412 r3 5. 325 r5 6. 346 r1 7. 127 r3 8. 145 r5 9. 244 r2
10. 251 r1

Unit 12 **240.** 1. 6 2. 7 3. 6 4. 5 5. 8 6. 4 7. 3 8. 5 9. 9 10. 8
243. 1. 5 r28 2. 7 r19 3. 8 r27 4. 6 r35 5. 6 r39 6. 9 r19 7. 9 8. 9 r38 9. 4 r49 10. 7 r55
244. 1. 9 r2 2. 3 r32 3. 6 r18 4. 6 r12 5. 3 r16 6. 6 r19 7. 4 r25 8. 4 r11 9. 6 10. 2 r13
247. 1. Yes 2. No 3. Yes 4. No 5. Yes 6. 7 r89 7. 7 r62 8. 5 r15 9. 6 r64 10. 8 r43
248. 1. 6 r21 2. 7 r83 3. 8 r21 4. 9 r30 5. 7 r32 6. 7 r30 7. 7 r43 8. 8 r33 9. 6 r21
10. 7 r21
251. 1. No 2. Yes 3. No 4. Yes 5. No 6. 9 7. 7 r2 8. 6 r13 9. 4 r16 10. 8 r11

Unit 13 **258.** 1. $\frac{1}{2}$ 2. $\frac{3}{4}$ 3. $\frac{5}{8}$ 4. $\frac{1}{3}$ 5. $\frac{7}{10}$ 6. $\frac{1}{5}$
261. 1. < 2. < 3. > 4. >
262. 1. $\frac{3}{5}$ 2. $\frac{1}{2}$ 3. $\frac{1}{3}$
265. 1. 2 2. 3
267. 1. 10 2. 12
269. 1. $\frac{2}{8}$ 2. $\frac{8}{10}$ 3. $\frac{4}{6}$
270. 1. $2\frac{1}{2}$ 2. $1\frac{5}{6}$ 3. $2\frac{2}{3}$

272. 1. $\frac{3}{8}$ 2. $\frac{7}{8}$ 3. $\frac{5}{8}$ 4. $\frac{9}{10}$ 5. $\frac{7}{10}$ 6. $\frac{9}{10}$

274. 1. $\frac{5}{8}$ 2. $\frac{5}{8}$ 3. $\frac{1}{8}$ 4. $\frac{7}{10}$ 5. $\frac{3}{10}$ 6. $\frac{3}{10}$

277. 1. $7\frac{2}{3}$ 2. $3\frac{4}{5}$ 3. $6\frac{3}{4}$ 4. $6\frac{5}{8}$ 5. $7\frac{5}{6}$ 6. $5\frac{5}{8}$ 7. $8\frac{7}{10}$ 8. $6\frac{5}{6}$ 9. $7\frac{7}{8}$ 10. $8\frac{5}{6}$

278. 1. $6\frac{2}{5}$ 2. $2\frac{1}{6}$ 3. $5\frac{1}{8}$ 4. $2\frac{1}{4}$ 5. $1\frac{1}{3}$ 6. $2\frac{1}{4}$ 7. $1\frac{3}{5}$ 8. $4\frac{3}{10}$ 9. $3\frac{1}{6}$ 10. $3\frac{5}{8}$

Unit 14 **287.** 1. One tenth 2. Four tenths 3. Seven tenths 4. Two and three tenths 5. Seven and five tenths 6. Nine and eight tenths 7. 0.3 8. 0.5 9. 0.2 10. 1.6 11. 4.9 12. 8.1 13. 0.7   5.4

289. 1. Four tenths 2. Nine and nine tenths 3. Ten and three tenths 4. Sixty-five and three tenths 5. Four hundred fifty-six and three tenths 6. Six hundred fifty-four and one tenth

291. 1. 1.5 2. 3.6

293. 1. Six hundredths 2. Seventy-five hundredths 3. One and forty-two hundredths 4. Thirty-four and eighty-five hundredths 5. Two hundred fifteen and thirty-eight hundredths 6. 0.05 7. 0.72 8. 16.61 9. 125.37

294. 1. 13.84 2. 14.16 3. 0.25 4. 30.70 5. 29.85 6. 0.82 7. 8.03 8. 99.97 9. 11.14 10. 27.72

296. 1. 5.58 2. 6.07 3. 9.14 4. 1.49 5. 10.04 6. 0.05 7. 0.58 8. 16.17 9. 51.04 10. 86.29

Unit 15 **303.** 1. No 2. Yes 3. No

305. 1. Ray *AB* 2. Ray *DC* 3. Ray *EF* 4. Angle *GHI* or *IHG* 5. Angle *KJL* or *LJK* 6. Angle *MNO* or *ONM*

307. 1. Yes 2. No 3. No 4. Yes

309. 1. Angles *ACB* or *BCA*, *CBA* or *ABC*, *BAC* or *CAB* 2. Angles *RST* or *TSR*, *STR* or *RTS*, *TRS* or *SRT* 3. Angles *XYZ* or *ZYX*, *YZX* or *XZY*, *ZXY* or *YXZ*

311. 1. Sides yes, polygons no 2. Sides no, polygons yes

313. 1. *P* 2. *DC* or *CD* 3. *PA*, *PB*, *PD*

314. 1. Cylinder 2. Cone 3. Rectangular prism 4. Sphere 5. Rectangular prism 6. Cylinder

326

Practice Sets

Practice Sets

Set 1 p. 10

Write the numeral.

1. 3 tens 9 ones   39

2. 1 hundred 5 ones

3. 2 thousands 8 hundreds 1 ten

4.
tens	ones
2	7

5.
hundreds	tens	ones
7	9	5

6.
hundreds	tens	ones
3	8	0

7. sixteen

8. sixty

9. six hundred ninety-two

10. 6 thousand, 572

11. 4 thousand, 99

12. 5 thousand, 800

13. 7 thousand, 36

14. 8 thousand, 8

15. 9 thousand, 5

Set 2 p. 10

Write > or <.

1. 9 > 7

2. 16 ● 60

3. 38 ● 42

4. 520 ● 420

5. 126 ● 136

6. 816 ● 813

7. 8264 ● 9264

8. 6018 ● 5918

9. 6007 ● 6003

10. 5833 ● 5733

11. 1217 ● 1270

12. 2870 ● 2780

13. 4267 ● 4276

14. 3445 ● 3454

15. 4509 ● 4590

16. 8321 ● 8312

17. 1010 ● 1001

18. 7654 ● 7645

Set 3 p. 14

Write the numeral.

1. 30 thousand, 200   30,200

2. 68 thousand

3. 756 thousand, 199

4. 309 thousand, 800

5. 100 thousand, 225

6. 970 thousand, 53

7. 1 million, 206 thousand, 400

8. 7 million, 24 thousand

9. 5 million, 800 thousand, 47

10. 1 million, 500

11. 2 million, 34 thousand, 116

12. 6 million

13. 9 million, 5 thousand, 25

14. 3 million, 4 thousand, 5

Set 4 p. 22

Add.

1. $2 + 7 = \underline{\ ?\ }$ 9

2. $9 + 3 = \underline{\ ?\ }$

3. $6 + 0 = \underline{\ ?\ }$

4. $8 + 3 = \underline{\ ?\ }$

5. $1 + 9 = \underline{\ ?\ }$

6. $5 + 6 = \underline{\ ?\ }$

7. 4	**8.** 2	**9.** 9	**10.** 8	**11.** 7	**12.** 8
+5	+9	+5	+1	+3	+9

13. 9	**14.** 0	**15.** 7	**16.** 9	**17.** 7	**18.** 9
+6	+7	+8	+9	+9	+7

Set 5 p. 24

Add.

1. 6	16	26		**2.** 5	15	25
+3	+ 3	+ 3		+5	+ 5	+ 5
9						

3. 28	38	48		**4.** 66	76	86
+ 9	+ 9	+ 9		+ 8	+ 8	+ 8

5. 14	**6.** 31	**7.** 62	**8.** 29	**9.** 54	**10.** 36
+ 3	+ 7	+ 8	+ 3	+ 9	+ 4

11. 25	**12.** 12	**13.** 48	**14.** 51	**15.** 17	**16.** 39
+ 8	+ 9	+ 3	+ 9	+ 8	+ 9

Set 6 p. 26

Add.

1. 5	**2.** 7	**3.** 7	**4.** 8	**5.** 5	**6.** 9
2	6	3	6	7	9
+8	+3	+8	+9	+8	+4
15					

7. 3	**8.** 9	**9.** 7	**10.** 7	**11.** 9	**12.** 5
9	5	5	9	1	8
5	5	2	8	7	9
+8	+6	+6	+5	+6	+6

Set 7 p. 28

Add.

1. 6230	**2.** 1708	**3.** 4005	**4.** 9316	**5.** 2781
+2160	+1031	+3753	+ 283	+ 116
8390				

6. $18.25	**7.** $10.13	**8.** $27.04	**9.** $62.19	**10.** $33.51
+ 11.04	+ .76	+ 1.84	+ 6.50	+ 16.35

11. 2651	**12.** 1205	**13.** 312	**14.** $16.15	**15.** $21.03
4003	520	6102	12.30	4.63
+ 243	70	435	+ 1.24	3.10
	+ 103	+1040		+ 1.22

Set 8 p. 34

Subtract.

1. 7 − 4 = ?   3   **2.** 9 − 8 = ?   **3.** 17 − 8 = ?

4. 16 − 9 = ?   **5.** 6 − 0 = ?   **6.** 15 − 6 = ?

7. 8	**8.** 4	**9.** 13	**10.** 16	**11.** 11	**12.** 12
−1	−4	− 6	− 8	− 3	− 8

13. 10	**14.** 14	**15.** 18	**16.** 13	**17.** 15	**18.** 10
− 1	− 6	− 9	− 9	− 8	− 9

Set 9 p. 38

Subtract.

1. 8629	**2.** 6045	**3.** 9798	**4.** 4900	**5.** 5786
−4601	−1042	−3178	−1300	−4503
4028				

6. 9885	**7.** 1766	**8.** 5428	**9.** 4193	**10.** 5749
− 265	− 305	− 13	− 20	− 438

11. $24.16	**12.** $78.75	**13.** $14.98	**14.** $17.36	**15.** $45.95
− 12.14	− 27.70	− 11.55	− 6.32	− 3.60

330

Set 10 pp. 66, 68

Estimate the sum. Use the nearest tens.

1. 12   10
  +38 +40
       50

2. 29
  +44

3. 56
  +21

4. 30
  +65

5. 87
  +57

6. 63
  +72

7. 39
   54
  +17

8. 16
   50
  +68

9. 18
   93
  +34

10. 65
    9
  +19

11. 49
   75
  +58

12. 51
   88
  +42

Estimate the sum. Use the nearest hundreds.

13. 231   200
  +168 +200
        400

14. 107
  +324

15. 125
  +372

16. 490
  +355

17. 532
  +256

18. 664
  +185

19. 453
   170
  +219

20. 97
   500
  +129

21. 138
   302
  +243

22. 149
   311
  +257

23. 350
   182
  +193

24. 167
   175
  +218

Set 11 p. 72

Add.

1. 25
  +46
   71

2. 16
  +68

3. 41
  + 9

4. 73
  +48

5. 98
  +17

6. 82
  +19

7. 34
  +27

8. 77
  +63

9. 9
  +68

10. 68
  +78

11. 96
  +57

12. 59
  +75

13. 127
  +317

14. 205
  +458

15. 619
  + 27

16. 345
  +125

17. 776
  +109

18. 432
  + 18

Set 12 p. 76

Add.

1. 134
  +493
   627

2. 670
  +288

3. 586
  +552

4. 725
  + 94

5. 41
  +677

6. 390
  +895

7. 458
  +271

8. 65
  +341

9. 972
  + 67

10. 977
  +890

11. 689
  +830

12. 713
  +295

331

Set 13 p. 78

Add.

1. 159 +176 335	2. 286 +335	3. 164 +557	4. 68 +357	5. 467 + 93	6. 414 +289
7. 897 +327	8. 242 +798	9. 378 + 49	10. 345 + 95	11. 696 +807	12. 898 +785
13. 778 +938	14. 71 +529	15. 803 +598	16. 897 +515	17. 488 +796	18. 994 + 96

Set 14 p. 80

Add.

1. 432 160 +296 888	2. 525 108 +217	3. 732 91 +344	4. 609 429 + 56	5. 518 32 +945	6. 932 97 + 80
7. 157 563 + 98	8. 78 207 +345	9. 9 168 + 75	10. 889 761 +287	11. 906 319 +278	12. 258 697 + 86
13. 185 71 220 +463	14. 600 127 448 +503	15. 98 637 34 + 58	16. 123 790 45 +418	17. 107 445 523 +625	18. 780 16 135 + 77

Set 15 p. 82

Add.

1. 1286 +2915 4201	2. 792 +6389	3. 1939 +3795	4. 2305 + 898	5. 6987 + 58	6. 5443 + 659
7. 3698 +7896	8. 7864 +4298	9. 8843 +1797	10. 1226 4531 + 969	11. 2045 9782 +1248	12. 9510 2684 + 706

Set 16 p. 84

Add.

1. $42.60
   + 43.65
   $86.25

2. $27.18
   +   2.57

3. $19.12
   + 65.86

4. $ 3.20
   + 29.88

5. $36.07
   + 27.59

6. $ 9.46
   + 10.95

7. $82.89
   + 27.31

8. $94.05
   +   8.08

9. $ 3.15
     18.25
   +   .50

10. $69.05
      1.38
   + 24.57

Set 17 p. 90

Estimate. Use the nearest tens.

1. 64
   −21
   60
   −20
   40

2. 49
   −36

3. 35
   −12

4. 86
   −54

5. 92
   −19

6. 31
   −15

7. 47
   −27

8. 74
   −35

9. 58
   −29

10. 90
    −43

11. 63
    −18

12. 88
    −63

Estimate. Use the nearest hundreds.

13. 423
    −190
    400
    −200
    200

14. 890
    −116

15. 681
    −479

16. 176
    −102

17. 560
    −163

18. 902
    −258

19. 545
    −184

20. 850
    −347

21. 738
    −259

22. 509
    −235

23. 650
    −275

24. 410
    −247

Set 18 p. 94

Subtract.

1. 54
   −28
   26

2. 26
   −17

3. 98
   − 9

4. 75
   −38

5. 40
   −11

6. 82
   −79

7. 421
   −107

8. 873
   −355

9. 650
   −128

10. 387
    −319

11. 745
    −237

12. 196
    − 68

13. 263
    −158

14. 534
    − 17

15. 960
    −424

16. 581
    −522

17. 730
    − 25

18. 912
    −903

333

Set 19 p. 98

Subtract.

1. 530	2. 629	3. 248	4. 319	5. 805	6. 717
−180	−453	− 64	−158	− 53	−285
350					

7. 421	8. 904	9. 645	10. 882	11. 217	12. 539
− 70	−892	− 95	−791	−122	−369

13. 368	14. 713	15. 809	16. 406	17. 958	18. 877
−286	− 61	−710	−363	−271	− 87

Set 20 p. 100

Subtract.

1. 420	2. 754	3. 591	4. 638	5. 976	6. 345
−148	− 95	−497	−169	−378	−169
272					

7. 213	8. 342	9. 680	10. 825	11. 463	12. 771
−185	−143	− 82	−377	− 98	−593

13. 651	14. 730	15. 824	16. 292	17. 567	18. 982
− 79	−286	− 97	−195	−268	−899

Set 21 p. 102

Subtract.

1. 307	2. 502	3. 705	4. 104	5. 408	6. 701
−118	− 44	−677	− 16	−209	−435
189					

7. 600	8. 200	9. 800	10. 200	11. 900	12. 400
−345	− 58	−701	− 39	−863	−266

13. 503	14. 900	15. 700	16. 602	17. 806	18. 500
−258	−192	−607	− 26	−347	−296

19. 707	20. 100	21. 601	22. 300	23. 705	24. 400
−209	− 57	− 93	− 7	− 9	−394

Set 22 p. 104

Subtract.

1. 5649 −1806 3843	**2.** 8105 −7503	**3.** 2568 − 745	**4.** 1297 − 692	**5.** 6025 −2315
6. 7332 −3912	**7.** 4770 −3860	**8.** 3006 − 802	**9.** 9818 − 917	**10.** 7484 −2612
11. 73,049 −10,518	**12.** 18,665 −15,934	**13.** 67,508 − 1,803	**14.** 43,165 −42,265	**15.** 31,297 − 927

Set 23 p. 106

Subtract.

1. 2485 −1729 756	**2.** 1367 − 558	**3.** 9652 −3662	**4.** 7834 −4972	**5.** 4036 − 728
6. 5136 − 869	**7.** 7240 −2364	**8.** 9755 −6768	**9.** 2316 −1717	**10.** 4985 −3996
11. 3040 − 246	**12.** 4600 −1821	**13.** 7008 −6379	**14.** 6000 −5525	**15.** 8000 − 714
16. 5200 −1298	**17.** 8975 −7988	**18.** 4300 − 621	**19.** 9044 − 165	**20.** 3000 −1507

Set 24 p. 108

Subtract.

1. $24.78 − 11.29 $13.49	**2.** $63.90 − 57.60	**3.** $59.09 − 48.72	**4.** $72.35 − 20.96	**5.** $20.62 − 9.28
6. $30.67 − 6.59	**7.** $21.54 − 9.64	**8.** $47.10 − 19.15	**9.** $85.23 − 79.66	**10.** $96.46 − 37.88
11. $15.06 − 3.99	**12.** $40.08 − 27.59	**13.** $10.00 − 1.96	**14.** $30.00 − 16.31	**15.** $20.00 − 18.25

Set 25 p. 136

Multiply.

1. 6 ×3 18	2. 3 ×6	3. 8 ×2	4. 2 ×7	5. 5 ×1	6. 4 ×4
7. 3 ×5	8. 9 ×2	9. 8 ×4	10. 3 ×3	11. 1 ×3	12. 8 ×5
13. 4 ×6	14. 6 ×5	15. 4 ×7	16. 5 ×9	17. 9 ×4	18. 5 ×2

Set 26 p. 148

Multiply.

1. 6 ×6 36	2. 0 ×9	3. 5 ×8	4. 1 ×7	5. 7 ×6	6. 9 ×5
7. 4 ×9	8. 8 ×8	9. 7 ×5	10. 3 ×9	11. 8 ×6	12. 9 ×8
13. 4 ×8	14. 7 ×8	15. 7 ×3	16. 8 ×0	17. 3 ×8	18. 7 ×9

Set 27 pp. 158, 160

Multiply.

1. 20 × 2 40	2. 70 × 3	3. 40 × 8	4. 50 × 2	5. 60 × 7	6. 50 × 9
7. 40 × 5	8. 30 × 9	9. 80 × 7	10. 50 × 6	11. 70 × 5	12. 90 × 4
13. 100 × 4	14. 900 × 3	15. 800 × 4	16. 500 × 6	17. 800 × 2	18. 300 × 8
19. 300 × 9	20. 700 × 3	21. 800 × 7	22. 900 × 4	23. 600 × 7	24. 900 × 5

336

Set 28 p. 164

Multiply.

1. 25 × 3 75	**2.** 16 × 4	**3.** 28 × 2	**4.** 92 × 5	**5.** 64 × 7	**6.** 89 × 3
7. 76 × 2	**8.** 37 × 8	**9.** 46 × 3	**10.** 68 × 6	**11.** 17 × 9	**12.** 75 × 5
13. 95 × 6	**14.** 28 × 9	**15.** 58 × 4	**16.** 25 × 8	**17.** 87 × 7	**18.** 94 × 9

Set 29 p. 166

Multiply.

1. 690 × 4 2760	**2.** 908 × 2	**3.** 506 × 5	**4.** 528 × 3	**5.** 361 × 2	**6.** 616 × 6
7. 360 × 2	**8.** 248 × 4	**9.** 153 × 6	**10.** 245 × 8	**11.** 439 × 3	**12.** 502 × 9
13. 675 × 8	**14.** 129 × 7	**15.** 862 × 5	**16.** 245 × 9	**17.** 730 × 7	**18.** 638 × 9
19. 728 × 5	**20.** 249 × 7	**21.** 904 × 6	**22.** 625 × 8	**23.** 794 × 9	**24.** 884 × 7

Set 30 p. 168

Multiply.

1. $.18 × 5 $.90	**2.** $.96 × 2	**3.** $1.15 × 6	**4.** $6.07 × 3	**5.** $3.19 × 8
6. $2.53 × 9	**7.** $1.08 × 7	**8.** $2.40 × 5	**9.** $5.38 × 2	**10.** $.28 × 9
11. $4.36 × 7	**12.** $.68 × 6	**13.** $9.02 × 4	**14.** $4.95 × 3	**15.** $3.94 × 6

337

Set 31 p. 178

Multiply.

1. 18 ×10 = 180	2. 35 ×10	3. 60 ×10	4. 29 ×10	5. 78 ×10	6. 99 ×10
7. 236 × 10	8. 460 × 10	9. 200 × 10	10. 605 × 10	11. 883 × 10	12. 700 × 10
13. 398 × 10	14. 170 × 10	15. 500 × 10	16. 507 × 10	17. 777 × 10	18. 990 × 10

Set 32 p. 180

Multiply.

1. 12 ×20 = 240	2. 16 ×50	3. 65 ×30	4. 60 ×70	5. 46 ×80	6. 90 ×40
7. 375 × 90	8. 136 × 60	9. 348 × 20	10. 274 × 30	11. 419 × 50	12. 160 × 90
13. 308 × 40	14. 745 × 60	15. 750 × 50	16. 258 × 70	17. 288 × 90	18. 952 × 80

Set 33 p. 182

Multiply.

1. 23 ×36 = 828	2. 56 ×28	3. 53 ×54	4. 72 ×64	5. 84 ×14	6. 37 ×23
7. 88 ×29	8. 35 ×83	9. 86 ×51	10. 49 ×32	11. 54 ×76	12. 90 ×15
13. 50 ×63	14. 92 ×59	15. 56 ×18	16. 68 ×78	17. 74 ×38	18. 26 ×94
19. 25 ×47	20. 39 ×60	21. 81 ×89	22. 97 ×41	23. 47 ×96	24. 75 ×48

Set 34 p. 184

Multiply.

1. 349 × 31 10,819	2. 366 × 54	3. 926 × 18	4. 507 × 35	5. 168 × 66	6. 385 × 24
7. 230 × 48	8. 367 × 72	9. 163 × 91	10. 275 × 52	11. 400 × 74	12. 385 × 12
13. 921 × 27	14. 297 × 63	15. 412 × 38	16. 162 × 93	17. 685 × 44	18. 198 × 56
19. 407 × 19	20. 325 × 81	21. 774 × 40	22. 124 × 85	23. 270 × 95	24. 925 × 84

Set 35 p. 186

Multiply.

1. $.18 × 20 $3.60	2. $.13 × 80	3. $.35 × 75	4. $.56 × 14	5. $.40 × 52
6. $2.38 × 50	7. $1.25 × 36	8. $3.62 × 17	9. $4.62 × 68	10. $1.08 × 92
11. $4.70 × 58	12. $2.22 × 83	13. $3.09 × 28	14. $4.75 × 89	15. $3.45 × 47

Set 36 p. 198

Find the quotient.

1. $3\overline{)9}$ 3	2. $2\overline{)8}$	3. $5\overline{)15}$	4. $4\overline{)12}$	5. $3\overline{)21}$	6. $5\overline{)5}$
7. $2\overline{)16}$	8. $4\overline{)16}$	9. $3\overline{)12}$	10. $5\overline{)25}$	11. $2\overline{)12}$	12. $3\overline{)24}$
13. $3\overline{)18}$	14. $5\overline{)40}$	15. $4\overline{)4}$	16. $2\overline{)14}$	17. $4\overline{)32}$	18. $5\overline{)45}$
19. $2\overline{)10}$	20. $4\overline{)36}$	21. $5\overline{)35}$	22. $3\overline{)27}$	23. $2\overline{)18}$	24. $4\overline{)28}$

Set 37 p. 202

Divide.

1. $6\overline{)30}$ (5)
2. $8\overline{)32}$
3. $9\overline{)36}$
4. $7\overline{)7}$
5. $7\overline{)21}$
6. $6\overline{)18}$

7. $7\overline{)28}$
8. $9\overline{)54}$
9. $6\overline{)42}$
10. $8\overline{)40}$
11. $8\overline{)16}$
12. $7\overline{)56}$

13. $9\overline{)72}$
14. $6\overline{)24}$
15. $7\overline{)49}$
16. $8\overline{)56}$
17. $9\overline{)9}$
18. $6\overline{)54}$

19. $9\overline{)27}$
20. $6\overline{)36}$
21. $7\overline{)35}$
22. $8\overline{)72}$
23. $9\overline{)63}$
24. $7\overline{)63}$

25. $8\overline{)48}$
26. $9\overline{)45}$
27. $6\overline{)48}$
28. $9\overline{)81}$
29. $7\overline{)42}$
30. $8\overline{)64}$

Set 38 p. 204

Find the mean.

1. 8, 4, 3 (5)
2. 8, 7, 0
3. 6, 12, 12

4. 4, 3, 4, 5
5. 3, 9, 9, 5, 9
6. 0, 8, 9, 3

7. 8, 9, 9, 6, 8
8. 8, 7, 1, 4
9. 10, 12, 6, 9, 8

10. 1, 7, 9, 8, 9, 8
11. 8, 1, 7, 9, 6, 5
12. 10, 9, 6, 6, 15, 8

Set 39 p. 210

Find the quotient and the remainder.

1. $2\overline{)9}$ (4 r1)
2. $5\overline{)8}$
3. $3\overline{)13}$
4. $8\overline{)18}$
5. $4\overline{)21}$
6. $6\overline{)28}$

7. $5\overline{)16}$
8. $7\overline{)22}$
9. $8\overline{)30}$
10. $2\overline{)13}$
11. $9\overline{)20}$
12. $6\overline{)32}$

13. $9\overline{)73}$
14. $4\overline{)19}$
15. $5\overline{)29}$
16. $7\overline{)60}$
17. $4\overline{)14}$
18. $8\overline{)68}$

19. $7\overline{)41}$
20. $5\overline{)47}$
21. $3\overline{)29}$
22. $7\overline{)39}$
23. $7\overline{)50}$
24. $9\overline{)59}$

340

Set 40 p. 218

Divide.

1. $2\overline{)60}$ (30)   2. $4\overline{)80}$ 3. $6\overline{)60}$ 4. $5\overline{)100}$ 5. $8\overline{)160}$

6. $7\overline{)420}$ 7. $4\overline{)120}$ 8. $9\overline{)180}$ 9. $3\overline{)150}$ 10. $2\overline{)140}$

11. $8\overline{)400}$ 12. $9\overline{)450}$ 13. $5\overline{)250}$ 14. $3\overline{)90}$ 15. $5\overline{)300}$

Set 41 p. 220

Divide.

1. $2\overline{)124}$ (62)   2. $4\overline{)368}$ 3. $3\overline{)63}$ 4. $2\overline{)44}$ 5. $9\overline{)189}$

6. $8\overline{)248}$ 7. $3\overline{)159}$ 8. $7\overline{)217}$ 9. $2\overline{)68}$ 10. $5\overline{)155}$

11. $7\overline{)77}$ 12. $6\overline{)486}$ 13. $4\overline{)88}$ 14. $5\overline{)205}$ 15. $3\overline{)276}$

16. $4\overline{)204}$ 17. $8\overline{)168}$ 18. $2\overline{)100}$ 19. $8\overline{)408}$ 20. $9\overline{)279}$

21. $5\overline{)400}$ 22. $5\overline{)455}$ 23. $9\overline{)549}$ 24. $2\overline{)186}$ 25. $8\overline{)648}$

Set 42 p. 222

Find the tens in the quotient.

1. $2\overline{)76}$ (30)   2. $5\overline{)165}$ 3. $4\overline{)252}$ 4. $3\overline{)78}$ 5. $6\overline{)198}$

6. $5\overline{)410}$ 7. $8\overline{)424}$ 8. $2\overline{)156}$ 9. $4\overline{)96}$ 10. $2\overline{)114}$

11. $3\overline{)255}$ 12. $6\overline{)312}$ 13. $7\overline{)455}$ 14. $4\overline{)188}$ 15. $9\overline{)504}$

16. $7\overline{)581}$ 17. $5\overline{)260}$ 18. $6\overline{)504}$ 19. $8\overline{)752}$ 20. $9\overline{)684}$

341

Set 43 p. 224

Divide.

1. $2\overline{)156}$ (78)

2. $5\overline{)165}$

3. $6\overline{)156}$

4. $3\overline{)87}$

5. $8\overline{)96}$

6. $7\overline{)168}$

7. $4\overline{)188}$

8. $9\overline{)108}$

9. $5\overline{)90}$

10. $3\overline{)201}$

11. $5\overline{)320}$

12. $8\overline{)264}$

13. $3\overline{)285}$

14. $6\overline{)438}$

15. $2\overline{)192}$

16. $4\overline{)232}$

17. $9\overline{)477}$

18. $9\overline{)783}$

19. $7\overline{)504}$

20. $8\overline{)360}$

Set 44 p. 226

Divide.

1. $2\overline{)157}$ (78 r1)

2. $5\overline{)118}$

3. $3\overline{)107}$

4. $6\overline{)85}$

5. $4\overline{)369}$

6. $4\overline{)97}$

7. $7\overline{)156}$

8. $2\overline{)75}$

9. $5\overline{)272}$

10. $3\overline{)82}$

11. $3\overline{)170}$

12. $2\overline{)171}$

13. $9\overline{)127}$

14. $4\overline{)118}$

15. $6\overline{)369}$

16. $5\overline{)309}$

17. $6\overline{)164}$

18. $8\overline{)506}$

19. $2\overline{)119}$

20. $7\overline{)507}$

21. $3\overline{)286}$

22. $6\overline{)430}$

23. $5\overline{)386}$

24. $8\overline{)666}$

25. $9\overline{)755}$

Set 45 p. 228

Find the hundreds in the quotient.

1. $2\overline{)915}$ (400)

2. $5\overline{)1728}$

3. $3\overline{)700}$

4. $6\overline{)4327}$

5. $4\overline{)1070}$

6. $4\overline{)3765}$

7. $8\overline{)936}$

8. $2\overline{)1361}$

9. $7\overline{)2039}$

10. $8\overline{)6617}$

11. $3\overline{)2366}$

12. $6\overline{)5000}$

13. $5\overline{)3432}$

14. $9\overline{)8500}$

15. $7\overline{)6619}$

342

Set 46 p. 230

Divide.

631 r1
1. $2\overline{)1263}$ 2. $5\overline{)4091}$ 3. $3\overline{)752}$ 4. $8\overline{)1448}$ 5. $6\overline{)1666}$

6. $7\overline{)2185}$ 7. $9\overline{)6489}$ 8. $5\overline{)1156}$ 9. $4\overline{)1769}$ 10. $9\overline{)6059}$

11. $6\overline{)3188}$ 12. $4\overline{)3234}$ 13. $2\overline{)937}$ 14. $7\overline{)4958}$ 15. $3\overline{)2505}$

16. $2\overline{)1977}$ 17. $5\overline{)2852}$ 18. $9\overline{)992}$ 19. $3\overline{)2840}$ 20. $7\overline{)1707}$

21. $4\overline{)2360}$ 22. $8\overline{)3845}$ 23. $6\overline{)5676}$ 24. $9\overline{)3605}$ 25. $8\overline{)4825}$

Set 47 p. 240

Divide.

3
1. $20\overline{)60}$ 2. $90\overline{)180}$ 3. $30\overline{)150}$ 4. $20\overline{)160}$ 5. $40\overline{)360}$

6. $50\overline{)200}$ 7. $60\overline{)120}$ 8. $10\overline{)60}$ 9. $80\overline{)720}$ 10. $30\overline{)240}$

11. $50\overline{)150}$ 12. $40\overline{)200}$ 13. $60\overline{)540}$ 14. $90\overline{)450}$ 15. $60\overline{)300}$

Set 48 p. 242

Divide.

4 r15
1. $40\overline{)175}$ 2. $50\overline{)329}$ 3. $80\overline{)302}$ 4. $60\overline{)253}$ · 5. $30\overline{)100}$

6. $70\overline{)654}$ 7. $40\overline{)286}$ 8. $20\overline{)101}$ 9. $70\overline{)506}$ 10. $90\overline{)450}$

11. $20\overline{)198}$ 12. $30\overline{)216}$ 13. $60\overline{)420}$ 14. $50\overline{)266}$ 15. $30\overline{)195}$

16. $50\overline{)425}$ 17. $80\overline{)500}$ 18. $90\overline{)179}$ 19. $70\overline{)490}$ 20. $90\overline{)770}$

343

Set 49 p. 244

Divide.

1. 22)156
    7 r2

2. 92)486

3. 41)350

4. 70)235

5. 81)648

6. 32)193

7. 43)260

8. 20)155

9. 80)346

10. 51)433

11. 23)119

12. 52)416

13. 31)253

14. 31)200

15. 22)198

16. 64)578

17. 74)596

18. 42)383

19. 84)180

20. 91)300

Set 50 p. 246

Divide.

1. 32)186
    5 r26

2. 44)251

3. 64)495

4. 83)656

5. 53)260

6. 63)249

7. 93)552

8. 22)165

9. 72)140

10. 43)368

11. 74)368

12. 94)839

13. 33)250

14. 52)410

15. 23)105

16. 62)544

17. 74)500

18. 53)462

19. 34)200

20. 84)748

Set 51 p. 248

Divide.

1. 36)241
    6 r25

2. 19)163

3. 27)160

4. 89)365

5. 45)352

6. 77)650

7. 56)425

8. 59)540

9. 26)181

10. 86)547

11. 67)495

12. 48)400

13. 75)725

14. 28)276

15. 79)644

16. 87)300

17. 68)500

18. 19)107

19. 55)481

20. 78)400

Set 52 p. 250

Divide.

1. $29\overline{)262}$ $\quad 9\ r1$
2. $47\overline{)331}$
3. $65\overline{)460}$
4. $58\overline{)352}$
5. $39\overline{)273}$

6. $87\overline{)526}$
7. $48\overline{)339}$
8. $75\overline{)304}$
9. $35\overline{)300}$
10. $65\overline{)600}$

11. $57\overline{)460}$
12. $89\overline{)802}$
13. $36\overline{)148}$
14. $78\overline{)546}$
15. $68\overline{)478}$

16. $26\overline{)156}$
17. $69\overline{)625}$
18. $66\overline{)267}$
19. $79\overline{)635}$
20. $87\overline{)700}$

Set 53 p. 270

Write a mixed numeral.

1. 5 and $\frac{5}{8}$ $\quad 5\frac{5}{8}$
2. 1 and $\frac{1}{2}$
3. 4 and $\frac{3}{8}$
4. 9 and $\frac{3}{4}$

5. 17 and $\frac{2}{5}$
6. 12 and $\frac{7}{10}$
7. 28 and $\frac{1}{10}$
8. 46 and $\frac{3}{5}$

9. $6 + \frac{1}{4}$
10. $7 + \frac{9}{10}$
11. $5 + \frac{1}{8}$
12. $8 + \frac{1}{5}$

13. $11 + \frac{1}{2}$
14. $19 + \frac{1}{10}$
15. $30 + \frac{5}{8}$
16. $52 + \frac{3}{10}$

Set 54 p. 272

Add.

1. $\frac{1}{4} + \frac{2}{4} = \underline{\ ?\ }$ $\quad \frac{3}{4}$
2. $\frac{1}{8} + \frac{4}{8} = \underline{\ ?\ }$
3. $\frac{1}{5} + \frac{3}{5} = \underline{\ ?\ }$

4. $\frac{2}{6} + \frac{3}{6} = \underline{\ ?\ }$
5. $\frac{1}{10} + \frac{2}{10} = \underline{\ ?\ }$
6. $\frac{6}{8} + \frac{1}{8} = \underline{\ ?\ }$

7. $\frac{2}{5} + \frac{2}{5} = \underline{\ ?\ }$
8. $\frac{5}{10} + \frac{2}{10} = \underline{\ ?\ }$
9. $\frac{2}{8} + \frac{3}{8} = \underline{\ ?\ }$

10. $\frac{2}{8} + \frac{5}{8} = \underline{\ ?\ }$
11. $\frac{8}{10} + \frac{1}{10} = \underline{\ ?\ }$
12. $\frac{2}{6} + \frac{3}{6} = \underline{\ ?\ }$

Set 55 p. 274

Subtract.

1. $\frac{2}{4} - \frac{1}{4} = $? $\frac{1}{4}$

2. $\frac{7}{10} - \frac{4}{10} = $?

3. $\frac{6}{8} - \frac{5}{8} = $?

4. $\frac{8}{10} - \frac{5}{10} = $?

5. $\frac{3}{5} - \frac{1}{5} = $?

6. $\frac{3}{8} - \frac{2}{8} = $?

7. $\frac{4}{10} - \frac{3}{10} = $?

8. $\frac{2}{2} - \frac{1}{2} = $?

9. $\frac{7}{8} - \frac{4}{8} = $?

10. $\frac{6}{6} - \frac{5}{6} = $?

11. $\frac{9}{10} - \frac{6}{10} = $?

12. $\frac{5}{5} - \frac{3}{5} = $?

Set 56 p. 276

Add.

1. $1\frac{1}{5}$ $+1\frac{2}{5}$ $2\frac{3}{5}$

2. $2\frac{1}{3}$ $+1\frac{1}{3}$

3. $3\frac{2}{4}$ $+3\frac{1}{4}$

4. $4\frac{1}{8}$ $+2\frac{2}{8}$

5. $1\frac{1}{10}$ $+5\frac{2}{10}$

6. $2\frac{3}{10}$ $+2\frac{4}{10}$

7. $3\frac{2}{8}$ $+4\frac{3}{8}$

8. $4\frac{5}{10}$ $+4\frac{4}{10}$

9. $5\frac{3}{5}$ $+\ \frac{1}{5}$

10. $1\frac{3}{10}$ $+\ \frac{6}{10}$

Set 57 p. 278

Subtract.

1. $4\frac{2}{4}$ $-1\frac{1}{4}$ $3\frac{1}{4}$

2. $7\frac{7}{8}$ $-4\frac{6}{8}$

3. $6\frac{9}{10}$ $-2\frac{2}{10}$

4. $8\frac{4}{5}$ $-3\frac{2}{5}$

5. $9\frac{7}{10}$ $-4\frac{4}{10}$

6. $9\frac{5}{8}$ $-3\frac{2}{8}$

7. $5\frac{3}{4}$ $-5\frac{2}{4}$

8. $4\frac{5}{10}$ $-4\frac{2}{10}$

9. $6\frac{3}{5}$ $-\ \frac{2}{5}$

10. $2\frac{6}{8}$ $-\ \frac{3}{8}$

Set 58 pp. 286, 292

Write the decimal.

1. $\frac{1}{10}$ 0.1   **2.** $\frac{7}{10}$ **3.** $\frac{9}{10}$ **4.** $1\frac{2}{10}$ **5.** $3\frac{8}{10}$ **6.** $7\frac{3}{10}$

7. $10\frac{6}{10}$ **8.** $51\frac{2}{10}$ **9.** $99\frac{9}{10}$ **10.** $125\frac{5}{10}$ **11.** $100\frac{6}{10}$ **12.** $166\frac{4}{10}$

13. Five tenths   **14.** One and seven tenths

15. Seven hundredths   **16.** Fifteen hundredths

17. Fifty-three hundredths   **18.** Nine and one hundredth

19. One hundred and thirty hundredths

20. Two hundred sixty-three and fifty-nine hundredths

Set 59 p. 294

Add.

1. 2.6 +1.3 3.9	**2.** 4.0 +7.5	**3.** 0.5 +0.4	**4.** 3.62 +5.16	**5.** 2.41 +9.07
6. 0.8 +0.9	**7.** 1.6 +2.7	**8.** 6.07 +1.18	**9.** 5.95 +6.13	**10.** 4.72 +0.75
11. 6.54 +2.87	**12.** 3.59 +1.65	**13.** 7.02 +5.18	**14.** 18.57 +10.56	**15.** 25.69 + 9.32

Set 60 p. 296

Subtract.

1. 3.9 −2.1 1.8	**2.** 0.8 −0.5	**3.** 7.6 −7.2	**4.** 0.75 −0.40	**5.** 8.97 −3.67
6. 1.5 −0.7	**7.** 7.0 −3.5	**8.** 7.08 −4.28	**9.** 9.25 −6.08	**10.** 8.12 −0.05
11. 7.24 −0.87	**12.** 5.06 −1.58	**13.** 6.32 −0.53	**14.** 18.00 −16.19	**15.** 25.96 − 7.29

Tables of Measurement

Metric System

Length

$$10 \text{ millimeters} = 1 \text{ centimeter}$$
$$100 \text{ centimeters} = 1 \text{ meter}$$
$$1000 \text{ meters} = 1 \text{ kilometer}$$

Area

$$100 \text{ square millimeters} = 1 \text{ square centimeter}$$
$$10{,}000 \text{ square centimeters} = 1 \text{ square meter}$$

Mass (weight)

$$1000 \text{ milligrams} = 1 \text{ gram}$$
$$1000 \text{ grams} = 1 \text{ kilogram}$$
$$1000 \text{ kilograms} = 1 \text{ metric ton}$$

Capacity

$$4 \text{ metric cups} = 1 \text{ liter}$$
$$1000 \text{ milliliters} = 1 \text{ liter}$$
$$1000 \text{ liters} = 1 \text{ kiloliter}$$

United States Customary System

Length

$$12 \text{ inches} = 1 \text{ foot}$$
$$36 \text{ inches} = 1 \text{ yard}$$
$$3 \text{ feet} = 1 \text{ yard}$$

Area

$$144 \text{ square inches} = 1 \text{ square foot}$$
$$9 \text{ square feet} = 1 \text{ square yard}$$

Weight

$$16 \text{ ounces} = 1 \text{ pound}$$
$$2000 \text{ pounds} = 1 \text{ ton}$$

Capacity

$$8 \text{ fluid ounces} = 1 \text{ cup}$$
$$2 \text{ cups} = 1 \text{ pint}$$
$$2 \text{ pints} = 1 \text{ quart}$$
$$4 \text{ quarts} = 1 \text{ gallon}$$

Glossary

Addition Numbers are added to find how many in all.

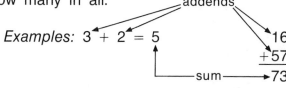

Examples: $3 + 2 = 5$

$$\begin{array}{r} 16 \\ +57 \\ \hline 73 \end{array}$$

addends — sum

Angle Two rays that have the same endpoint. The endpoint is the **vertex** of the angle.

vertex

rays

Area The number of square units needed to cover a given surface.

Circle A simple closed path. All the points on the path are the same distance from a point inside, called the **center.**

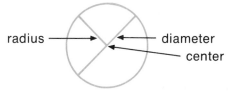

radius — diameter — center

Cone If an ice-cream cone had a round lid, it would have the shape of a *cone* in geometry.

Congruent line segments Line segments that are the same length.

Congruent polygons Polygons that are the same size and shape.

Cylinder A can for soup has the shape of a *cylinder.*

Decimal A numeral that uses place value and a **decimal point.** Any digits to the left of the decimal point name a whole number. Digits to the right stand for a fraction.

Example: 4.25, which means $4\frac{25}{100}$.

decimal point

Degree Celsius A standard unit used to measure temperature.

Denominator In the fraction $\frac{2}{3}$, 3 is the *denominator.*

Diameter of a circle Any line segment that goes through the center of the circle, and whose endpoints are on the circle.

Digit Any one of the ten symbols used to write our numerals:

0, 1, 2, 3, 4, 5, 6, 7, 8, 9

Division Numbers are divided to answer questions such as:

1. How many fives in 37?

quotient ⟶ 7 r2 ⟵ remainder

divisor ⟶ $5\overline{)37}$ ⟵ dividend

2. If there are 36 in all, how many are there in each of 9 fair shares?

quotient ⟶ 4

divisor ⟶ $9\overline{)36}$ ⟵ dividend

Division-addition property (the distributive property of division over addition) To divide a sum of addends by a number, you may divide each addend by the number and then add the answers.

Example: This property is used in division. For $2\overline{)64}$, think of 64 as $60 + 4$. Divide each addend by 2 and then add the answers.

$$\frac{30}{2\overline{)60}} + \frac{2}{2\overline{)4}} = \frac{32}{2\overline{)64}}$$

Equivalent fractions Fractions that name the same number.

Even number A whole number whose numeral ends in 0, 2, 4, 6, or 8.

Expanded notation A way to show the number named by each digit in a numeral.

Example: These are expanded notations for 634.

$$\begin{array}{r} 600 \\ 30 \\ +\ \ 4 \end{array} \qquad 600 + 30 + 4$$

Factors Numbers that are to be multiplied.

Fraction A numeral that shows how to compare a part of a whole (or of a group) with all the parts.

Example: 2 of the 3 fair shares of a candy bar is $\frac{2}{3}$ of the candy bar.
Example: 2 of the 3 people in a family are $\frac{2}{3}$ of the family.
Example: 2 of the 3 dimes are $\frac{2}{3}$ of the dimes.

Grouping property of addition (associative property of addition) To add, numbers can be grouped differently. The sum is always the same.

Example:
$$\underline{(3 + 2)} + 4 = \underline{?} \qquad 3 + \underline{(2 + 4)} = \underline{?}$$
$$\ \ \ \ 5\ \ \ + 4 = 9 \qquad 3 + \ \ \ 6\ \ \ = 9$$

Grouping property of multiplication (associative property of multiplication) To multiply, numbers can be grouped differently. The product is always the same.

Example:
$$\underline{(4 \times 3)} \times 2 = \underline{?} \qquad 4 \times \underline{(3 \times 2)} = \underline{?}$$
$$\ \ \ 12\ \ \ \times 2 = 24 \qquad 4 \times \ \ \ 6\ \ \ = 24$$

Line A *line* can be thought of as a straight path that never ends. It has no endpoints.

Line of symmetry A line that separates a flat figure into two parts that can be matched exactly.

Line segment Two **endpoints** and the straight (shortest) path between them.

Mean The *mean* of a group of numbers is found by dividing the sum of the numbers by the number of addends. The mean can replace each original number to give the same sum.

Example: $8 + 3 + 2 + 7 + 10 = 30$, and $30 \div 5 = 6$.
6 is the mean of these five numbers because: $8 + 3 + 2 + 7 + 10 = 30$, and $6 + 6 + 6 + 6 + 6 = 30$.

Median The middle number of a group of numbers, when they are arranged in order.

  Example: 3 is the median of:
        0, 2, 2, 3, 4, 5, 5

Mixed numeral A numeral that uses a name for a whole number and a fraction.
  Example: $1\frac{1}{4}$, which means $1 + \frac{1}{4}$.

Multiplication Two numbers are multiplied to find how many in all. One number tells how many groups. The other number tells how many in each group.
  Example: How many in 3 boxes, if each box has 4?

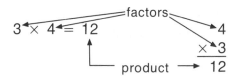

Multiplication-addition property (distributive property of multiplication over addition) To multiply a sum of addends by a number, you may multiply each addend by the number and then add the answers.
  Example: This property is used in multiplication. For 4×368, think of 368 as $8 + 60 + 300$. Multiply each addend by 4 and then add the answers.

```
     368                    23
   ×   4           or      368
      32 ← 4 × 8         ×   4
     240 ← 4 × 60         1472
    1200 ← 4 × 300
    1472
```

Numerals Names (symbols) for numbers.
  Examples: $\frac{3}{4}$; 4.6; 20; XX

Numerator In the fraction $\frac{2}{3}$, 2 is the *numerator.*

Octagon A polygon that has eight sides.

Odd number A whole number whose numeral ends in 1, 3, 5, 7, or 9.

One as a factor (identity property for multiplication) The product of any number and 1 is that number.
  Example: $5 \times 1 = 5$

Order property of addition (commutative property of addition) Two numbers can be added in either order. The sums are the same.
  Example: $3 + 5 = 8$ and $5 + 3 = 8$.

Order property of multiplication (commutative property of multiplication) Two numbers can be multiplied in either order. The products are the same.
  Example: $3 \times 5 = 15$ and $5 \times 3 = 15$.

Ordinal number A whole number, when it is used to tell if something is first, second, third, fourth, and so on.

Parallel lines Lines in the same flat surface that do not cross (intersect).·

Pentagon A polygon that has five sides.

Perimeter The sum of the lengths of the sides of a polygon.

Place value The value of a position (place) for a digit in a numeral. In our system, the value of each place is ten times the value of the place at its right.
Examples: The 2 in 42 names 2.
The 2 in 21 names 20.

Point An exact location. A dot is often drawn to stand for a *point.*

Polygon A simple closed path formed by line segments. The segments are called **sides** of the polygon.

Probability A number from 0 to 1 that tells how likely it is that a thing will happen.

Product The number found by multiplying.

Quadrilateral A polygon that has four sides (and four angles).

Quotient In a division answer, the *quotient* tells the greatest number of times the divisor can be subtracted from the dividend.

$$\overset{\text{quotient}}{5\,r4}$$
Example: divisor ⟶ $7\overline{)39}$ ⟵ dividend
$$\underline{-35}$$
$$4$$

Radius of a circle Any line segment with endpoints that are the center of the circle and a point on the circle.

Ray A part of a line that has one **endpoint.** It goes on without end in only one direction.

352

Rectangle A quadrilateral that has four right angles.

Rectangular prism A shoe box has the shape of a *rectangular prism.*

Related facts These addition and subtraction facts are related. They use the same three numbers.
$$3 + 4 = 7 \qquad 4 + 3 = 7$$
$$7 - 4 = 3 \qquad 7 - 3 = 4$$
These multiplication and division facts are related.
$$3 \times 6 = 18 \qquad 6 \times 3 = 18$$
$$18 \div 6 = 3 \qquad 18 \div 3 = 6$$

Remainder (in division) The number that is left after the divisor has been subtracted from the dividend as many times as possible.

$$\overset{\text{remainder}}{3\,r2}$$
Example: divisor ⟶ $12\overline{)38}$ ⟵ dividend
$$\underline{-36}$$
$$2 ⟵$$

Renaming numbers Thinking of numbers in different ways.
Example (addition): Group ten tens to make one more hundred.
$$\overset{1}{531}$$
$$\underline{+294}$$
$$825$$

Example (subtraction): Show one fewer hundred and ten more tens.
$$\overset{7\ 13}{8\!\!\!/47}$$
$$\underline{-364}$$
$$473$$

Right angle An angle whose rays form a square corner.

Roman numerals A system for naming numbers that does not use place value. The basic symbols are:

I	V	X	L	C	D	M
(1)	(5)	(10)	(50)	(100)	(500)	(1000)

Simple closed path If you can trace a path (in a flat surface), and without turning back, return to where you started, it is a **closed path.** A closed path that does not cross over (intersect) itself is a simple closed path.

Closed paths

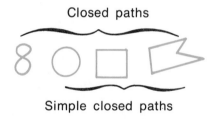

Simple closed paths

Sphere A hollow ball has the shape of a *sphere.*

Square A rectangle that has four congruent sides.

Standard units of measure Units that people, through their government, agree to use when they measure things.
  Examples: meter, gram, liter
  See also Tables of Measurement, page 348.

Subtraction Numbers are subtracted to answer questions such as:
1. How many are left when 4 is taken from 7?

$$7 - 4 = 3 \quad \underset{\text{addends}}{\overset{\text{sum}}{}} \quad \begin{array}{r} 7 \\ -4 \\ \hline 3 \end{array}$$

2. What must be added to 8 to have 14?
   $14 - 8 = 6$ (Think: $8 + \underline{\ ?\ } = 14$)
3. 9 is how much greater than 6?
   $9 - 6 = 3$

Sum The number found by adding.

Triangle A polygon that has three sides.

Whole number Any one of the numbers 0, 1, 2, 3, 4, 5, 6, and so on. No matter how long you count, you cannot come to the last *whole number.*

Zero property of addition (identity property) When one of two addends is 0, the sum equals the other addend.
  Example: $59 + 0 = 59$

Zero property of multiplication When one of the numbers to be multiplied is 0, the product is 0.
  Example: $0 \times 9 = 0$

Zero properties of subtraction When 0 is subtracted from a number, the answer is the number.
  Example: $7 - 0 = 7$
When a number is subtracted from itself, the answer is 0.
  Example: $7 - 7 = 0$

353

Table of Symbols

		Page
>	is greater than	6
<	is less than	6
+	plus	8
=	is equal to	20
$1.30	one dollar and thirty cents	28
−	minus	30
×	times	130
÷	divided by	196
4⟌12	twelve divided by four	198

Index

B 8
C 9
D 0
E 1
F 2
G 3
H 4
I 5
J 6